The Fiqh of Islam:

A Contemporary Explanation of Principles of Worship

Volume 2

The Fiqh of Islam:

A Contemporary Explanation of Principles of Worship

Volume 2

Shaykh Muhammad Hisham Kabbani

Published by the
Institute for Spiritual & Cultural Advancement

Published and Distributed by:

Institute for Spiritual and Cultural Advancement (ISCA)
17195 Silver Parkway, #201
Fenton, MI 48430 USA
Tel: (888) 278-6624
Fax: (810) 815-0518
Email: staff@naqshbandi.org
Web: http://www.naqshbandi.org

First Edition: April 2015
The Fiqh of Islam: A Contemporary Explanation of Principles of Worship, Volume 2
ISBN: 978-1-938058-25-7

Library of Congress Cataloging-in-Publication Data

Kabbani, Muhammad Hisham.
The fiqh of Islam / Shaykh Muhammad Hisham Kabbani.
volumes cm
Projected to be complete in 2 volumes--ECIP data.
Includes bibliographical references.
ISBN 978-1-938058-25-7 (alk. paper)
1. Islamic law. I. Title.
KBP144.K33 2014
340.5'9--dc23

2014019237

PRINTED IN THE UNITED STATES OF AMERICA
15 14 13 12 11 05 06 07 08 09

Cyprus, 2005. The author receiving blessing and support to fulfill his mission from his spiritual guide and father-in-law, the founder of the Naqshbandiyya-Nazimiyya Sufi Order, as-Sayyid Shaykh Muḥammad Nazim Adil an-Naqshbandi (1922-2014).

July 2014. The author giving a *ṣuḥbah* (discourse) in the pre-dawn hours of the holy month Ramadan at the Michigan *zawiya* dedicated by as-Sayyid Shaykh Nazim Adil an-Naqshbandi in 1993.

Contents

About the Author i

Preface iii

Publisher's Notes v

Masters of the Naqshbandi Golden Chain ix

Recitation before Every Association xi

Allāh Orders Us to Remember Him (Dhikrullāh) 1

- Remember Allāh throughout Your Day 3
- Dhikrullāh Focuses the Mind and Calms Anger 5
- Dhikrullāh Increases Heavenly Light in the Heart 7
- How Shaytan Takes Hold 11

Dhikrullāh Mentioned in the Holy Traditions (Aḥādīth) 13

- Dhikrullāh Polishes the Heart Like a Mirror 13
- Dhikrullāh Increases the Hidden Knowledge of Realities (Ḥaqāiq) 15
- Allāh Appoints Special Angels to Attend Circles of Dhikr 19
- Prophet ﷺ Said Dhikrullāh is the Best of Deeds 21
- Who Remembers Allāh is Alive and Who does not is Dead 24

Rust of the Heart 27

- Allāh Defines the Heedless as Those Who Abandon Dhikrullāh 27
- Darkness Dwells in the Heedless Heart and Leads to Unbelief 29
- The Best Dhikrullāh is "Lā ilāha illa-Llāh" 33

The Signs of a Worthy Teacher 41

- Ibn Qayyim al-Jawziyya Describes His Shaykh 42
- Remember Allāh Excessively Until People Say You Are Insane 45

Nine Miraculous Benefits of Dhikrullāh 53

Dhikrullāh Represents You in the Divine Presence 65

- Your Dhikr Remembers You at the Arsh 65
- Allāh Sends Difficulty to Raise Your Station 68
- Angels Praise Who Makes Dhikrullāh and Deny Who Doesn't 69
- More Benefits of Dhikrullāh 72

Allāh's Light is in the Hearts of Believers 75

- The Many Redeeming Rewards of Dhikrullāh 75

How to Remain Connected to Allāh 78
Majlis of Dhikr is the Majlis of Angels 84
All Worship was Decreed Because of Dhikrullāh 91
"If Only They Had Come to You and Asked Allāh's Forgiveness" 91
"They Never Saw Me, but They Believe in Me" 93
Allāh is with the One Who Remembers Him 96
The Prayer Begins with Dhikrullāh 100
More on Dhikrullāh from Ibn Qayyim 103
Dhikr Surpasses Supplication 105
Dhikrullāh Brought Yūnus out of the Belly of the Whale 107
Dhikrullāh is by ʿAsmaullāh wa 'l-Husna 109
Evidence of Various Forms of Remembering Allāh 115
All Creations Praise Allāh and Seek His Forgiveness 115
Istighfār is Dhikrullāh 119
We Uphold the Sunnah of Prophet's Many Adhkār 122
Who is Touched by Allah's Light is Guided 125
Religion is Based on Advice and to Accept Advice is Sunnah 129
Faith is to Love for Your Brother what You Love for Yourself 132
Overwhelming Benefits of Sadaqa 134
Dhikr is the Head of Shukr 139
"If You Remember Me, You Have Thanked Me" 144
Traits of a Believer 147
From Darkness into Light 151
Dhikrullāh Brings Favors, Heedlessness Brings Miseries 151
Dhikrullāh Increases Divine Protection from Shayṭān 157
Some of the Magnificent Benefits of Dhikr 163
From Our Dhikrullāh, Allāh Will Say "My Servant Said the Truth!" 164
Heavenly Palaces are Built on Our Dhikrullāh 165
Heavenly Trees Sprout from Our Dhikrullāh 167
The Fence between You and Hellfire and the Dhikr of Stones 168
Angels Ask Allāh for Our Forgiveness and Continue our Dhikr 169
Dhikrullāh Brightens Your Face 175
Important Holy Days of Fasting 176
Redeeming Acts in the Ḥadīth, "I Saw a Man from my Ummah" 180
Ṣalawāt al-Fātiḥ 188

About the Author

World-renowned religious scholar Shaykh Muḥammad Hisham Kabbani has been featured in the ground-breaking book published by Georgetown University, *The 500 Most Influential Muslims* in *the World* annually since its inaugural printing in 2006. For decades, he has promoted traditional Islamic principles of peace, tolerance, love, compassion and brotherhood, while rigorously opposing extremism in all its forms. He hails from a respected family of traditional Islamic scholars, which includes the former head of the Association of Muslim Scholars of Lebanon and the present grand mufti (highest Islamic religious authority) of Lebanon.

Shaykh Kabbani is highly trained, both as a western scientist and as an Islamic scholar. He received a Bachelor's degree in Chemistry and later studied medicine. Under the instruction of Shaykh 'AbdAllāh ad-Dāghestānī of Damascus, he holds a degree in Islamic Divine Law. Shaykh Muḥammad Nazim Adil al-Ḥaqqānī, founder of the Naqshbandiyya Nazimiyya Sufi Order, authorized him to teach and counsel students in Sufism.

In his long-standing effort to promote a better understanding of traditional Islam, in February 2010, Shaykh Kabbani hosted HRH Charles, the Prince of Wales at a cultural event at the revered Old Trafford Stadium in Manchester, U.K. The shaykh has hosted two ground-breaking international conferences in the U.S. and other international and regional conferences on a host of contemporary issues that featured moderate Muslim scholars from Asia, the Far East, Middle East, Africa, U.K. and Eastern Europe. His counsel is sought by media outlets, academics, policymakers and government leaders.

For thirty years, Shaykh Kabbani has consistently promoted peaceful cooperation among people of all beliefs. Since the early 1990s, he launched numerous endeavors to bring moderate Muslims into the mainstream. Often at great personal risk, he has been instrumental in awakening Muslim social consciousness regarding the religious duty to stand firm against extremism and terrorism, for the benefit of all. His bright, hopeful outlook, with a goal to honor and serve all humanity, has helped millions understand the difference between moderate mainstream Muslims and minority extremist sects.

In the United States, Shaykh Kabbani serves as Chairman, Islamic Supreme Council of America; Founder, Naqshbandi Sufi Order of America; Advisor, World Organization for Resource Development and Education; Chairman, As-Sunnah Foundation of America; Founder, The Muslim Magazine. In the United Kingdom, Shaykh Kabbani is an advisor to Sufi Muslim Council, which consults to the British government on public policy and social and religious issues.

Other titles by Shaykh Kabbani include: *The Illuminations Series* (5 volumes on Islamic spirituality & law) (2014), *The Benefits of Bismillāhi 'r-Raḥmāni 'r-Rahīm & Surat al-Fātiḥah* (2013), *The Importance of Prophet Muḥammad in Our Daily Life* (2013), *The Dome of Provisions* (2013), *The Hierarchy of Saints* (2013, also in French), *Healing Verses in the Holy Qur'an and Sunnah* (2013), *Ṣalawāt of Tremendous Blessings* (2012, also in Turkish/Spanish), *The Heavenly Power of Divine Obedience and Gratitude* (2012), *The Sufilive Series* (2010-2012), *The Prohibition of Domestic Violence in Islam* (2011, also in French, Spanish), *At the Feet of My Master* (2010), *The Nine-fold Ascent* (2009), *Banquet for the Soul* (2008), *Illuminations* (2007), *Universe Rising* (2007), *Symphony of Remembrance* (2007), *A Spiritual Commentary on the Chapter of Sincerity* (2006), *The Sufi Science of Self-Realization* (Fons Vitae, 2005), *Keys to the Divine Kingdom* (2005), *Classical Islam and the Naqshbandi Sufi Order* (2004), *The Naqshbandi Sufi Tradition Guidebook* (2004), *The Approach of Armageddon? An Islamic Perspective* (2003), *Encyclopedia of Muḥammad's Women Companions and the Traditions They Related* (1998, with Dr. Laleh Bakhtiar), *Encyclopedia of Islamic Doctrine* (7 vols. 1998), *Angels Unveiled* (1996), *The Naqshbandi Sufi Way* (1995), and *Remembrance of God Liturgy of the Sufi Naqshbandi Masters* (1994).

Preface

This prestigious series, *The Fiqh of Islam*, is based on legal explanations taken from preeminent Muslim scholars throughout history and includes further elucidation from venerable Sufi masters. This approach underscores the wisdom of examining both legal and spiritual teachings to reach the best possible outcome.

Compiled by a globally recognized Muslim scholar and teacher of Islam's spiritual side, Sufism (*Taṣawwuf*), this series is written for those who seek a better understanding of Islamic tenets.

The Fiqh of Islam, Volume 1 examines the foundation of Islamic jurisprudence and its symbiotic relationship with Islamic spirituality. The priority to develop good manners, the prerequisite and wisdom of obeying divine law, and the indisputable role of the ongoing guidance of Prophet Muhammad, may the peace and blessing of God be upon him, are integral parts in the journey of receiving Heavenly knowledge, upon which *Fiqh* is based.

Volume 2 broadens the discussion with an in-depth examination of divine remembrance, known as *dhikrullāh*, including: its description in the sacred Islamic texts, the Holy Qur'ān and *Sunnah*; depictions of *dhikrullāh* as practiced by Prophet Muḥammad and his Companions; and, illustrious examples from the Saints (*awlīyāullāh*) of its protective, redeeming, purifying and uplifting powers.

For fifty years, the author has sought to serve his master and promote these ancient teachings for the good of all, a spirit we hope is reflected in this book. These universal lessons will make a fine addition to any study of Islam, Islamic law, Prophet Muḥammad, Sufism, Islamic mysticism, spirituality and New Age teachings.

Publisher's Notes

This series is directed to those familiar with the Sufi Way; however, to accommodate lay readers unfamiliar with Sufi terminology and practices, we have provided English translations of Arabic texts and a comprehensive glossary. Where Arabic terms are crucial to the discussion, we have included transliteration and explanations. For readers familiar with Arabic and Islamic teachings, for further clarity please consult cited sources.

The original material is based on transcripts of a series of holy gatherings known as *ṣuḥbah,* a divinely inspired talk given by the "shaykh," a highly trained spiritual guide. To present the authentic flavor of such rare teachings, great care was taken to preserve the speaking styles of both the author and the illustrious shaykhs upon whose notes this book is based.

Translations from Arabic to English pose unique challenges that we have tried our best to make understandable to Western readers. Please note our application of the common Arabic oral tradition of omitting definite articles such as "the Prophet" and "the Holy Qur'ān," as practiced by Muslims around the world as intimate references.

We apply contemporary American English publishing standards and italicize foreign proper nouns (*Fātiḥah, Quṭb az-Zamān, Rasūlullāh, Sūratu 'n-Naml),* but not commonly known foreign-language nouns (jihād, Qur'ān, shaykh) unless they appear in transliterations.

Quotes from the Holy Qur'ān and Holy Traditions of Prophet Muḥammad are offset, italicized and cited.

The pronoun "they" is frequently used by Sufi guides to reference Heavenly beings and holy souls who support them and give them orders, a usage that appears throughout this book. Where gender-specific pronouns such as "he" and "him" are applied in a general sense, no discrimination is intended towards women, upon whom The Almighty bestowed great honor.

Islamic teachings are primarily based on four sources, in this order:

- **Holy Qur'ān**: the Islamic holy book of divine revelation (God's Word) granted to Prophet Muḥammad. Reference to Holy Qur'ān appears as "4:12," which indicates "Chapter 4, Verse 12."
- ***Sunnah*:** holy traditions of Prophet Muḥammad ﷺ; the systematic recording of his words and actions that comprise the *ḥadīth.* For fifteen centuries, Islam has applied a strict, highly technical standard, rating

each narration in terms of its authenticity and categorizing its "transmission." As this book is not highly technical, we simplified the reporting of *ḥadīth,* but included the narrator and source texts to support the discussion at hand.

- ***Ijma*'**: The adherence, or agreement of the experts of independent reasoning *(āhl al-ijtihād)* to the conclusions of a given ruling pertaining to what is permitted and what is forbidden after the passing of the Prophet, Peace be upon him, as well as the agreement of the Community of Muslims concerning what is obligatorily known of the religion with its decisive proofs. Perhaps a clearer statement of this principle is, "We do not separate (in belief and practice) from the largest group of the Muslims."
- **Legal Rulings**: highly trained Islamic scholars form legal rulings from their interpretation of the Qur'ān and the *Sunnah,* known as *ijtihād.* Such rulings are intended to provide Muslims an Islamic context regarding contemporary social norms. In theological terms, scholars who form legal opinions have completed many years of rigorous training and possess degrees similar to a doctorate in divinity in Islamic knowledge, or in legal terms, hold the status of a high court or supreme court judge, or higher.

The following universally recognized symbols have been respectfully included in this work and are deeply appreciated by a vast majority of our readers.

ﷻ *Subḥānahu wa Taʿalā* (may His Glory be Exalted), recited after the name "Allāh" and any of the Islamic names of God.

ﷺ *ṢallAllāhu ʿalayhi wa sallam* (God's blessings and greetings of peace be upon him), recited after the holy name of Prophet Muḥammad.

ﷳ *ʿAlayhi ʿs-salām* (peace be upon him/her), recited after holy names of other prophets, names of Prophet Muḥammad's relatives, the pure and virtuous women in Islam, and angels.

رضي الله عنها/رضي الله عنه *RaḍīAllāhu ʿanh(um)* (may God be pleased with him/her), recited after the holy names of Companions of Prophet Muḥammad; plural: *raḍīAllāhu ʿanhum.*

ق QaddasAllāhu *sirrah* (may God sanctify his secret), recited after names of saints.

Transliteration

Transliteration from Arabic to English poses challenges. To show respect, Muslims often capitalize nouns which, in English, appear in lowercase. To facilitate authentic pronunciation of names, places and terms, use the following key:

Symbol	**Transliteration**	**Symbol**	**Transliteration**	**Vowels: Long**	
ء	'	ط	ṭ	آ ى	ā
ب	b	ظ	ẓ	و	ū
ت	t	ع	ʿ	ي	ī
ث	th	غ	gh	**Short**	
ج	j	ف	f	َ	a
ح	ḥ	ق	q	ُ	u
خ	kh	ك	k	ِ	i
د	d	ل	l		
ذ	dh	م	m		
ر	r	ن	n		
ز	z	ه	h		
س	s	و	w		
ش	sh	ي	y		
ص	ṣ	ة	ah; at		
ض	ḍ	ال	al-/'l-		

Masters of the Naqshbandī Golden Chain

May Allāh ﷻ preserve their secrets.

1. Prophet Muḥammad ibn ʿAbdAllāh ﷺ
2. Abū Bakr aṣ-Ṣiddīq ؓ
3. Salmān al-Fārsī ؓ
4. Qāsim bin Muḥammad bin AbūBakr ؓ
5. Jaʿfar aṣ-Ṣādiq ؑ
6. Ṭayfūr Abū Yazīd al-Bistāmī ق
7. Abūl-Ḥassan ʿAlī al-Kharqānī ق
8. Abū ʿAlī al-Farmadī ق
9. Abū Yaʿqūb Yūsuf al-Ḥamadānī ق
10. Abūl-ʿAbbās, al-Khiḍr ؑ
11. ʿAbdul-Khāliq al-Ghujdawānī ق
12. ʿArif ar-Riwakrī ق
13. Khwāja Maḥmūd al-Anjīr al-Faghnawī ق
14. ʿAlī ar-Ramitānī ق
15. Muḥammad Bābā as-Samāsī ق
16. As-Sayyid Amīr Kulāl ق
17. Muḥammad Bahāuddīn Shāh Naqshband ق
18. ʿAlāuddīn al-Bukhārī al-ʿAṭṭār ق
19. Yaʿqūb al-Charkhī ق
20. ʿUbaydullāh al-Ahrār ق
21. Muḥammad az-Zāhid ق
22. Darwish Muḥammad ق
23. Muḥammad Khwāja al-Amkanakī ق
24. Muḥammad al-Bāqī bilLāh ق
25. Āḥmad al-Farūqī as-Sirhindī ق
26. Muḥammad al-Maʿṣūm ق
27. Muḥammad Sayfuddīn al-Fārūqī al-Mujaddidī ق
28. As-Sayyid Nūr Muḥammad al-Badawānī ق
29. Shamsuddīn Ḥabīb Allāh ق
30. ʿAbdAllāh ad-Dahlawī ق
31. Khālid al-Baghdādī ق
32. Ismāʿīl Muḥammad ash-Shirwānī ق
33. Khāṣ Muḥammad Shirwānī ق
34. Muḥammad Effendī al-Yarāghī ق
35. Jamāluddīn al-Ghumūqī al-Ḥusaynī ق
36. Abū Aḥmad aṣ-Ṣughūrī ق
37. Abū Muḥammad al-Madanī ق
38. Sharafuddīn ad-Dāghestānī ق
39. ʿAbdAllāh al-Fā'iz ad-Dāghestānī ق
40. Muḥammad Nāẓim ʿAdil al-Ḥaqqānī ق

Recitation before Every Association

بسم الله الرحمن الرحيم

Aʿūdhu billāhi min ash-Shayṭān ir-rajīm.
Bismillāhi' r-Raḥmāni 'r-Raḥīm.
Nawaytu 'l-arbāʿīn, nawaytu 'l-ʿitikāf,
nawaytu 'l-khalwah, nawaytu 'l-ʿuzlah,
nawaytu 'r-riyāḍa, nawaytu 's-sulūk,
lillāhi Taʿalā fī hādhā 'l-masjid.

Atiʿūllāha wa atiʿ ūr-Rasūla
wa ūli'l-amri minkum.

I seek refuge in Allāh from Satan, the rejected.
In the Name of Allāh, the Merciful,
the Compassionate.
I intend the forty (days of seclusion);
I intend seclusion in the mosque,
I intend seclusion, I intend isolation,
I intend discipline (of the ego); I intend to travel
in God's Path for the sake of God,
in this mosque.

Obey Allāh, obey the Prophet,
and obey those in authority among you.
Sūratu 'n-Nisā
(The Women), 4:59

Allāh Orders Us to Remember Him (Dhikrullāh)

Aʿūdhu billāhi min ash-Shayṭāni 'r-rajīm. Bismillāhi' r-Raḥmāni 'r-Raḥīm.
Nawaytu 'l-arbāʿīn, nawaytu 'l-ʿitikāf, nawaytu 'l-khalwah, nawaytu 'l-ʿuzlah,
nawaytu 'r-riyāḍa, nawaytu 's-sulūk, lillāhi Taʿalā fī hādhā 'l-masjid.
Atīʿūllāha wa atīʿū 'r-Rasūla wa ūli 'l-amri minkum. (4:59)

As-salāmu ʿalaykum wa raḥmatullāhi wa barakātuh. Bismillāhi 'r-Raḥmāni 'r-Raḥīm.

وَمَا آتَاكُمُ الرَّسُولُ فَخُذُوهُ وَمَا نَهَاكُمْ عَنْهُ فَانتَهُوا

Whatever the Prophet brought take it and leave whatever he forbade.[1]

أَطِيعُواْ اللهَ وَأَطِيعُواْ الرَّسُولَ وَأُوْلِي الأَمْرِ مِنكُمْ

Obey Allāh, obey the Prophet, and obey those in authority among you.[2]

As-salāmu ʿalaykum yā ʿibādullāh, viewers, brothers and sisters wherever you are. Today we begin the chapter on *dhikrullāh* and the importance of *dhikr* in Islam and what is meant by *dhikrullāh.* First of all we will mention some *āyahs* of Holy Qur'an regarding *dhikrullāh,* and there are too many of them.

فَاذْكُرُونِي أَذْكُرْكُمْ وَاشْكُرُواْ لِي وَلاَ تَكْفُرُو

Remember Me, I will remember you. Give thanks to Me
and do not be ungrateful towards Me. [3]

"Remember Me, I will remember you. Thank Me and don't be an unbeliever, *wa lā takfurūn,* don't be a person who has no belief."

وَاذْكُر رَّبَّكَ فِي نَفْسِكَ تَضَرُّعاً وَخِيفَةً وَدُونَ الْجَهْرِ
مِنَ الْقَوْلِ بِالْغُدُوِّ وَالآصَالِ وَلاَ تَكُن مِّنَ الْغَافِلِينَ

---

[1] Sūrat al-Hashr, 59:7.
[22] Sūrat an-Nisa, 4:59.
[3] Sūrat al-Baqarah, 2:152.

And remember your Lord within yourself in humility and in reverence, without loudness in words, in the mornings and evenings. And do not be among the heedless.[4]

"Remember Allāh ﷻ within yourself, asking Him, begging Him, requesting Him as a weak servant, as a humble person, not as a proud person." And when you remember Allāh, remember what the Allāh ﷻ said to Prophet ﷺ in *Sūrat al-Kahf*:

قُلْ إِنَّمَا أَنَا بَشَرٌ مِّثْلُكُمْ يُوحَى إِلَيَّ

Say, "I am but a man like yourselves."[5]

The Prophet ﷺ said, "I am only a human being like you." Look how much he humbled himself. The one whom Allāh brought to *Qāba Qawsayni aw Adnā* is saying, "I am only a human being like you." Look how much he brought himself down to make sure that he is not praising himself. He ﷺ also said in a *ḥadīth*:

اللَّهُمَّ لَا تَكِلْنِي إِلَى نَفْسِي طَرْفَةَ عَيْنٍ وَلَا أَقَلَّ مِنْ ذَلِكَ

O Allāh! Don't leave me to my ego for the blink of an eye or even less.

If the Prophet ﷺ is saying, "Don't leave me to myself for the blink of an eye," what do we have to say? So humbleness is necessary to express that we are weak servants in front of Allāh ﷻ, we are helpless without Allāh's support. So the verse says, "Remember Allāh *in* your self," *tadarruʿan wa khīfatan*, requesting and asking and fearing from Him, *wa dūn al-jahri min al-qawl*, without disturbing the people, without making *dhikr* in a loud voice in order that people will say, "Look what this person is doing!" For example, in common places or in a *masjid* when you are doing *dhikr* with a loud voice, if other people are reciting Qur'ān you will disturb them, so try to do it in a lower voice and remember Allāh *"bi 'l-ghudūwwi wa'l-āsāl."* It means, whenever you leave your house to go to work, remember Allāh on your way to your work, *wa 'l-āsāl*, and at *Maghrib* time when people come back from work you remember Allāh ﷻ.

---

[4] Sūrat al-ʿAraf, 7:205.
[5] Sūrat al-Kahf, 18:110.

Remember Allāh throughout Your Day

There is a kind of bird, *al-ghurāb*, a black crow. They move together and you can see them after *Fajr* as soon as the light begins to appear, then they move from the trees they are in by the hundreds and they go...Allāh knows where they go. They go and then return to these trees in the evening. This is the seeking of work, when you go in the morning, as mentioned by Allāh, *"bi'l-ghudūwwi,"* and when you come back from your work you remember Allāh. "Remembering Allāh" means remember Allāh when you go to work and remember Him when you come home, and of course while you are working and *wa lā takun min al-ghāfilīn*, "Don't be a heedless person." May Allāh forgive us, like us, we are heedless, we forget and Allāh says, "Don't forget, don't forget! Remember Him when you are going and when you are coming," but we forget. May Allāh forgive us.

فِي بُيُوتٍ أَذِنَ اللَّهُ أَن تُرْفَعَ وَيُذْكَرَ فِيهَا اسْمُهُ يُسَبِّحُ لَهُ فِيهَا بِالْغُدُوِّ وَالْآصَالِ

(Lit is such a Light) in houses that Allāh permitted to be raised to honor (and) for the celebration in them of His Name. In them is He glorified in the mornings and in the evenings, (again and again).[6]

Allāh gave permission *fī buyūtin,* "in homes." It's not a home, it's Allāh's House, which means "in *masājid*," in places where people pray for Allāh ﷻ. He permits, *an turfaʿa wa yudhkkara fīhā 'smuhu,* "to raise in it *dhikrullāh* and for the people who are there to remember Him and to remember His Name." *Yusabbiḥu lahu fīhā bi 'l-ghudūwwi wa 'l-āṣāl,* "People praise Allāh ﷻ in these *masājid* in the morning when they go to work and in the evening when they come," which means they pass by the *masājid* for *Fajr* prayer and *Maghrib* and *ʿIshā* prayer.

رِجَالٌ لَّا تُلْهِيهِمْ تِجَارَةٌ وَلَا بَيْعٌ عَن ذِكْرِ اللَّهِ وَإِقَامِ الصَّلَاةِ
وَإِيتَاءِ الزَّكَاةِ يَخَافُونَ يَوْمًا تَتَقَلَّبُ فِيهِ الْقُلُوبُ وَالْأَبْصَارُ

(Are) men whom neither commerce nor sale distracts from the remembrance of Allāh and performance of prayer and giving of zakāt. They fear a Day in which the hearts and eyes will (fearfully) turn about.[7]

---

[6] Sūrat an-Nūr, 24:36.

By 'men' it means men and women, anyone, "They will never be distracted and lose, they are never distracted by their businesses from *dhikrullāh.*" Even if they are buying or selling, or speaking with customers, still they remember Allāh ﷻ. They are a special group of 'men.'

Bismillāhi 'r-Raḥmāni 'r-Raḥīm.

يَا أَيُّهَا الَّذِينَ آمَنُوا اذْكُرُوا اللهَ ذِكْرًا كَثِيرًا وَسَبِّحُوهُ بُكْرَةً وَأَصِيلًا

O you who believe! Remember Allāh with much remembrance and glorify Him early and late. [8]

"O Believers!" Allāh is calling on us in the Holy Qur'ān, *udhkurallāh,* "remember Allāh," remember Him and what He gave you during the day. Remember Him, how He gave you eyes, ears, nose, hands, legs, and how He gave you a mind. Today you see many children come, people come to ask *du'ā* for their children to be healed from what is called high-functioning or low-functioning autism. They didn't find it before as it was very rare, but now you are seeing it everywhere. You cannot control such patients and they keep screaming. Low-functioning is where you can control these patients, but they talk too much and in high-functioning they talk, but they scream and you cannot control them, they hurt themselves and hurt others.

That is because people forgot *dhikrullāh.* Before there was *dhikrullāh,* more than now, and one *masjid* will be mercy for the whole area, but now although you have *masājid,* that mercy is lifted up because there is too much *ẓulmah* and too many people reject *dhikrullāh.* They say, "O no need, it's too much! What is *dhikrullāh*? Read Qur'ān!" Allāh ﷻ says, "Remember Me, I remember you." He said:

وَرَتَّلْنَاهُ تَرْتِيلًا

And We have rehearsed it to you in slow, well-arranged stages, gradually. [9]

This means, "We have recited the Qur'ān to Prophet ﷺ." So for sure, you have to read Qur'ān, but you have to remember Allāh ﷻ. Some people

---

[7] Sūrat an-Nūr, 24:37.

[8] Sūrat al-Aḥzāb, 33:41,42.

[99] Sūrat al-Furqan, 25:32.

read Holy Qur'an and their mind is not on the Holy Qur'ān, because it is a habit to read Qur'ān and they read one chapter a day, but their mind is somewhere else. But when you do *dhikrullāh* with your tongue or with your heart, you will be always focusing.

Dhikrullāh Focuses the Mind and Calms Anger

We never saw autism in the past; the condition brings instability in the mind, because people are losing their *dhikrullāh.* He ﷻ is saying *w'adhkurullāha dhikran kathīra, "Remember Allāh excessively," wa sabbihūhu bukratan wa aṣīla, "and praise Him in the morning, bukratan, and asīla, in the evening."*

And Allāh ﷻ said:

ا أَيُّهَا الَّذِينَ آمَنُوا لَا تُلْهِكُمْ أَمْوَالُكُمْ وَلَا أَوْلَادُكُمْ عَن ذِكْرِ اللَّهِ
وَمَن يَفْعَلْ ذَٰلِكَ فَأُولَٰئِكَ هُمُ الْخَاسِرُون

O Believers! Let not your wealth and your children divert you from remembrance of Allāh, and whoever does that, then those are the losers. [10]

Allāhumma ṣalli ʿalā Sayyīdinā Muḥammad! Bismillāhi 'r-Raḥmāni 'r-Raḥīm:

يَا أَيُّهَا الَّذِينَ آمَنُواْ إِذَا لَقِيتُمْ فِئَةً فَاثْبُتُواْ وَاذْكُرُواْ اللهَ كَثِيرًا لَّعَلَّكُمْ تُفْلَحُونَ

O Believers! When you encounter a company (from the enemy forces), stand firm and remember Allāh much that you may be successful.[11]

"O Believers! If you see a group of people attacking you, you must do *dhikrullāhi kathīran.*" If you see a group of people who are angry, they want to fight with you and make a problem, what should you do? Remember Allāh ﷻ, make *ṣalawāt* on Prophet ﷺ, make *dhikrullāh* and try to cool yourself down. Try not to answer and hold together, hold yourself well by making *dhikrullāh* not to come against them.

Bismillāhi 'r-Raḥmāni 'r-Raḥīm.

وَالذَّاكِرِينَ اللَّهَ كَثِيرًا وَالذَّاكِرَاتِ أَعَدَّ اللَّهُ لَهُم مَّغْفِرَةً وَأَجْرًا عَظِيمًا

---

[10] Sūrat al-Munāfiqūn, 63:9.
[11] Sūrat al-Anfāl, 8:45.

And men who remember Allāh much and women who remember,
for them has Allāh prepared forgiveness and great reward.[12]

Those men who remember Allāh, *"kathīran,"* meaning excessively. *Wa 'dh-dhākirāt,* He adds here women as well, not only men, but men and women; "those who are remembering Allāh excessively."

Bismillāhi 'r-Raḥmāni 'r-Raḥīm.

فَإِذَا قَضَيْتُم مَّنَاسِكَكُمْ فَاذْكُرُواْ اللهَ كَذِكْرِكُمْ آبَاءكُمْ أَوْ أَشَدَّ ذِكْرًا فَمِنَ النَّاسِ
مَن يَقُولُ رَبَّنَا آتِنَا فِي الدُّنْيَا وَمَا لَهُ فِي الآخِرَةِ مِنْ خَلاَقٍ

So when you have accomplished your holy rites, celebrate the praises of Allāh, as you used to celebrate the praises of your fathers, or with far more heart and soul. There are men who say, "Our Lord! Give us (Your bounties) in this world!" but they will have no portion in the Hereafter. [13]

Fa idhā qadaytum manāsikakum fadhkuru 'Llāha, "When you finished all the rites of *Hajj,* remember Allāh ﷻ." When you are coming down from 'Arafāt, because this is the peak of the *Hajj* rites, it is the 'cream of the coffee.' When you are coming down and you leave in the evening, it is the peak of the *Hajj.* So He is saying, *fadhkuru 'Llāha kadhikrikum ābā'akum,* "When this happens, mention Allāh as you mention your parents." How do you mention your parents? By name, by name; for example, it's not related here, but you say, "O father, father!" you mention his name, "Dad! Daddy!" or, "Yassir," or "'Omar," or "'Alī," or "Fatima," you mention the name. So that means *dhikrullāh* is through Allāh's Name. When you do *dhikrullāh,* you do it through His Beautiful Names and Attributes, which is important for us in a *jama'ah* or by yourself, in a loud voice together when in *jama'ah* or by yourself when there is no one there, by mentioning Allāh's Ninety-Nine Beautiful Names and Attributes.

You cannot only mention Allāh's verses of Holy Qur'ān; if you do that, that is *dhikrullāh,* but *dhikrullāh* is also mentioning Allāh, *ka-dhikrikum,* "in the same way that you mention your parents," with all kind of emotion and love, or as He said, *aw ashadda dhikrā,* "or more!" It must be more, more than

---

[12] Sūrat al-Aḥzāb, 33:35.
[13] Sūrat al-Baqarah, 2:200.

what you mention of your parents or your children or your babies. They mention babies more than they mention anything today and mentioning Allāh ﷻ is better.

Dhikrullāh Increases Heavenly Light in the Heart

So these are some of the verses of Holy Qur'an that Allāh mentioned *dhikrullāh* in them. Also, there is the *āyah, "Allāhu nūru 's-samāwāti wa 'l-ʿarḍ."*

اللَّهُ نُورُ السَّمَاوَاتِ وَالْأَرْضِ مَثَلُ نُورِهِ كَمِشْكَاةٍ فِيهَا مِصْبَاحٌ الْمِصْبَاحُ فِي زُجَاجَةٍ الزُّجَاجَةُ كَأَنَّهَا كَوْكَبٌ دُرِّيٌّ يُوقَدُ مِن شَجَرَةٍ مُّبَارَكَةٍ زَيْتُونِةٍ لَّا شَرْقِيَّةٍ وَلَا غَرْبِيَّةٍ يَكَادُ زَيْتُهَا يُضِيءُ وَلَوْ لَمْ تَمْسَسْهُ نَارٌ نُّورٌ عَلَى نُورٍ يَهْدِي اللَّهُ لِنُورِهِ مَن يَشَاء وَيَضْرِبُ اللَّهُ الْأَمْثَالَ لِلنَّاسِ وَاللَّهُ بِكُلِّ شَيْءٍ عَلِيمٌ

Allāh is the Light of the Heavens and Earth. The parable of His Light is as if there were a niche and within it a lamp: the lamp is in a glass, the glass like a Brilliant Star lit from a blessed tree, an olive tree that is neither of the East nor of the West, the oil of which is so bright that it would certainly give light of itself. Light upon Light! Allāh guides whom He will to His Light: Allāh sets forth Parables for men: and Allāh knows all things.[14]

"Allāh is the Light of Heavens and Earth. *Mathala nūrihi ka mishkāthin fīhi miṣbāh,* His Light is like a bundle that carries." Allāh ﷻ knows what it carries, but scholars say it is like a bundle of different lights and in the middle is a huge *miṣbāh,* lamp." *Mathala nūrihi ka mishkāthin fīhi miṣbāh,* "(The example of His Light) is a bundle that inside it is a Lamp. That Lamp is inside a glass, *zujāja, ka-annahā kawkabun durrīyy,* and it looks like a white, shining pearl, *kawkabun.*"

"Kawkab" is a star or planet. Allāh ﷻ is describing that Lamp like a star, a great star. You can see stars bigger than the Sun, you can see stars bigger than this galaxy. Allāh ﷻ is giving an example and we can go further into that later, but He is saying, "That Lamp is shining like a pearl, like a star, shining like a pearl," *yūqadu min shajaratin mubārakatin,* "it is ignited from an olive tree," *lā sharqīyyatin wa lā gharbīyyatin,* "that is neither from the East nor from the West," but it is in this universe, "and the oil of this Lamp is as

[14]. Sūrat an-Nūr, 24:35.

if it is going to burst into a Shining Star, even though not touched by fire that makes light, but as if glowing by itself," *nūrun ʿalā nūr*, "Light over Light," *yahdīya'Llāhu li-nūrihi man yashā*, "Allāh guides whom He likes to His Light," *wa yaḍribu 'Llāhu'l-amthāla li 'n-nāsi*, "and Allāh gives examples for people." And Allāh knows best.

That Light, "*Allāhu nūru 's-samāwāti wa 'l-ʿarḍi mathala nūrihi kamishkātin*," that *mishkāt*, that Lamp, that Light as said by scholars, by *ʿulamā*, is *Rasūlullāh* ﷺ, and Allāh ﷻ gave from His Light to the Prophet ﷺ when He created him before Creation as a Light. Before He created any Creation, Allāh created the Light of Prophet ﷺ and that is why the Prophet ﷺ said:

كنت نبي و ادم بين الماء و الطين

I was a prophet when Ādam was between water and clay.

كنت نبيا وآدم بين الروح والجسد

I was a prophet while Ādam was between soul and body.

So that Light, as it is said, and we will explain later about that Light, is an example of Prophet's ﷺ Light.

قال أبي بن كعب: (مثل نوره في قلب المسلم) وهذا هو النور الذي اودعه في قلبه من معرفته ومحبته والايمان به وذكره وهو نوره الذي انزله اليهم فأحياهم به وجعلهم يمشون به بين الناس وأصله في قلوبهم ثم تقوى مادته فتتزايد حتى يظهر على وجوههم وجوارحهم وابدانهم بل وثيابهم ودورهم يبصره من هو من جنسهم وسائر الخلق له منكر فإذا كان يوم القيامة برز ذلك النور وصار بايمانهم يسعى بين ايديهم في ظلمة الجسر حتى يقطعوه وهم فيه على حسب قوته وضعفه في قلوبهم في الدنيا فمنهم من نوره كالشمس واخر كالقمر واخر كالنجوم واخر كالسراج واخر يعطي نورا على ابهام قدمه يضئ مرة ويطفأ اخرى، اذا كانت هذه حال نوره في الدنيا فأعطي على الجسر بمقدار ذلك بل هو نفس نوره ظهر له عيانا ولما لم يكن للمنافق نور ثابت في الدنيا بل كان نوره ظاهرا لا باطنا اعطى نورا ظاهرا مآله إلى الظلمة والذهاب.

Ubay Ibn Kaʿb ؓ said, "The example of His Light...." Allāh is the Light of Heavens and Earth, but, "the example of that Light is the Light that He sent...." meaning, "the evidence of that Light is the Light He sent to a person who is a Muslim and who is a Believer. He fills his heart with that Light, the Light that is shining in Heavens and Earth, Allāh ﷻ put from that Light."

Allāhu nūru 's-samāwāti wa 'l-ʿarḍi. Nūr is one of the Beautiful Names and Attributes of Allāh ﷻ:

وقد ضرب سبحانه وتعالى النور في قلب عبده مثلا لا يعقله إلا العالمون

Wa qad ḍaraba subḥāna wa taʿalā an-nūr fī qalbi ʿabdihi mathalan lā yaʿqiluhu illa 'l-ʿAlīmūn, "So that *Nūr*, that Light, describes Allāh's Greatness in the metaphor of Light that goes into the heart of His servant. No one will understand that metaphor except *al-ʿAlīmūn*, the Knowers"

He wants to introduce here that not everyone can see this Light, only those who are *ʿulamā*. Here it is not '*ʿulamā*' in the meaning of scholars, but in the meaning of "Knowers," the People of Gnosticism, the People of *Maʿrifah*, those can understand, because he said, *fa qāla Subḥānahu wa Taʿalā Allāhu nūru 's-samāwāti wa 'l-ʿarḍ*, "Allāh is the Light of Heavens and Earth." That Light, no one can understand except the people whom Allāh ﷻ gave the power of understanding through the cleanliness of their hearts. Allāh ﷻ gave it to them because their hearts are clean.

وهو نوره الذي انزله اليهم فأحياهم به وجعلهم يمشون به بين الناس وأصله في قلوبهم

"It is that Light that is put in their hearts that makes them to shine like a spotlight between people and the origin of that Light is in their hearts."

مادته فتتزايد حتى يظهر على وجوههم وجوارحهم وابدانهم بل وثيابهم ودورهم يبصره من هو من جنسهم وسائر الخلق له منكر فإذا كان يوم القيامة برز ذلك النور وصار بايمانهم يسعى بين ايديهم في ظلمة الجسر

He (Ubay Ibn Kaʿb) said, "So when that Light increases in their heart by dhikrullāh, slowly, slowly, increasing through dhikrullāh it appears in their faces and their limbs and their bodies and even on their clothes."

You see the Light, because the Light will take over, like today we see through light, different colors and things you see through light. It depends on how the light goes through the different things you are looking at and how that light is absorbed, and once it is absorbed you see the color. So *awlīyāullāh*, anyone who looks at them can see the Light in their faces.

So you can detect, people can see, "O, this person looks different! He is like us, but there is something on his face, *nūr al-īmān*, the Light of Faith, there is something that we don't have that he has." That's why people are attracted to him. I heard from Grandshaykh ق that there are *awlīyāullāh* that they don't do that, but if they want, they only have to say, "*Yā Rabbī*, open to us for people to come and listen to us," and people would be *yashafūna zaḥfan*, crawling on their chests to reach these *awlīyāullāh*, about whom Allāh ﷻ mentioned in a Holy Ḥadīth:

من عادا لي وليا فقد آذنته بالحرب

(Allāh [swt] said) Whoever comes against a Friend of Mine, I declare war on him.[15]

Such as these are the Friends of Allāh ﷻ, that Allāh gave them power. What did the Prophet ﷺ mention about *dhikrullāh*?

وَآمُرُكُمْ أَنْ تَذْكُرُوا اللهَ فَإِنَّ مَثَلَ ذَلِكَ كَمَثَلِ رَجُلٍ خَرَجَ الْعَدُوُّ فِي أَثَرِهِ سِرَاعًا حَتَّى إِذَا أَتَى
عَلَى حِصْنٍ حَصِينٍ فَأَحْرَزَ نَفْسَهُ مِنْهُمْ كَذَلِكَ الْعَبْدُ لاَ يُحْرِزُ نَفْسَهُ مِنَ الشَّيْطَانِ إِلاَّ بِذِكْرِ اللهِ

And He commands you to remember Allāh, for indeed the parable of that is a man whose enemy quickly tracks him until he reaches an impermeable fortress in which he protects himself from them. This is how the worshiper is: he does not protect himself from Shayṭān except by the remembrance of Allāh."[16]

"*Dhikrullāh* is like a man who went out somewhere and enemies knew that person went that way, and ran after him to catch and kill him, until he is running away from them and reaches a very strong fortress that is in a safe position so that they cannot come inside." The enemy cannot come inside, so he saved himself from them trying to kill him. *Dhikrullāh* is your safety from Shayṭān; it is as if you have run to Allāh ﷻ and He will protect you so that Shayṭān cannot reach you.

It is said, "If there were nothing in *dhikrullāh* except to save you from Shayṭān, then that is the great favor that Allāh ﷻ has given to you." If there is nothing else, if *dhikrullāh* didn't do anything else, this is the biggest benefit or favor that you can achieve. That is why it is our obligation, because Allāh is protecting us through *dhikrullāh*. The Prophet ﷺ said, "You have to keep your tongue always mentioning and remembering Allāh ﷻ."

Ibn Qayyim continues his explanation:

---

[15] Ḥadīth Qudsī ; Bukhārī, from Abū Hurayrah.
[16] Tirmidhī, Āḥmad .

فإنه لا يحرز نفسه من عدوه إلا بالذكر ولا يدخل عليه العدو إلا من باب الغفلة فهو يرصده
فإذا غفل وثب عليه وافترسه

He cannot save himself from the enemy except by dhikrullāh. The enemy will not enter the heart except through the door of heedlessness. He is observing you and when he sees you neglectful he pounces on you and devours you.

How Shaytan Takes Hold

How does the enemy, Shayṭān, enter you? When he sees you are heedless of *dhikrullāh,* he immediately penetrates your heart and tries to take you away from Allāh ﷻ, and that's how we forget. Today they call that sickness for people who forget, "Alzheimer's." Alzheimer's makes you forget until you don't remember anything. Also, when Shayṭān enters your heart, he makes you forget. When you remember, then immediately do *dhikrullāh* and he will run away. With Alzheimer's, sometimes you remember and sometimes you don't. From the religious or spiritual point of view, we are all sick with Alzheimer's; Shayṭān makes that possible by entering our hearts.

Ibn Qayyim said, "The enemy will not enter the heart except through the door of heedlessness." Shayṭān is observing you, like he has cameras. Like today they have cameras everywhere, they know you, and not only that, but through your telephone, through your TV, through your credit card, through your computer, they can know anywhere you are going and they can find you as they have GPS.

One time I went in a car with someone and he was pushing some buttons...this was six or seven years ago, because the one who invented the GPS is from California, he is a convert through us and his name is Simon. He is the one who invented the GPS navigation used in cars. So I was in a car with him and heard a lady, and there was no lady in the car, and she was saying to him, "Drive right, drive left," then, "You reached your destination."

I asked him, "What is that?"

He said, "That is the GPS, navigation system." He didn't show it to me at the beginning.

So Shayṭān has a GPS and when we are heedless he runs in our direction searching for us. Angels have GPS, but a Heavenly GPS, and when we are in *dhikrullāh* they come and join us. So *dhikrullāh* is very important to protect ourselves from Shayṭān, not to jump on us and kill us.

Ibn Qayyim states:

وإذا ذكر الله تعالى انخنس عدو الله تعالى وتصاغر وانقمع حتى يكون كالوصع وكالذباب ولهذا سمي الوسواس الخناس أي يوسوس في الصدور

> When Allāh is mentioned, Shayṭān will shrink and shrink until he has no power, until he becomes smaller than a bird, and more than that, *ka 'dh-dhubāb*, he becomes like a fly, very small. For that reason he was called *al-waswāsu 'l-khannās*, "the fly that gossips in the hearts of people."

That's why when you see a black fly, be careful from Shayṭān, try to protect yourself (from it).

قال ابن عباس : الشيطان جاثم على قلب أبن آدم فإذا سها وغفل وسوس فإذا ذكر الله تعالى خنس

> Ibn 'Abbās said, "The Shayṭān is always standing on the heart of human beings. If one forgets and becomes heedless, he begins to gossip in his ear, *waswasa*, but if he mentions Allāh [by His Divine Names and Attributes] immediately he (Shayṭān) weakens."

May Allāh forgive us and may Allāh bless us.

Wa min Allāhi 't-tawfīq, bi ḥurmati 'l-ḥabīb, bi ḥurmati 'l-Fātiḥah. And with Allāh is success. For the sake of the Beloved, for his sake we recite the opening chapter of Holy Qur'ān.

Dhikrullāh Mentioned in the Holy Traditions (Aḥādīth)

*A'ūdhu billāhi min ash-Shayṭāni 'r-rajīm. Bismillāhi' r-Raḥmāni 'r-Raḥīm.
Nawaytu 'l-arbā'īn, nawaytu 'l-'itikāf, nawaytu 'l-khalwah, nawaytu 'l-'uzlah,
nawaytu 'r-riyāḍa, nawaytu 's-sulūk, lillāhi Ta'alā fī hādhā 'l-masjid.
Atī'ūllāha wa atī'ū 'r-Rasūla wa ūli 'l-amri minkum. (4:59)*

As-salāmu 'alaykum wa raḥmatullāhi wa barakātuh. Bismillāhi 'r-Raḥmāni 'r-Raḥīm. Alḥamdulillāhi Rabbī 'l-'ālamīn, wa 'ṣ-ṣalātu wa 's-salāmu 'alā ashrafi 'l-mursalīn Sayyīdinā Muḥammadin wa 'alā ālihi wa ṣaḥbihi wa sallam.

Dhikrullāh Polishes the Heart Like a Mirror

Dhikrullāh is very important for us and for every *mu'min* and Muslim, because it is the instrument or the way to polish the heart that has already been 'oxidized' and too much dirtiness is on it.

عَنْ مُعَاذٍ ، قَالَ : قَالَ رَسُولُ اللَّهِ صَلَّى اللَّهُ عَلَيْهِ وَسَلَّمَ : " مَا عَمِلَ ابْنُ آدَمَ مِنْ عَمَلٍ أَنْجَى لَهُ مِنَ النَّارِ مِنْ ذِكْرِ اللَّهِ عَزَّ وَجَلَّ " ، قَالُوا : يَا رَسُولَ اللَّهِ ، وَلا الْجِهَادُ فِي سَبِيلِ اللَّهِ ، قَالَ : " وَلا الْجِهَادُ فِي سَبِيلِ اللَّهِ إِلا أَنْ تَضْرِبَ بِسَيْفِكَ حَتَّى يَنْقَطِعَ ، ثُمَّ تَضْرِبَ بِهِ حَتَّى يَنْقَطِعَ " ، قَالَهَا ثَلاثًا

> As it is narrated by Mu'adh ibn Jabal that the Prophet said, "No work will more surely save a man from the punishment of Allāh than the remembrance of Allāh." They said, "not even striving in the Way of Allāh?" and he said, "not even striving in the Way of Allāh, except to strike with one's sword until it breaks, then to strike with it until it breaks." and he repeated it thrice.[17]

"No one did a better *'amal* than *dhikrullāh* to save him from difficulties; *dhikrullāh* will save him from Punishment and save him from being away from Allāh's Presence on Judgment Day," which is due to being far from the Prophet's presence on Judgment Day, in a position that he is going to feel shy. Why? Because *dhikrullāh*, as mentioned, will take away all dirtiness from the heart.

---

[17] Īmām Aḥmad, 'Abd bin Ḥumayd in his *Musnad*.

ولا ريب أن القلب يصدأ كما يصدأ النحاس والفضة وغيرهما وجلاؤه بالذكر، فإنه يجلوه حتى يدعه كالمرآة البيضاء فإذا ترك صدئ فإذا جلاه وصدأ القلب بأمرين بالغفلة والذنب وجلاؤه بشيئين بالاستغفار والذكرفمن كانت الغفلة أغلب أوقاته كان الصدأمتراكباعلى قلبه وصداه بحسب غفلته وإذاصدئ القلب لم تنطبع فيه صورالمعلوماتعلى ماهيعليه

There is no doubt that the heart becomes covered with rust, just as metal dishes, silver, and their like become rusty. So the rust of the heart is polished with dhikr (remembrance of Allāh), for dhikr polishes the heart until it becomes like a shiny mirror. However, when dhikr is abandoned, the rust returns; and when it commences then the heart again begins to be cleansed. Thus the heart becoming rusty is due to two matters: sins and neglecting remembrance of Allāh. Likewise, it is cleansed and polished by two things: istighfār and dhikr.[18]

"It is known that the heart will get rusted just as copper and silver get rusted." Gold doesn't rust, but silver and copper get rusted due to oxygen in the atmosphere, and the atmosphere of the heart is the body. So the body has its own environment and atmosphere which affect the purity and cleanliness of the heart. If that environment within the body is rusted, then for sure the heart will begin to rust slowly, slowly.

As we are children, we say as the Prophet ﷺ said:

يولد الانسان على الفطرة وانما ابواه يهودانه او ينصرانه او يمجسانه

Human beings are born on Fiṭrah, innocence;
either his parents make him Jewish or Christian or Zoroastrian. [19]

Children are born on innocence, their heart is not rusted; they are born on *īmān*, as Allāh ﷻ does not create anyone except on *īmān*. So the child is clean, but when the mother gives birth she reflects her negativity and bad character onto the child as she is feeding him, or the father, or the reflection of the home is reflected on the child. So that darkness is reflected onto the child, although he didn't do anything, but his heart will be affected and he can no longer see what he was seeing when he came to *dunyā*.

---

[18] Ibn Qayyim al-Jawzīyya, al-Wābil aṣ-Ṣayyib.
[19] Muslim.

When the child comes to *dunyā*, his heart's eyes are open; he can hear and can see, because he is innocent, he has no sins. That's why they say today that the child hears the mother and can respond. So slowly while growing up in the environment around him, especially youngsters, as teenagers have many things that they discuss amongst each other that they should not, and they reflect on each other and make the heart rusted and veil the heart with that bad character and veil it with all kinds of sins and *ma'asiyya*.

So for copper and silver you need to polish it, and the way to polish the heart is you need an instrument that can polish, and it is by *dhikrullāh*. *Wa jalāuhu bi 'dh-dhikr*, "The heart's cleanliness is through *dhikrullāh*." So *dhikrullāh* will make the heart clean and back to normal, and make it like a mirror. When you are a mirror, you reflect; if I put a mirror in front of you, it reflects your picture. The heart becomes a mirror and reflects what you cannot see into the heart, because the heart is clean. So all these realities around us that we cannot see are reflected on your heart when you polish your heart with *dhikrullāh*, which brings you to see the realities that you cannot see through anything else except through *dhikrullāh*.

Dhikrullāh Increases the Hidden Knowledge of Realities (Ḥaqāiq)

'Abdul-Wahhāb ash-Sha'rānī ق who was a famous scholar of Egypt one-thousand years ago, the author of *Kāshif al-Ghummah*, was asked, "What do you speak about *'Ilm aẓ-Ẓāhir* and *'Ilm al-Bāṭin*, Knowledge of Books (this one said this, this one said that, teachings of *fiqh* and so on) and Knowledge of the Hidden?"

He said, "No, there are no two kinds of knowledge, *'Ilm aẓ-Ẓāhir* or *'Ilm al-Bāṭin*, knowledge of what you see and that which is hidden, that is not true. For us everything is appearing, it is Realities. There is only one knowledge, which is the Knowledge of Realities, *Ḥaqāiq*. For us it is open, for you it is closed, you cannot see behind the wall."

Yes, of course you cannot see behind the wall, but there are some people for whom that wall is not an obstacle in front of them.

That is why the Prophet ﷺ said:

اتقوا فراسة المؤمن فإنه ينظر بنور الله

Beware the vision of the Believer,
for he sees with the light of Allāh. [20]

That is the answer. "Be aware of the piercing vision of the Believer, for surely, he looks with Allāh's Light," that means Allāh ﷻ dressed him with that Attribute that darkness becomes daylight for him. We cannot see in the dark, but he can see according to what the Prophet ﷺ said in the *ḥadīth*. So that person who has *firāsah* can see what we cannot see, can hear what we cannot hear, because he has cleaned his heart with *dhikrullāh*. So why do *shuyūkh* ask their followers to follow the *ḥadīth* of Prophet ﷺ and assign their followers *dhikrullāh*? Because it is the way of polishing the heart and will take away all kinds of sickness from you.

Abū Hurayrah ؓ narrated that the Prophet ﷺ said:

إِنَّ لِلَّهِ تِسْعَةً وَتِسْعِينَ اسْمًا مِائَةً غَيْرَ وَاحِدٍ مَنْ أَحْصَاهَا دَخَلَ الْجَنَّةَ "

Indeed Allāh has Ninety-Nine Names, one hundred less one.
Whoever counts them shall enter Paradise.[21]

"Allāh has Ninety-Nine Names, one hundred less one, and anyone who knows them or has counted them or read them will enter Paradise." That is why at *Ṣalāt al-Fajr*, after *Sūrat Yāsīn, mashaykh* encourage their students to memorize, read or count all these Ninety-Nine Beautiful Names and Attributes of Allāh, because it will make you enter Paradise. And (in the continuation of the above *ḥadīth*) the Prophet ﷺ began mentioning these Names: *Hūwa-Llāhu 'l-ladhī lā ilāha illā Hūwa ar-Raḥmān, ar-Raḥīm, al-Mālik, al-Quddūs, as-Salām*...up to the end, *aṣ-Ṣabūr*.

هُوَ اللهُ الَّذِي لاَ إِلَهَ إِلاَّ هُوَ الرَّحْمَنُ الرَّحِيمُ الْمَلِكُ الْقُدُّوسُ السَّلاَمُ الْمُؤْمِنُ الْمُهَيْمِنُ الْعَزِيزُ
الْجَبَّارُ الْمُتَكَبِّرُ الْخَالِقُ الْبَارِئُ الْمُصَوِّرُ الْغَفَّارُ الْقَهَّارُ الْوَهَّابُ الرَّزَّاقُ الْفَتَّاحُ الْعَلِيمُ الْقَابِضُ
الْبَاسِطُ الْخَافِضُ الرَّافِعُ الْمُعِزُّ الْمُذِلُّ السَّمِيعُ الْبَصِيرُ الْحَكَمُ الْعَدْلُ اللَّطِيفُ الْخَبِيرُ الْحَلِيمُ

[20] Tirmidhī.
[21] Tirmidhī.

الْعَظِيمُ الْغَفُورُ الشَّكُورُ الْعَلِيُّ الْكَبِيرُ الْحَفِيظُ الْمُقِيتُ الْحَسِيبُ الْجَلِيلُ الْكَرِيمُ الرَّقِيبُ الْمُجِيبُ
الْوَاسِعُ الْحَكِيمُ الْوَدُودُ الْمَجِيدُ الْبَاعِثُ الشَّهِيدُ الْحَقُّ الْوَكِيلُ الْقَوِيُّ الْمَتِينُ الْوَلِيُّ الْحَمِيدُ
الْمُحْصِي الْمُبْدِئُ الْمُعِيدُ الْمُحْيِي الْمُمِيتُ الْحَيُّ الْقَيُّومُ الْوَاجِدُ الْمَاجِدُ الْوَاحِدُ الصَّمَدُ الْقَادِرُ
الْمُقْتَدِرُ الْمُقَدِّمُ الْمُؤَخِّرُ الأَوَّلُ الآخِرُ الظَّاهِرُ الْبَاطِنُ الْوَالِي الْمُتَعَالِي الْبَرُّ التَّوَّابُ الْمُنْتَقِمُ الْعَفُوُّ
الرَّءُوفُ مَالِكُ الْمُلْكِ ذُو الْجَلاَلِ وَالإِكْرَامِ الْمُقْسِطُ الْجَامِعُ الْغَنِيُّ الْمُغْنِي الْمَانِعُ الضَّارُّ النَّافِعُ
النُّورُ الْهَادِي الْبَدِيعُ الْبَاقِي الْوَارِثُ الرَّشِيدُ الصَّبُورُ

Hūwa-Llāhu 'l-ladhī lā ilāha illā Hūwa ar-Raḥmānu 'r-Raḥīmu 'l-Māliku 'l-Quddūsu 's-Salāmu 'l-Mu'minu 'l-Muhayminu 'l-ʿAzīzu 'l-Jabbāru 'l-Mutakabbiru 'l-Khāliqu 'l-Bāri'u 'l-Muṣawwiru 'l-Ghaffāru 'l-Qahhāru 'l-Wahhābu 'r-Razzāqu 'l-Fattāḥu 'l-ʿAlīmu 'l-Qābiḍu 'l-Bāsiṭu 'l-Khāfiḍu 'r-Rāfiʿu 'l-Muʿizzu 'l-Mudhillu 's-Samīʿu 'l-Baṣīru 'l-Ḥakamu 'l-ʿAdlu 'l-Laṭīfu 'l-Khabīru 'l-Ḥalīmu 'l-ʿAẓīmu 'l-Ghafūru 'ash-Shakūru 'l-ʿAlīyyu 'l-Kabīru 'l-Ḥafiẓu 'l-Muqītu 'l-Ḥasību 'l-Jalīlu 'l-Karīmu 'r-Raqību 'l-Mujību 'l-Wāsiʿu 'l-Ḥakīmu 'l-Wadūdu 'l-Majīdu 'l-Bāʿithu 'sh-Shahīdu 'l-Ḥaqqu 'l-Wakīlu 'l-Qawīyyu 'l-Matīnu 'l-Walīyyu 'l-Ḥamīdu 'l-Muḥṣīyu 'l-Mubdīʿu 'l-Muḥīyyu 'l-Mumītu 'l-Ḥayyu 'l-Qayyūm. Al-Wājidu 'l-Mājidu 'l-Wāḥidu 'l-Āḥadu 'ṣ-Ṣamadu 'l-Qādiru 'l-Muqtadiru 'l-Muqaddimu 'l-Mu'akhkhiru 'l-Āwwalu 'l-Ākhiru 'ẓ-Ẓāhiru 'l-Bāṭinu 'l-Wāli 'l-Mutaʿālu 'l-Barru 't-Tawwābu 'l-Muntaqimu 'l-ʿAfūwwu 'r-Ra'ūf, Māliku 'l-mulki Dha 'l-Jalāli wa 'l-Ikrām. Al-Muqsiṭu 'l-Jāmiʿu 'l-Ghanīyyu 'l-Mughnīyyu 'l-Muʿtīyu 'l-Māniʿu 'ḍ-Ḍārru 'n-Nāfiʿu 'n-Nūr.[22]

قال الإمام البيهقي: باب بيان أن لله جل ثناؤه أسماء أخرى، وليس في قول النبي صلى الله عليه وسلم: لله تسعة وتسعون اسماً نفي غيرها

Imam Bayhaqī said, "He didn't say, 'Allāh has only Ninety-nine Names and the other Names are non-existent.'"

ونقل ابن بطال عن القاضي أبي بكر بن الطيب قال: ليس في الحديث دليل على أنه ليس لله من الأسماء إلا هذه العدة، وإنما معنى الحديث أن من أحصاها دخل الجنة، ويدل على عدم الحصر أن أكثرها صفات وصفات الله لا تتناهى

He said, 'The more known Names are these Ninety-Nine, but Allāh ﷻ has infinite Names: *wa man aḥṣāhā dakhal al-jannah*, who counted them and memorized them, who undertook as a principle for himself to take from each name a wisdom shall enter Paradise.'" From every Name there is a

[22] Tirmidhī.

meaning, not just one meaning, but according to scholars there are infinite number of meanings in each name, many different types of description of these Names, depending on the environment. If we say, *"as-Salām,"* many things come under that Name, it is not only one thing. Same as if you say, *"al-Ghaffār," "al-Muṣawwir," "Al-Khāliq," "al-Mutakabbir."* Like *"al-Khāliq,"* every moment He is creating, Creation cannot stop. If you say, "He created, then stopped," it doesn't befit Allāh's Greatness.

So rusting of the heart mainly comes from one major issue: the sins we do by *ghaflah,* heedlessness. When your heart is heedless Shayṭān quickly attacks and enters in order to rust your heart. So slowly, slowly, it is rusting and veiling and the heart becomes blind; the heart does not have the light it had when you were born. Like you come as an innocent, pure child with that light; there is a 'pilot light' in your heart, it is always there: *yūlidu 'l-insānu ʿalā 'l-fiṭra,* "Human beings are born on innocence." *Fiṭra* is a pilot light that never disappears, but what happens? We are veiling it slowly, slowly. That's why our heart becomes blind, our eyes become blind and we cannot see the Truth anymore, but if we polish it, it will become like a mirror; it will take all the information and it will be reflected on the mirror.

Like in the old Persian time, the king made a competition between two big artists and he said, "The one who will draw the best artwork will get this and this and this rewards from me." The one on the right side had a huge wall to draw on it and the one on the left side also had a huge wall to draw on it, and he gave them each six months to do it. One of them was drawing, drawing very nicely, working hard, and the other one was working very hard in scrubbing, polishing, polishing the wall, and between them was a curtain, they could not see each other.

And the sultan came when time had arrived, and said, "Show me your work."

He said, "Let the one on the left show you first, I will show you after."

So they opened the curtain and he was showing the sultan, then he finished looking and turned and saw the same artwork reflected on the other wall from the other one. This one was tired working day and night, and this one was clever, polishing the wall to become a mirror. So in the mirror it reflected and the sultan didn't know what to do, both of them the same artwork, the same design, the same nice artwork. So he gave them both rewards. The one who worked hard had a nice picture, and the one who didn't work hard, it was reflected on the mirror by polishing the wall. So polishing the heart will reflect all kind of Realities, there is no obstacle in front of the heart, there is nothing more to block the Vision of Realities.

Allāh Appoints Special Angels to Attend Circles of Dhikr

Ibn Qayyim said:

وإذا صدئ القلب لم تنطبع في صور المعلومات على ما هي عليه

When the heart becomes dark from too much rust, then it is impossible for that information that appears from realities around us that we cannot see; it will not appear in that heart because it's rusted, so we need to clean our heart.

The Prophet ﷺ said, "When the heart is clean angels will come and sit with you." They will not run away because you smell like the smell of Paradise, and you are mentioning *dhikrullāh* with Allāh's Beautiful Names and Attributes, and you polish your heart. Even if you did not polish it completely, even if you polish a little bit and there is a little light appearing from it, angels are attracted to that.

It is said that Abū Hurayrah ؓ and Abū Saʿīd ؓ bore witness that the Prophet ﷺ said:

لا يقعد قوم يذكرون الله عز وجل إلا حفتهم الملائكة، وغشيتهم الرحمة ونزلت عليهم السكينة، وذكرهم الله فيمن عنده

No people sit in a gathering remembering Allāh, but the angels surround them, mercy covers them, tranquility descends upon them and Allāh remembers them before those who are with Him.[23]

Lā yaqʿudu qawmun yadhkurūna 'Llāha illa ḥaffatumu 'l-malā'ikah, "No group of people sit to mention Allāh ﷻ except the angels surround them." *"Haffathum"* has two meanings: surrounding or rubbing. Sometimes you feel goose bumps suddenly, that is caused by an angel's touch when you are listening to Allāh's Words. So we can translate it as "angels touch them and they feel goose bumps." So angels will encompass them or rub them, and *ghashyatuhum ar-raḥmāh,* "mercy will overtake them," *Raḥmātullāh* will be

[23] Muslim.

there and when someone has *raḥmah* and it dressed him, he becomes like Sayyīdinā Khidr ﷺ:

فَوَجَدَا عَبْدًا مِّنْ عِبَادِنَا آتَيْنَاهُ رَحْمَةً مِنْ عِندِنَا وَعَلَّمْنَاهُ مِن لَّدُنَّا عِلْمًا

So they found one of Our Servants, on whom We had bestowed Mercy from Ourselves and whom We had taught knowledge from Our Own Presence.[24]

Sayyīdinā Mūsā ﷺ was looking for *maʿarifah* and Allāh ﷻ sent him to Sayyīdinā Khidr ﷺ to learn, to take wisdom from Sayyīdinā Khidr ﷺ. "We found a servant who was dressed with *raḥmāh,* mercy," like here *ghashiyatuhum ar-raḥmāh,* "angels will be with you and *raḥmāh* will dress you." So when *raḥmāh* dresses you, then *wa ʿallamnāhu min ladunnā ʿilma,* "We taught him from Heavenly knowledge," He will teach you from Heavenly knowledge just as He taught Sayyīdinā Khidr ﷺ from Heavenly knowledge.

Here the angels will be with you and dress you, *wa nazalat ʿalayhim as-sakīnah,* "and tranquility will descend on them." So it means tranquility is a kind of stillness, let us say how clouds come: sometimes it is high, sometimes it is coming down. So it means here it is descending from Heavens, that stillness, that tranquility, in order to take them inside and take them up with it. So when you are doing *dhikrullāh,* you are not sitting where you are sitting, but they take you somewhere else, to Paradise; you turn the place you are sitting into a Paradise.

إِذَا مَرَرْتُمْ بِرِيَاضِ الْجَنَّةِ فَارْتَعُوا " . قَالَ وَمَا رِيَاضُ الْجَنَّةِ قَالَ " حِلَقُ الذِّكْرِ

The Prophet ﷺ said, "When you pass by the gardens of Paradise, then feast."
They said, "And what are the gardens of Paradise?"
He said, "The circles of remembrance[25]

The Prophet ﷺ said, "When you pass places of Paradise, sit there." They asked him, *wa mā hīya rīyāḍu 'l-jannah,* "What are these gardens of Paradise?" He ﷺ said, *majālis adh-dhikr,* "The circles of *dhikr,*" places where people are making *dhikrullāh.* So when angels come to you and dress you

---

[24] Sūrat al-Kahf, 18:65.
[25] Tirmidhī.

with the *raḥmāh* that Allāh ﷻ sends on you, *wa nazalat as-sakīna,* and this peacefulness, this tranquility dresses them, *wa dhakkarahumullāh fī man ʿindahu,* when all this process occurs—first the angels come, second *raḥmātullāh,* mercy will cover you—and at that time you can carry that tranquility that comes from Heaven as now you are ready, pure. Then, *wa dhakkarahumullāh fī man ʿindahu,* "Allāh ﷻ will mention you in front of whoever is in Allāh's Presence." What kind of presence Allāh knows, but we can say, *Allāhu fī man ʿindallāhu,* "You will be mentioned to whom He has in His Presence." Those who remember Allāh standing, sitting or laying down, meaning, when you are standing or walking, going to work, or sitting when you are at home resting, and all those times you are remembering Allāh ﷻ.

Prophet ﷺ Said Dhikrullāh is the Best of Deeds

عن عبد الله بن بشر أن رجلا قال : يا رسول الله إن أبواب الخير كثيرة ولا أستطيع القيام بكلها فأخبرني بما شئت أتشبث به ولا تكثر علي فأنسى وفي رواية : أن شرائع الإسلام قد كثرت علي وأنا كبرت فأخبرني بشئ أتشبث به قال : لا يزال لسانك رطبا بذكر الله تعالى

It is narrated by ʿAbdullāh bin Bishr ؓ that a person came to the Prophet ﷺ and said, "O Prophet! The ways of favors are too many. Tell me something easy and don't give me too much, because I will forget." The Prophet ﷺ said, "Keep your tongue wet with dhikrullāh." [26]

In this *ḥadīth* the man is saying, "O Prophet! There are too many doors of good deeds to do: do this, do this, do this and you enter Paradise. Give me something simple." It means, "I am not a scholar with mind to do too much, I am a Bedouin from the desert."]

He put these conditions for the Prophet ﷺ, but it is for us, *raḥmāh* for us in this time! If ʿAbdullāh bin Bishr ؓ hadn't said that, it would not have reached us. Look at the mercy of Prophet ﷺ that Allāh has given to him! When you are speaking to a president you design every word you want to say. So look how humble the Prophet ﷺ is to give such answers; he was entering and asking, "*Yā Rasūlullāh*! There are too many doors of goodness, give me something easy, because I forget all of them the next day. Don't

---

[26] Ṣaḥiḥ at-Tirmidhī.

give me too much, give me something that I can hold on to." The Prophet ﷺ said, "Keep your tongue wet with *dhikrullāh.*"

وفي رواية : أن شرائع الإسلام قد كثرت علي وأنا كبرت فأخبرني بشئ أتشبث به قال : لا يزال لسانك رطبا بذكر الله تعالى.

In another narration, "The conditions and principles of Islam are too many, give me something easy that I can hold onto as I am an old man now and I forget easily." The Prophet ﷺ said, "Keep your tongue wet with *dhikrullāh.*"

Silence here is for a private person. "Keep your tongue wet with *dhikrullāh*" means you are by yourself doing your *dhikr,* which gives us an idea that this person is doing *dhikrullāh* not *jahran,* out loud, but *qalban aw sirran,* hidden *dhikr* within himself, in order to clean himself. When the *mashaykh* give you to recite different *dhikrs,* you are by yourself, so it will be a *dhikr khafī,* hidden *dhikr.*

The Prophet ﷺ said:

يد الله مع الجماعة

Allāh's Hand is with the group of people.[27]

يد الله على الجماعة

Allāh's Hand is over the group of people. [28]

So the rewards are multiplied in *jama'ah,* as the prayer in *jama'ah* is 27 times better than without *jama'ah,* so similarly, the *dhikr* in *jama'ah* is 27 times better than *dhikr* by oneself, it's reward is 27 times more. That shows us that there is *dhikr* which is loud and *dhikr* which is hidden. When you do *dhikrullāh* by yourself, that is hidden. Although sometimes you may raise your voice for yourself to hear, it is still hidden from others as no one knows you are doing *dhikrullāh,* but the other one is when you sit with people it gives you an understanding that it is loud *dhikr* because everyone can hear each other.

---

[27] Tirmidhī.
[28] Ṭabarānī.

Also mentioned in <u>Tirmidhī</u> and many other *aḥādīth* in different ways, that the Prophet ﷺ was asked:

أَنَّ رَسُولَ اللَّهِ صلى الله عليه وسلم سُئِلَ أَيُّ الْعِبَادِ أَفْضَلُ دَرَجَةً عِنْدَ اللَّهِ يَوْمَ الْقِيَامَةِ قَالَ " الذَّاكِرُونَ اللَّهَ كَثِيرًا وَالذَّاكِرَاتُ " . قُلْتُ يَا رَسُولَ اللَّهِ وَمِنَ الْغَازِي فِي سَبِيلِ اللَّهِ قَالَ " لَوْ ضَرَبَ بِسَيْفِهِ فِي الْكُفَّارِ وَالْمُشْرِكِينَ حَتَّى يَنْكَسِرَ وَيَخْتَضِبَ دَمًا لَكَانَ الذَّاكِرُونَ اللَّهَ كَثِيرًا أَفْضَلَ مِنْهُ دَرَجَةً " .

> "Which of the worshippers is superior in rank with Allāh on the Day of Judgment?" He said, "Those men and women who remember Allāh much." I said, "O Messenger of Allāh! What about the fighter in the cause of Allāh?" He said, "If he were to strike with his sword among the disbelievers and the idolater, until it breaks, and he (or it) is dyed with blood, those who remember Allāh much would still be superior in rank."[29]

Ayyu 'l-'ibādi afḍalu darajatan 'inda 'Llāhi yawma 'l-qiyāmah, "Who are the people who are best and higher on the Day of Judgment?" He said, *adh-dhākirūna 'Llāha kathīrā*, "Those who remember or mention Allāh ﷻ too much in their coming and going and sitting," as Allāh said in Holy Qur'ān:

الَّذِينَ يَذْكُرُونَ اللَّهَ قِيَامًا وَقُعُودًا وَعَلَىٰ جُنُوبِهِمْ

> Those who remember Allāh (always, and in prayers) standing, sitting and lying down on their sides.[30]

"Standing" is when you are walking, which means going to work. "Sitting" is when you are at home resting, lying down or when you are sleeping. All these times when you are remembering Allāh ﷻ, "those are the people who are the high-level people, the best of the people." They asked, *yā Rasūlullāh wa min al-ghāzī fī sabīli 'Llāhi*, "Even the one going for jihad?" and the Prophet ﷺ said, *law ḍaraba bi ṣayfihi fī 'l-kuffāri wa al-mushrikīna ḥattā yankaṣira yakhtadiba daman kāna 'dh-dhākirūna 'Llāha kathīran afḍala minhu darajah*, "Even if he were to fight the unbelievers and broke his sword in fighting, killing to defend his people, even that person hitting right and left and saving his people from *mushrikīn* (their enemy) until his sword is broken," means he fought a lot and struggled a lot to defend his people,

---

[29] Tirmidhī.
[30] Sūrat Āli 'Imrān, 3:191.

"still the one who is doing *dhikrullāh* is better to Allāh ﷻ." This is showing us how much *dhikrullāh* is important in our life!

Who Remembers Allāh is Alive and Who does not is Dead

This is mentioned in *al-Bukhārī*, comparing the one who remembered Allāh ﷻ.

مَثَلُ الَّذِي يَذْكُرُ رَبَّهُ وَالَّذِي لاَ يَذْكُرُ مَثَلُ الْحَيِّ وَالْمَيِّتِ

Abū Mūsā al-Ashaʿari ؓ related from the Prophet ﷺ: The example of the one who celebrates the Praises of his Lord in comparison to the one who does not celebrate the Praises of his Lord, is that of a living creature compared to a dead one.[31]

The one who remembered Allāh ﷻ and mentioned Him through His Beautiful Names and Attributes versus the one who does not, is like someone who is alive and someone who is dead. Look how big is the difference. That means those who make *dhikrullāh*, their minds and hearts are alive. *Yandhurūna bi nūrillāh*, "They look around them with Allāh's Light." It's like the one who is alive and the one who is dead.

And we will mention this *ḥadīth* and stop.

عن أَبَا هُرَيْرَةَ ، يَقُولُ : قَالَ رَسُولُ اللهِ صَلَّى اللهُ عَلَيْهِ وَسَلَّمَ : " قَالَ اللهُ عَزَّ وَجَلَّ : أَنَا عِنْدَ ظَنِّ عَبْدِي بِي وَأَنَا مَعَهُ حِينَ يَذْكُرُنِي ، إِنْ ذَكَرَنِي فِي نَفْسِهِ ذَكَرْتُهُ فِي نَفْسِي ، وَإِنْ ذَكَرَنِي فِي مَلَإٍ ذَكَرْتُهُ فِي مَلَإٍ خَيْرٍ مِنْهُمْ ، وَمَنْ تَقَرَّبَ إِلَيَّ شِبْرًا تَقَرَّبْتُ إِلَيْهِ ذِرَاعًا ، وَمَنْ تَقَرَّبَ إِلَيَّ ذِرَاعًا تَقَرَّبْتُ إِلَيْهِ بَاعًا ، وَمَنْ جَاءَنِي يَمْشِي جِئْتُهُ مُهَرْوِلًا . "

From Abū Hurayrah that the Prophet ﷺ said, Allāh the Praised and Glorified said: "I am as My servant thinks I am. I am with him when he mentions Me. If he mentions Me to himself, I mention him to Myself, and if he mentions Me in an assembly, I mention him in an assembly better than it, and if he draws near to Me a hand's span, I draw near to him an arm's length, and if he draws near to Me an arm's length, I draw near to him a fathom's length, and if he comes to Me walking, I go to him running!"[32]

---

[31] Bukhārī.

[32] Ḥadīth Qudsī .

Yaqūl Allāhu ʿazza wa jalla anā ʿinda dhanna ʿabdī bī, Allāh says, "I am according to My servant's thinking about Me." That means, "If he thinks good of Me and remembers Me, than I will be happy with him and give him everything and open My Treasures to him, open My Light to him and open My Realities and give him what he wants." *Anā maʿahu ḥīna dhakaranī,* "and I am with him when he remembers Me." *in dhakaranī fī nafsihi dhakartahu fī nafsī,* "If he remembers me in his heart, I remember him through My Presence." *wa in dhakaranī fī malā'in dhakartahu fī malā'in khayran minhum,* "If he remembers Me in a group, then I mention him in a group/gathering that is Mine." Allāh's gatherings, who are in these gatherings?

Fī malā'in khayran minhum, "In a group better than his group." What kind of group? It might be a group that is in front of the Prophet ﷺ or angels, *yatabahā bī ʿabdī,* where Allāh ﷻ boasts and shows off His servant, He is happy with His servant and He mentioned him to His Prophet ﷺ, because the Prophet ﷺ is always standing at the Divine Presence. Allāh ﷻ will be happy, saying, "Look, *yā* Muḥammad, your *Ummah*! The one who is believing in you, believing in the Message of Islam. Look how much I bring him up when he remembers Me. I remember him in a nice presence, your presence or the presence of angels." Allāh knows what kind of presence; we don't know, we are guessing. To guess good is good, *ḥusna 'dh-dhann,* always keep good thoughts about Allāh ﷻ that He is The Forgiver, He will forgive us and bless us.

Wa in taqarraba ilayya shibran taqarrabtu ilayhi dhirāʿan, "If My servant comes to me one hand, I will approach him one arm." Allāh ﷻ is saying, "Approach Me by one hand, I will approach you by one arm," meaning, "Do something small, I will give you something bigger."

Wa in taqarraba ilayya dhirāʿan taqarrabtu ilayhi bāʿan, "If he approaches Me one arm, I approach him more than one meter or one yard."

Wa man jā'anī yamshī ji'tuhu muharwalan, "If he comes to me walking, I will go to him running." Does Allāh ﷻ run? No. Allāh ﷻ is Allāh ﷻ. It means, "If you are first in coming one hand, I will come one arm, giving you more; if you come one arm, I will come with a full extended arm; if you come walking to Me, (i.e. showing more interest), I will come to you running." When He comes running, it means He is sending you the manifestations of His Beautiful Names and Attributes, He is sending you knowledge that you never expect. That is why *awlīyāullāh* or scholars say, "Our duty as servants of Allāh ﷻ and followers of Prophet ﷺ is *ittiba'*, to follow." This is where the *āyah* comes:

قُلْ إِن كُنتُمْ تُحِبُّونَ اللهَ فَاتَّبِعُونِي يُحْبِبْكُمُ اللهُ وَيَغْفِرْ لَكُمْ ذُنُوبَكُمْ وَاللهُ غَفُورٌ رَّحِيمٌ

Say (O Muḥammad), "If you (really) love Allāh, then follow me! Allāh will love you and forgive your sins, and Allāh is Oft-Forgiving, Most Merciful.[33]

"Say to them, *yā* Muḥammad, that if they really love Allāh let them follow you, I will love them." If you follow Muḥammad ﷺ, Allāh ﷻ will love you. When He loves us, it means He comes *muharwala*, running, as the *ḥadīth* mentioned. So it means He will dress you, He will make you...our duty is to follow. Now if we get it or we don't, that is not our job and we must not think about it, because our duty is to remember Allāh ﷻ all the time and follow, to go on the highway, *aṣ-Ṣirāṭ al-Mustaqīm*, following the Prophet ﷺ. *Al-ittiba'* is very important, to go following the Prophet ﷺ. It might be that you go one hand and Allāh ﷻ will give you a full arm, but show interest, show eagerness, don't be lazy! We are lazy! One day we do, one day we don't do. It means one hour we do and one hour we don't; we remember Allāh ﷻ one moment and we forget the next. No, keep running, don't stop. Allāh ﷻ will take you, because He comes running to you, and that means the distance gets shorter and shorter in reaching to where Allāh ﷻ wants you to reach.

May Allāh forgive us and may Allāh bless us.

Wa min Allāhi 't-tawfiq, bi ḥurmati 'l-ḥabīb, bi ḥurmati 'l-Fātiḥah.
And with Allāh is success. For the sake of the Beloved, for his sake we recite the opening chapter of Holy Qur'ān.

[33] Sūrat Āli-'Imrān, 3:31.

Rust of the Heart

Aʿūdhu billāhi min ash-Shayṭāni 'r-rajīm. Bismillāhi' r-Raḥmāni 'r-Raḥīm.
Nawaytu 'l-arbāʿīn, nawaytu 'l-ʿitikāf, nawaytu 'l-khalwah, nawaytu 'l-ʿuzlah,
nawaytu 'r-riyāḍa, nawaytu 's-sulūk, lillāhi Taʿalā fī hādhā 'l-masjid.
Atīʿūllāha wa atīʿū 'r-Rasūla wa ūli 'l-amri minkum. (4:59)

As-salāmu ʿalaykum wa raḥmatullāhi wa barakātuh. Inshā-Allāh we continue about *dhikrullāh* and the benefit of *dhikrullāh*. From the most things that punish the heart is for the heart to get rusted and rusted from the effect of Shayṭān on the heart. Like how copper rusts, also the heart rusts and it will be layer over layer over layer of darkness. It is very difficult to do *ʿibādah* pure to Allāh ﷻ when the heart is completely dominated by veils of darkness, one veil over the other veil that Shayṭān puts on the heart when he is going in and going out. Every moment that he sees us heedless, he enters and throws in our heart some gossips and dirt that are not correct, to make us listen to him and not to Allāh ﷻ, and all this comes from heedlessness, when you are heedless of remembering Allāh ﷻ. When you are in *ghaflah*, heedlessness, it is easy for Shayṭān to enter.

Allāh Defines the Heedless as Those Who Abandon Dhikrullāh

Allāh mentioned in Holy Qur'an a verse that is warning you, and all of us, to be careful. Allāh said to the Prophet ﷺ:

وَاصْبِرْ نَفْسَكَ مَعَ الَّذِينَ يَدْعُونَ رَبَّهُم بِالْغَدَاةِ وَالْعَشِيِّ يُرِيدُونَ وَجْهَهُ وَلَا تَعْدُ عَيْنَاكَ عَنْهُمْ
تُرِيدُ زِينَةَ الْحَيَاةِ الدُّنْيَا وَلَا تُطِعْ مَنْ أَغْفَلْنَا قَلْبَهُ عَن ذِكْرِنَا وَاتَّبَعَ هَوَاهُ وَكَانَ أَمْرُهُ فُرُطًا

And keep yourself patient (by being) with those who call upon their Lord in the morning and the evening, seeking His Countenance. And let not your eyes pass beyond them, desiring adornments of the worldly life, and do not obey one whose heart We have made heedless of Our remembrance and who follows his desire and whose affair is ever (in) neglect.[34]

"O Muḥammad ﷺ, don't obey…" means to us mainly. The Prophet ﷺ is receiving the Revelation, but Allāh is giving the examples for us to

[34] Sūrat al-Kahf, 18:28.

understand through Prophet ﷺ. "Don't obey those heedless ones because they are worth nothing." People who are heedless are so immersed in all kinds of *fitna* and confusion, and the Prophet ﷺ said:

الفتنه نائمه لعن الله من ايقضها

Fitna is dormant and Allāh cursed the one who awoke it.

Through heedlessness you wake up the *fitna,* because in that moment you forget Allāh ﷻ and instead you remember Shayṭān, Satan, and are listening to what he whispers to you. So that heedlessness is the major...it is like putting a seed and watering it, and later it becomes a tree. So heedlessness is like a seed planted in the heart; every time he comes and waters it and it begins to grow and grow and takes over all the heart with all its branches. That is why the Prophet ﷺ said:

انما بعثت لاتمم مكارم الاخلاق

I have been sent to perfect the best of conduct (your behavior and character).[35]

"I have been sent to complete and perfect the character of human beings," because when we fix the character we reach the level of chasing Shayṭān away from our heart, because at that time we know what is correct and what is not correct and we are keeping Allāh ﷻ in the heart. So heedlessness, *ghaflah,* and bad desires, the combination of the two, *yaṭmisa nūr al-qalb,* will extinguish and compress the light of the heart. Finished! That heart is 'dead' before it dies, that heart is completely gone. That's why you become so involved in *dunyā* and don't remember anything from *Ākhirah.* That is why you see many people don't pray, and as the Prophet ﷺ mentioned and we mentioned in the Chapter of *Ṣalāt,* that *ṣalāt* is the pillar of the religion:

الصلاةُ عمودُ الدين

Prayer is the pillar of the religion.[36]

---

[35] Bazzār.
[36] Bayhaqī.

Darkness Dwells in the Heedless Heart and Leads to Unbelief

And what is between heedlessness, *kufr*, unbelief, and *īmān*, faith, is to drop the prayers:

بَيْنَ الْكُفْرِ وَالإِيمَانِ تَرْكُ الصَّلَاةِ

What is between disbelief and belief is the leaving of prayers.[37]

So when the heart becomes dark by not letting Allāh ﷻ send inspirations to your heart, as you let Shayṭān send whispers, you become heedless and you follow your bad desires, and your heart becomes darkened and darkened, until the heart is completely under the control of Shayṭān.

So Allāh ﷻ is saying, *wa lā tuṭiʿ man aghfalnā qalbahu,* "Don't obey those whose hearts have become heedless." From what do they become heedless? *ʿAn dhikrinā,* "from Our remembrance," because He mentioned *dhikr* there. So if anyone is heedless of *dhikrullāh,* don't obey that person, don't listen to that person, run away from that person who follows his desires. So the Holy Qur'an is saying *"aghfalnā"* and *"hawā,"* where *ghaflah* is heedlessness and *hawā* is bad desires. So those who have bad desires and *ghaflah,* heedlessness in their hearts, you cannot listen to them and you cannot obey them. Today, unfortunately we are lost because there are too many different parties or groups that people are lost between them, but to bring you back is to remember Allāh ﷻ. Allāh doesn't want anything from us except to remember Him! He ﷻ said:

أَنَا جَلِيسُ مَنْ ذَكَرَنِي

I sit with him who remembers Me.[38]

"I am sitting," means, "I am with the one who remembers Me." When we remember Him, He is with us and when we don't remember, He is away from us. Who is with us when we don't remember, when we are heedless? Shayṭān. So you have a mind to choose: do you choose to be with Allāh ﷻ, with Prophet ﷺ, *awlīyā* and *ʿulamā,* or you want to be with Shayṭān? It's in

---

[37] Tirmidhī.
[3838] Aḥmad, Bayhaqī.

your hands, it's included in freedom of religion. Which do you want? You want Islam, you want *īmān*? Okay, then you are saved. You want something else? We don't know, but it's in Allāh's Hands, Allāh ﷻ will judge people.

So He said, *wa lā tuṭiʿ man aghfalnā qalbahu ʿan dhikrinā,* "Don't obey those who are heedless of *dhikrullāh,*" *w 'attabaʿa hawāhu,* "and follows his desires," *wa kāna amruhu furuṭā,* "his matters, his business is going to lose, he is going to be losing." *Lā tuṭiʿ*, "Don't listen to him, don't obey him; he will never take your hand and succeed!"

So always, when you look at someone who has a shaykh or guide, or if you don't have a guide and you are looking for a guide to teach you, look for one because you are not coming from the womb of the mother knowledgeable. They study and go to university, it takes at least twenty-five years to become a master, and to become a professor add ten years, or an assistant professor add three or four years. To study and become an intellectual in your major and to know what to teach takes from you twenty-five years of your life. Today studying in schools up to university is one-third of your life. If this is for *dunyā* knowledge, what about for *Ākhirah* knowledge? If for *dunyā,* we have how many professors every semester? Count! After high school, how many professors for O Level or A Level, how many semesters in university? Every time two or three semesters a year, and every time you take three or four courses and every course is three credits. Four courses means four professors every semester, two semesters, ten professors, approximately with summer. For one year you put ten professors. For *dunyā* you put ten professors, but for Eternal Life, for *Ākhirah,* to have someone to guide us to remember Allāh ﷻ they don't accept even one, they say, "Don't follow *shuyūkh*, don't follow *awlīyāullāh*! Who are these *awlīyāullāh*? Where is this *awlīyā*?"

Allāh ﷻ mentioned in the Holy Qur'ān:

أَلا إِنَّ أَوْلِيَاء اللهِ لاَ خَوْفٌ عَلَيْهِمْ وَلاَ هُمْ يَحْزَنُونَ الَّذِينَ آمَنُواْ وَكَانُواْ يَتَّقُونَ

Behold! Verily, on the Friends of Allāh there is no fear, nor shall they grieve; they who have attained faith and have always been conscious of Him.[39]

[39] Sūrah Yunus, 10:62-63.

He ﷻ put a condition that *awlīyā* will not have to fear anything or be sad in anything: *alladhīnā āmanū*, "Those who believed! Even if you are a *mu'min* or you are a *walī*, you have to have good belief." *Lā khawfun ʿalayhim*, "For those *awlīyāullāh*, there is nothing to make them fear." *Alladhīna āmanū wa kānū yattaqūn,* "Those who believed and they have *taqwā*." Those who believed, the Believer is the one who remembers his Creator. What is a Believer? The definition, a small definition of a Believer, is one who says, "*Lā ilāha illa-Llāh Muḥammadun Rasūlullāh,*" one who remembers Allāh ﷻ is the Creator and we are His servants.

Ibn Qayyim states:

أن الله سبحانه وتعالى نهى عن طاعة من جمع هذه الصفات

Surely, Allāh has forbidden to follow one with the following attributes: isrāf, wastefulness and heedlessness.

So you have to look: if he is heedless and follows his desires and did not make *dhikr, kāna amruhu furuṭā,* means his matters or his way is all in *dayaʿ*, faded or lost, completely lost! You are not going in the right direction anymore, you exited from *Sirātu 'l-Mustaqīm*, so you have to come quickly back. How to come back? By *dhikrullāh*!

عَنْ أَبِي هُرَيْرَةَ، قَالَ كَانَ رَسُولُ اللَّهِ صلى الله عليه وسلم يَسِيرُ فِي طَرِيقِ مَكَّةَ فَمَرَّ عَلَى جَبَلٍ يُقَالُ لَهُ جُمْدَانُ فَقَالَ " سِيرُوا هَذَا جُمْدَانُ سَبَقَ الْمُفَرِّدُونَ". قَالُوا وَمَا الْمُفَرِّدُونَ يَا رَسُولَ اللَّهِ قَالَ " الذَّاكِرُونَ اللَّهَ كَثِيرًا وَالذَّاكِرَاتُ " .

Abū Hurayrah ؓ reported that Allāh's Messenger ﷺ was travelling along the path leading to Mecca that he happened to pass by a mountain called Jumdān. He said (to his Companions), "Move on, it is Jumdan, it has overtaken the Mufarridūn."
They said, "O Allāh's Messenger! Who are Mufarridūn?"
He said, "They are those males and females who remember Allāh much." [40]

Kāna Rasūlullāh ﷺ yasīru fī ṭarīqi Mecca, "The Prophet ﷺ was walking on his journey on the way to Mecca," *fa marra ʿalā jabalin yuqālu lahu jumdān,* "and he passed by a mountain called *'al-Jumdān'* (or *'Jamdān'*). *Fa qāla sīrū hādhā jumdān sabaqa 'l-mufarridūn,* "Quickly move! This mountain has

[40] Related by Abū Hurayrah in *Ṣaḥiḥ Muslim.*

overpassed the *Mufarridūn.*" They said, "Who are the *Mufarridūn, yā Rasūlullāh*?" He said, *adh-dhākirūna 'Llāha kathīran wa 'dh-dhākirāt,* "Those who do *dhikr,* men and women."

Who are the *Mufarridūn* and how did the mountain overpass them, was it walking? They were walking, the mountain is firm in its place. How was it able to overcome everyone, although they were walking quickly?

He ﷺ said to the *Ṣaḥābah* ؓ, *sīrū,* "Move quickly, that mountain has overpassed all of you!" They said, "How?" He said, "By *dhikrullāh.*"

O People! It means the mountain is doing *dhikr*! If the mountain is doing *dhikr,* then what about us? If the mountain is doing *dhikr,* is it not out of wisdom to do more *dhikrullāh* than the mountain? *Dhikrullāh,* that mountain has overcome everyone because he is doing *dhikr* more than anyone, by Prophet ﷺ mentioning the *āyah, "adh-dhākirūna 'Llāha kathīran."* He said *"kathīran,"* the *Mufarridūn* are those who remember Allāh ﷻ too much. It means that mountain is remembering Allāh ﷻ more than 'too much' as it overtook the *Mufarridūn,* those who make *dhikr*; he overcame and won over them. So Allāh ﷻ mentioned that in the Holy Qur'ān, "Those who remember Allāh ﷻ excessively, non-stop."

وَالذَّاكِرِينَ اللَّهَ كَثِيرًا وَالذَّاكِرَاتِ

And for men and women who engage much in Allāh's praise.[41]

Abū Hurayrah ؓ narrated that the Prophet ﷺ said:

ما من قوم يقومون من مجلس لا يذكرون الله تعالى فيه، إلا قاموا عن مثل جيفة حمار، وكان لهم حسرة.

Those people who leave a gathering in which they have not remembered Allāh will conclude it as if it has foul odor similar to that of a rotten carcass of a donkey and it will be a cause of grief to them.[42]

Any group of people sitting together and they leave without *dhikrullāh,* it is as if they have left like a donkey which died and now has a bad smell.

[41] Sūrat al-Ahzab, 33:35.
[42] Abū Dāwūd.

Any group of people sitting together and they are not making *dhikrullāh* or remembering Allāh ﷻ through the Holy Qur'an, *ḥadīth* and *dhikr* of Allāh's Beautiful Names and Attributes, they are like a donkey's carcass with its bad smell, *jīfatu ḥimār*. *Wa kāna ʿalayhim ḥasrah*, "and they are going to be too sorry on the Day of Judgment that they didn't sit in an association and do *dhikrullāh*."

وذكر عن معاذ بن جبل يرفعه أيضا : ليس يتحسر أهل الجنة إلا على ساعة مرت بهم لم يذكروا الله عز وجل فيها

From Muʿadh ibn Jabal, who related (marfuʿan): "Those who will be saved on the Day of Judgment and go to Paradise, their only regret will be one hour they did not spend in dunyā making dhikrullāh."

That means they were doing *dhikrullāh* twenty-three hours, and one hour they did not do that. Although they will be in Heaven, they will be so sorry that they did not do *dhikrullāh* for that one hour that they lost it from their life. Today what do we do? We are twenty-three hours in *dunyā* and might be one hour of *dhikrullāh* in our life! They are *Āhlu 'l-Jannah*, the People of Paradise, means the people who are saved, they were doing twenty-three hours *dhikrullāh* and for one hour that they didn't do *dhikr* they will get very sorry. What about those who are doing *dhikr* only one hour and twenty-three hours of their day they were not doing *dhikrullāh*?

O People! *Dhikrullāh* is very important for us to do! *Allāhumma ṣalli ʿalā Sayyīdinā Muḥammad* ﷺ *ḥattā yarḍā Sayyīdinā Muḥammad* ﷺ.

The Best Dhikrullāh is "Lā ilāha illa-Llāh"

Jābir ؓ said, *qāl samiʿtu Rasūlullāh* ﷺ *yaqūl afḍalu 'dh-dhikr*, "I heard the Prophet ﷺ saying, 'What is the best of *dhikrullāh*?" What do you want to recite? We can recite anything, but the Prophet ﷺ is telling, "What is the best of *dhikr*?" teaching his *Ṣaḥābah* ؓ how to approach Allāh ﷻ and Allāh will be happy with their *dhikr*. So he said:

افضل الذكل لا اله الاّ الله

The best remembrance of Allāh is to say, "There is no god but Allāh."[43]

Lā ilāha illa-Llāh. So say, *"Lā ilāha illa-Llāh Muḥammadan Rasūlullāh."* Raise your voice: *Lā ilāha illa-Llāh Muḥammadan Rasūlullāh!* He didn't say how many times. He said it is the best of *dhikr*, and say it even one time.

من قال لا اله الا الله دخل الجنة

Whoever says 'Lā ilāha illa-Llāh' enters Paradise.

"Whoever says, *Lā ilāha illa-Llāh* enters Paradise." He didn't say how many times and all Muslims around the world say, *"Lā ilāha illa-Llāh,"* or else what is the meaning of Muslim? If you ask a person, "What is your religion," and he says, "I am Muslim," what does that mean? It means *"Lā ilāha illa-Llāh,"* whether he said it or not. When he says, "I am a Muslim," it means he is saying, *"Lā ilāha illa-Llāh Muḥammadun Rasūlullāh."* You cannot be a Muslim by praying and fasting without saying, *"Lā ilāha illa-Llāh,"* no; you say, *"Lā ilāha illa-Llāh,"* and if you are not fasting or praying you are still a Muslim. If you fast and pray, because you are with a group of Muslims and you do like them, but you are not yet a Muslim until you say, *"Lā ilāha illa-Llāh Muḥammadun Rasūlullāh."* So the best of *dhikrullāh* that saves you from Hellfire is *"Lā ilāha illa-Llāh Muḥammadun Rasūlullāh."*

Abū Hurayrah ؓ said that Sayyīdinā Muḥammad ﷺ said:

كلمتان خفيفتان على اللسان، ثقيلتان في الميزان، حبيبتان إلى الرحمن: سبحان الله وبحمده، سبحان الله العظيم

There are two statements that are light on the tongue, heavy in the Scales and are beloved to the Merciful: SubḥānAllāhi wa bi-ḥamdihi, SubḥānAllāhi 'l-ʿAẓīm (Glory be to Allāh and His is the praise, (and) Allāh, The Greatest is free from imperfection).[44]

The Prophet ﷺ said to the Ṣaḥābah ؓ, "I am going to teach you two words very light on the tongue, that you can say easily, but are very heavy in the scale," *kalimatān khafīfatān ʿalā al-lisān thaqīlatān fī 'l-mīzān,* where

---

[43] Tirmidhī.
[44] Bukhārī and Muslim.

"thaqīl" means "heavy; they are very heavy." *Ḥabībatān ila 'r-Raḥmān*, "Allāh loves these two words: *SubḥānAllāh wa bi-ḥamdihi, SubḥānAllāhi 'l-ʿAẓīm."* Say, *"SubḥānAllāh wa bi-ḥamdihi, SubḥānAllāhi 'l-ʿAẓīm,"* as Allāh loves the one who says these two words! So we have to say these two words.

So we say *"Lā ilāha illa-Llāh,"* daily as much as you like. Some *awlīyā* say it one-hundred times to one-thousand times, or if you want to say it one-million times, what's the problem? And to make Allāh ﷻ love you, say these two words that are very heavy in the scale as Allāh loves them and loves the one who says them, because when you mention something He loves you will be loved. When you say something that is *ḥabībatān ila 'r-Raḥmān*, very dear to Allāh ﷻ, you become very dear to Allāh ﷻ. What are these? *SubḥānAllāh wa bi-ḥamdihi, SubḥānAllāhi 'l-ʿAẓīm.* Say it!

وعن أبي موسى رضي الله عنه قال: قال لي رسول الله صلى الله عليه وسلم: "ألا أدلك على كنز من كنوز الجنة ؟"

فقلت: بلى يا رسول الله قال: "لا حول ولا قوة إلا بالله" (متفق عليه).

Abū Mūsā al-Ashʿarī ؓ related from the Prophet ﷺ: The Messenger of Allāh ﷺ said to me, "Shall I not guide you to a treasure from the treasures of Paradise?" I said, "Yes, O Messenger of Allāh!" Thereupon he ﷺ said, 'Lā ḥawla wa lā quwwata illa billāh (There is no change of a condition nor power except by Allāh)."[45]

"Do you like me to tell you, *yā* Abū Mūsā al-ʿAshʿarī ؓ," he was the one that recited Holy Qur'an very beautifully. One time he was reciting with a very strong, beautiful voice, *tajwīd*, not *tartīl, tajwīd* of Qur'ān, meaning, *yataghanna fi 'l-Qur'ān*, melodious recitation, and the Prophet ﷺ was behind him. He was not seeing the Prophet ﷺ, who was behind him listening and was very happy from this melodious way of recitation. He finished, looked and saw the Prophet ﷺ and said, *"Yā Rasūlullāh*! I didn't know you were there. If I knew you were listening, I would have made it more melodious for you to be happy." So that *Ṣaḥābī* ؓ, the Prophet ﷺ was telling him, "Do you want me to tell you about a treasure from the treasures of Paradise?"

[45] Bukhārī and Muslim.

Allāh ﷻ is giving us treasures, we have to...if someone were to tell you that there is a treasure in this land, too many like that in countries around the world, they come to you and tell you there is a treasure in your house, treasure hunters, so you hunt the treasure. You might find or you might not find it, but if you want to find then there are codes, a password, if there is really a treasure. People dig and dig and don't find anything if they don't have the password. If you have the password, you will find it.

So the Prophet ﷺ was asking Abū Mūsā al-Ashʿarī ؓ, "Do you want me to give you a treasure from Heavenly treasures?" What is he going to say? *"Balā, yā Sayyīdī, yā Rasūlullāh,* yes of course! This is what I am waiting for!" And this what we are all waiting for, to get one of these Heavenly treasures, which means Heavenly knowledge, *maʿrifah,* that Allāh gives you in *dunyā* and raises you in *Ākhirah.*

What is the treasure? To raise you to be with the Prophet ﷺ, this is the highest treasure and Prophet ﷺ will be in the Divine Presence, *Qāba Qawsayni aw Adnā,* so he takes you with him to *Qāba Qawsayni aw Adnā* in *Ākhirah.* "Do you want that?" for Abū Mūsā al-Ashʿarī ؓ and of course for all of us. This is what we are expecting, why not? We are saying, *"Yā Sayyīdī, yā Rasūlullāh*! Take our hands, we are children; even if we reach 100 years age and die, we are still children and we need you to take us by the hands."

So he said, "Yes, *yā Rasūlullāh.*" The Prophet ﷺ said, "To recite, you have to say, *'Lā ḥawla wa lā quwatta illa billāh,'* there is no power or no way except with Allāh."

So now what do we have?

1. *Afḍalu 'dh-dhikr: Lā ilāha illa-Llāh Muḥammadun Rasūlullāh*
2. *Kalimatān khafīfatān ʿalā al-lisān: SubḥānAllāh wa bi-ḥamdihi, SubḥānAllāhi'l-Aẓīm.*
3. *And now Lā ḥawla wa lā quwatta illāh billāhi 'l-ʿAlīyyu 'l-ʿAẓīm,* if you want to end it like that.

Abū Ayyūb al-Anṣārī ؓ said that the Prophet ﷺ said:

من قال لا إله إلا الله وحده لا شريك له، له الملك وله الحمد، وهو على كل شيء قدير، عشر مرات، كان كمن أعتق أربعة أنفس من ولد إسماعيل (متفق عليه).

He who utters ten times, "Lā ilāha illa-Llāhu waḥdahu lā sharīka lah, lahu 'l-mulku wa lahu 'l-ḥamdu wa ʿalā kulli shay'in Qadīr. There is no true god except Allāh. He is One and He has no partner with Him. His is the sovereignty and His is the praise, and He is Omnipotent," he will have a reward equal to that for freeing four slaves from the progeny of Prophet Ismāʿīl.[46]

"Whoever says, 'Lā ilāha illa-Llāhu waḥdahu lā sharīka lah, lahu 'l-mulku wa lahu 'l-ḥamdu wa Hūwa ʿalā kulli shay'in Qadīr,' ʿashara marrāt, ten times..." There are numbers now, increasing now, before no numbers, now there are numbers. There are many aḥādīth that mention numbers, so they cannot say there are no numbers on how many times you recite, because one of their sayings is, "You don't count numbers."

This ḥadīth is muttafaqun ʿalayhi, accepted by Bukhārī and Muslim, and it has numbers. Why do you reject numbers? I don't understand why they reject, they say, "Don't do 100 times, don't do 3,000, or 1,100, don't do 330." They are numbers; the Prophet ﷺ mentioned numbers, so we follow the numbers. So he said, "Say one time, 'Lā ilāha illa-Llāhu waḥdahu lā sharīka lah, lahu 'l-mulku wa lahu 'l-ḥamdu wa Hūwa ʿalā kulli shay'in Qadīr,' ten times."

What benefit will you get? The one that was before you get one of the treasures of Paradise, the one that was before that, he said, "The best of dhikr is 'lā ilāha illa-Llāh.'" So this one, what will you get? Kāna kaman aʿataqa arbaʿta anfusin min waladi Ismāʿīl, "It is as if that person has freed four people, slaves, from the Children of Ismāʿīl." Sayyīdinā Ismāʿīl ؑ is the grand, grand, grand, grandfather to Sayyīdinā Muḥammad ﷺ. If, from that line, four people were kidnapped or taken into slavery, or it might be they did not become slaves, but they were taken to be tortured by the ignorant people for being Muslim, it is as if you have freed four of them. How difficult it is to free someone innocent from the death penalty, not because he did something, but only because he says, "Lā ilāha illa-Llāh Muḥammadun Rasūlullāh." They were torturing them in the beginning of Islam, in the beginning of the Message. How many people have Abū Lahab and Abū Jahl, uncles of the Prophet ﷺ, tortured of the Believers? So it will be as if you have freed four!

---

[46] Bukhārī and Muslim.

If you free one, the Prophet ﷺ said in a *ḥadīth,* in the meaning we can apply that *ḥadīth* on this to give understanding:

فوالله لأن يهدي الله بك رجلا واحدا خير من حمر النعم

By Allāh, for Allāh to guide one man by you is better for you than (possessing a whole lot of) red camels.[47]

"If Allāh ﷻ will guide one person through you, if you guide one person to Islam it is better for you than the wealth of this *dunyā,"* which means it is as if you are freeing him by bringing him from *kufr* to *īmān,* so you are converting him back to his normal destiny which Allāh has written for him to be a revert, to be a Muslim. So you're bringing him from *kufr,* means you are freeing him from *kufr* and bringing him to Islam, and this is better than the wealth of all this *dunyā.* So it is as if you guided four of them, or as if you freed four of them.

These are some benefits that we are sharing from the *ḥadīth* of the Prophet ﷺ on *dhikrullāh,* and *inshā-Allāh* we will continue more in the next session. *Wa min Allāhi 't-tawfiq, bi hurmati 'l-habīb, bi hurmati 'l-Fātiḥah.*

So in summary:

1. *Afḍalu 'dh-dhikri: Lā ilāha illa-Llāh.*
2. Two words that are light on the tongue, heavy on the Scale: *SubḥānAllāh wa bi-ḥamdihi, SubḥānAllāhi 'l-ʿAẓīm.* All of us recite it! *(SubḥānAllāh wa bi-ḥamdihi, SubḥānAllāhi 'l-ʿAẓīm.)*
3. The Prophet ﷺ is telling Abū Mūsā al-Ashʿarī ؓ about a treasure from Allāh's treasures, from the treasures of Paradise, to say, "*Lā ḥawla wa lā quwatta illa billāh.*"
4. He ﷺ is telling Abū Ayyūb ؓ that it is as if you freed four (slaves) from the Children of Ismāʿīl ؑ by saying this ten times: *Lā ilāha illa-Llāhu waḥdahu lā sharīka lah, lahu 'l-mulku wa lahu 'l-ḥamdu wa Hūwa ʿalā kulli shay'in Qadīr.*

So recite them, don't forget them! This is from the sayings of Prophet ﷺ and all of them are strong *aḥādīth* that we have to *inshā-Allāh* do as much as we can. We cannot say we are going to do, but we say, "May Allāh give us

---

[47] Bukhārī and Muslim.

power to do and may Allāh give us love to Prophet ﷺ and to *awlīyāullāh* to do."

May Allāh forgive us and may Allāh bless us.

Wa min Allāhi 't-tawfiq, bi ḥurmati 'l-ḥabīb, bi ḥurmati 'l-Fātiḥah.
And with Allāh is success. For the sake of the Beloved, for his sake we recite the opening chapter of Holy Qur'ān.

The Signs of a Worthy Teacher

Aʿūdhu billāhi min ash-Shayṭāni 'r-rajīm. Bismillāhi' r-Raḥmāni 'r-Raḥīm.
Nawaytu 'l-arbāʿīn, nawaytu 'l-ʿitikāf, nawaytu 'l-khalwah, nawaytu 'l-ʿuzlah,
nawaytu 'r-riyāḍa, nawaytu 's-sulūk, lillāhi Taʿalā fī hādhā 'l-masjid.
Atīʿūllāha wa atīʿū 'r-Rasūla wa ūli 'l-amri minkum. (4:59)

As-salāmu ʿalaykum. All of you here and wherever people are seeing through the Internet, may Allāh ﷻ bless you all.

Dhikrullāh cannot be defined in our language because it is the life; *dhikrullāh* is the life of the angels. Angels are continuously in *dhikrullāh,* so *dhikrullāh* is a Heavenly issue that we have to do it and to remember The One Who created everything, to remember the Greatness of Allāh ﷻ and to know how much we are dependent on Him and how much we are so like nothing in comparison to whom Allāh ﷻ loves!

He loves the people of *dhikrullāh,* so if we are from the people of *dhikrullāh* then Allāh ﷻ will honor us. If we are not of that then Allāh will dishonor us, because *dhikrullāh* is related to Allāh directly. You are remembering Him, no one else, and this is part of *tawḥīd,* that you are remembering the Oneness and declaring the Oneness of Allāh ﷻ. So as much as we are remembering as much as we are approaching the Divine Presence and as much as we are forgetting is that much we approach someone whom Allāh doesn't like, Shayṭān.

And that is why, as mentioned in the previous session, you have to have a teacher, a guide, someone you take as a role model. But you have to look at him: is he following his ego or following Allāh ﷻ, because the Prophet ﷺ said:

أخوف ما أخاف على أمتي الشرك الخفي

What I fear most for my Ummah is hidden shirk.[48]

In your eyes he might be doing well, but in reality he might be trying to promote himself, by doing something in front of you and when he is away

[48] Aḥmad mentioned like it.

from you doing what is heedless and following his own bad desires. So it is said that you have to know from whom you are taking *dhikrullāh.*

Ibn Qayyim writes in his :

والمقصود أن الله سبحانه وتعالى نهى عن طاعة من جمع هذه الصفات فينبغي للرجل أن
ينظر في شيخه وقدوته ومتبوعه فإن وجده كذلك فليبعد منه

Allāh prohibited us to follow those who carry the character of heedlessness and the character of bad desires, so whoever possesses these two characteristics, you must run from him. Therefore when the student needs a guide, "He must look carefully, is that guide always in dhikrullāh or is he not in dhikrullāh; rather, is he following his desires?"

It means if he see his shaykh is not always in *dhikrullāh* then leave him, don't follow him. If you see him following *dhikrullāh* then follow him.

A story that I saw myself and Grandshaykh, may Allāh bless his soul, Grandshaykh ʿAbdAllāh al-Fa'iz ad-Dāghestānī ق—whose line is coming from the Prophet ﷺ all the way to Āḥmad al-Farūqī ق to Ḥabībullāh Jani-Janān ق of India, then to Sayyīdinā Khālid al-Baghdādī ق then to some *awlīyāullāh* and then it came to him—said, and this is what I saw, speaking about Mawlana Shaykh Muḥammad Nazim, may Allāh give him long life, "I never saw him except in *dhikrullāh.*" And I am more than fifty years with Mawlana Shaykh Nazim and always he is doing *dhikrullāh* and his *dhikr* beads are in his hand until he wants to refresh his *wuḍū,* then he drops the beads from his hand. Otherwise, always his hands are moving, meaning that his heart is working, it is not necessary to make *dhikrullāh* by his tongue, it can be from his heart.

Ibn Qayyim al-Jawziyya Describes His Shaykh

That shows importance of *dhikrullāh* for everyone. Unfortunately today some people say, "O don't do that, O that is *bidʿa,* O don't count [your *Dhikr*]!" etc., but I will quote a story of someone whose ideology *Āhlu 's-Sunnah wa 'l-Jamaʿah* is not okay with, and that is Ibn Taymiyya. Ibn Qayyim al-Jawziyya, his student, related a story about him:

و حضرت شيخ الإسلام ابن تيمية مرة صلى الفجر ثم جلس يذكر الله تعالى إلى قريب من
انتصاف النهار ثم التفت الي وقال هذه غدوتي ولو لم أتغد الغداء سقطت قوتي أو كلاما

قريبا من هذا وقال لي مرة : لا أترك الذكر إلا بنية إجمام نفسي وإراحتها لأستعد بتلك الراحة لذكر آخر أو كلاما هذا معناه

> Once I went to my shaykh, Ibn Taymiyya. He sat after praying *Fajr ṣalāt*, doing the *dhikr* of Allāh until midday. He said to me, "This *dhikr* is my breakfast in the morning. If I do not eat this food (i.e., *dhikr*), I will become weak and I only avoid *dhikr* to give my *nafs* some breath to prepare it for *dhikr* at another time."[49]

He said, "One time I came to the *masjid* and we prayed *Fajr* with my teacher, Ibn Taymiyya, and he sat after *Fajr* and was making *dhikrullāh*." This is for those who deny *dhikr*. Do they deny *dhikr* or not? They say, "No, this is Sufi stuff, don't do it." This is Ibn Taymiyya doing it, whose ideology the Salafis follow. We pray for them, that Allāh guides them to *Āhlu 's-Sunnah wa 'l-Jamaʿah*. He was sitting there, so at least O Salafi, don't criticize the Sufis when they do *dhikr* as your teacher was doing *dhikr*. If you want to criticize, then criticize Ibn Taymiyya first! Is that not fair? It is fair for everyone.

So continuing Ibn Qayyim al-Jawziyya's description of his shaykh:

> I came and prayed *Fajr* with him and then my teacher was sitting after *Fajr* prayer and in one sitting making *dhikrullāh* up to *Ẓuhr* time, not moving or going anywhere but in one sitting, remembering Allāh ﷻ until the middle of the day.

This is mentioned in strong hadiths from *Bukhārī* and *Muslim* which we mentioned many of them yesterday and we will mention some today. How many hours is that? From *Fajr*, say 5 o'clock to 12 o'clock, that is seven hours sitting making *dhikrullāh*.

> *Thumma 'l-tafata ilayh, wa qāla hādhihī ghudwatī,* "And then he looked at me and said, 'This is my food. If I don't do that my power will drop. If I don't eat my food, my power, my energy will drop down.' And he said one time, *'Adh-dhikru li 'l-qalbī mathalu 'l-mā'i li 's-samak,'* he compared the heart to the fish."

---

[49] Related by Ibn Qayyim in Al-Wābil as-Ṣayyib.

The heart is swimming in water, like fish swim in water; if you take the fish out of water, what happens? It struggles. Put it back in water, it survives. If you take the heart out of water it struggles and becomes rusted. If you put it back in the water it surrenders. What is that water? It is *Mā al-Ḥayāt, wa Ḥaqq al-Ḥayāt wa Ḥayāt al-Abadī,* "That is the Fountain of Heavenly Youth," the fountain of water that gives you life and the heart likes to swim in that Heavenly fountain of water, and at that time it will be submitting to Allāh ﷻ. You cannot come to Allāh ﷻ like you are entering somewhere, you must first clean your heart and then enter.

You cannot visit a leader like it is a normal situation, you must first shower and dress well and then go. Why when we pray our five prayers a day and remembering Allāh ﷻ through these prayers, why do we not dress well like when we go to see a leader or our boss? Do you dress like that? No, you dress your best dress and then go. The best dress is *dhikrullāh*. The heart is always yearning to go back to its water and cannot enter without *dhikrullāh* and to drop bad desires, the ego from the heart.

That is why Bayāzīd al-Bistāmī ق asked, "*Yā Rabbī!* How can I reach you?" *kayfa 'l-wuṣūlu ilayk*, and he heard a voice that came, *al-wuṣūlu ilaynā an tatruka nafsaka wa taʿal*, "*Yā* Abā Yazīd! You want to come to Us, okay, but leave your self and come," which means "leave your desires and heedlessness and come, then you will find Us." So if you see the shaykh is not engaged in *dhikrullāh,* which is the food, provision of your soul, as the big teacher of Salafis, Ibn Taymiyya acknowledged that *dhikrullāh* is necessary in order that you can give strength to your body, to your energy. And he said, I am quoting that because it is important for *Āhlu 's-Sunnah wa 'l-Jamaʿah* to have an argument for those Salafis who deny *dhikrullāh* when their teacher is committing to *dhikrullāh*!

And one time Ibn Taymiyya said, as Ibn Qayyim al-Jawziyya relates, *lā atruku 'dh-dhikra illa bi nīyyati ijmāmi nafsī,* "He said to me, 'I don't leave *dhikrullāh* except to give myself a little rest.'" Because when you make *dhikrullāh,* entering into it is not easy. You are struggling with Shayṭān and Shayṭān doesn't want you to enter in it, so he tries to pull you away. It is a fight within your heart when you are doing *dhikrullāh.* Try, begin making *dhikrullāh* and you see how difficult it becomes. You make first 100, second 100, third 100, and then it becomes heavy, heavy, and heavy, not because it's *dhikrullāh,* but because you are fighting your desires. Your desire doesn't want you to make *dhikrullāh*. So he said, "I sometimes stop doing the *dhikrullāh, bi niyyati ijmāmi nafsī,* in order to give myself some time of rest, then I will have my power back and I begin another time to do *dhikrullāh*."

Remember Allāh Excessively Until People Say You Are Insane

It is related in Imam Āḥmad's *Musnad, marfuʿan, ḥadīth* from Prophet ﷺ, *Akhthirū dhikrullāhi taʿalā*, "Do *dhikrullāh* excessively," and what is the ceiling of 'excessively'? The Prophet ﷺ put a ceiling, "Do it excessively," excessively, excessively, excessively, like someone who is among people doing *dhikrullāh "lā ilāha illa-Llāh, lā ilāha illa-Llāh, lā ilāha illa-Llāh,"* not paying any attention to anyone: that is excessively. Keep doing, going up and up, until people begin to see he is crazy:

أَكْثِرُوا ذِكْرَ اللهِ حَتَّى يَقُولُوا مَجْنُونٌ

Remember Allāh ﷻ *so much that people start saying, "He has gone mad."*[50]

Until they say about you, "You are crazy!" *Akthirū dhikrullāhi taʿalā ḥattā yaqūlū majnūn*. Don't stop until you hear a word saying, "O! This one is crazy, leave him alone." And today if you want to sit to do your *awrād* and be busy with that, people come and say to you, "What are you doing? Leave, come sit with us. You are crazy, it is too much praying."

And it is said in some places and I heard it from people who are leading the Muslim community in America, but they are Salafi, and many people follow them. Every year they hold a conference and you know who they are. One of their leaders, who was a president of that organization said, "If the Prophet ﷺ comes in this time, he will wear jeans." And also, "Don't do too much prayers. You are only obliged for five prayers, do your five prayers and go to the mall and entertain yourself." That is a guide, a shaykh, they call him (by the title) "*ʿAllāmah. ʿAllāmah Muftī Ṣāhib*," I don't want to give names, but they are like that. He says, "Do your prayers," of course do your prayers, but do you want to be in first Paradise or with the Prophet ﷺ? There is a big difference. If you pray and fast you are in the first Paradise, but to be with the Prophet ﷺ you have to struggle!

---

[50] Aḥmad, *Musnad*.

وعن أبي هريرة رضي الله عنه أن فقراء المهاجرين أتوا رسول الله صلى الله عليه وسلم فقالوا: "ذهب أهل الدثور بالدرجات العلى، والنعيم المقيم: يصلون كما نصلي، ويصومون كما نصوم، ولهم فضل من أموال: يحجون، ويعتمرون، ويجاهدون، ويتصدقون. فقال: "ألا أعلمكم شيئًا تدركون به من سبقكم، وتسبقون به من بعدكم، ولا يكون أحد أفضل منكم إلا من صنع مثل ما صنعتم؟ قالوا: بلى يا رسول الله، قال: "تسبحون، وتحمدون، وتكبرون، خلف كل صلاة ثلاثًا وثلاثين

Abū Hurayrah ﷺ related:
The Muhājirūn (Emigrants) came to the Messenger of Allāh ﷺ and said, "The wealthy have gone with the highest ranks and lasting bliss." He asked, "How is that?" They replied, "They offer ṣalāt as we offer it, they observe fast as we do, (and as they are wealthy) they perform Hajj and ʿUmrah and go for jihad, and they spend in charity but we cannot, and they free the slaves but we are unable to do so." The Messenger of Allāh ﷺ said, "Shall I not teach you something with which you may overtake those who surpassed you and with which you will surpass those who will come after you? None will excel you unless he who does which you do." They said, "Yes, please do, O Messenger of Allāh!" He ﷺ said, "You should recite 'Tasbīḥ (SubḥānAllāh), taḥmīd (Alḥamdulillāh), takbīr (Allāhu Akbar)' thirty-three times after each ṣalāt.'"[51]

There were *Ansār* of Madīnah and the people who migrated from Mecca to Madīnah, the *Muhājirūn*. So the poor people of *Muhājirūn* came to the Prophet ﷺ and said, *dhahaba āhl ad-duthūri bi 'd-darajāti 'l-ūlā,* "The people of richness, the rich people, took the high rewards," because they have money, they have wealth, and they gave it to Prophet ﷺ without count, like today people give but they don't know where they are giving. They like to give, but they don't know where they are giving. It might fall into wrong hands. So today, it's dangerous to give if you don't know where you are giving. So they said, "They people of richness went with all the rewards and *'n-naʿīmu 'l-muqīm*, the best, highest levels of Paradises," and they were saying to Prophet ﷺ, *yusallūna kamā nuṣallū*, "They pray like us and fast like us," *wa yaṣūmūna kamā naṣūm, wa lahum faḍlun min amwālin yaḥajjūna yaʿtamarūn*, "and they have favors of money that Allāh granted that they use for *Hajj* and for *ʿUmrah*," *wa yujāhidūna wa yataṣadaqūn*, "and they give charity and fight for Allāh's sake."

---

[51] Bukhārī and Muslim.

And they were sad. A poor one is a sad person when he sees the rich ones have everything from *mata' ad-dunyā*, of material wealth. You see they have cars today, bank accounts, they have nice places, they go and come. Allāh gave and you cannot say no: to whom Allāh gives, He gives. So the poor are sad as they cannot be like that. These people can give everywhere, they are giving, helping, they pray, they fast, they make *Hajj* and *'Umrah*, they have the facility and the money. The poor don't have that, so they get sad.

So they are telling Prophet ﷺ, "The people of richness took everything! They took *dunyā* and from *dunyā* they are going to take *Ākhirah* also!" and the Prophet ﷺ said, *alā u'allimukum shay'an tudrikūna bihi man sabaqakum*, "Do you like me to teach you something that if you learn it, Allāh will make you ahead of those whom you think are ahead of you? You will be ahead of the rich people or will be like them in Allāh's Eyes, and He will dress you and favor you and no need to be sad." *Wa tasbiqūna bihi man ba'dikum*, "And not only you will overtake those in your time, but you will surpass those who come after you, you will be ahead of everyone!" *wa lā yakūna āḥadun afḍala minkum*, "and no one will better than you! You will be the best," *illā man sana' mithla mā sana'tum*, "unless they do the same of what I am teaching you, they will be like you and you will be like them." They said, *balā yā Rasūlullāh*, "Yes, of course, *yā Sayyīdī, yā Rasūlullāh!*" He ﷺ said, *tusabbiḥūna wa tuḥammidūn wa tukabbirūna khalfa kulla ṣalātin thalātha wa thalāthīna marrat*, "After every prayer is done, you recite each 33 times, "*SubḥānAllāh, Alḥamdulillāh, Allāhu Akbar*, 33 times; you will be richer than those people who got all these rewards, you will be ahead of them."

So we are poor, what should we do? Say "*subḥānAllāh*" 33 times! Say "*alḥamdulillāh*" 33 times! Say "*Allāhu Akbar*" 33 times. If you do that after every *ṣalāt*, you will be ahead of everyone. That is *dhikrullāh*, that is what the Prophet ﷺ is teaching and those *Ṣaḥābah* ؓ whom he was addressing, *fuqarā al-Muhājirūn*, the poor *Muhājirūn* who left Mecca and came with nothing but their clothes, nothing else, they didn't take anything with them, they are poor and Allāh is granting them richness!

We are poor! We ask, "*Yā Rabbī!* Grant us richness in *dunyā* and *Ākhirah*!

This *ḥadīth* from *Bukhārī* and *Muslim* is *mutaffaqun ʿalayh,* agreed upon. ʿAlī ibn Abī Ṭālib ﷺ reported that the Prophet ﷺ said to his daughter, Sayyida Fāṭima az-Zahra ﷺ and to Sayyīdinā ʿAlī, *raḍiAllāhu ʿanhumā wa karramAllāhu wajhahumā wa ʿalayhimā ʿs-salām*:

وعن علي رضي الله عنه أن رسول الله صلى الله عليه وسلم قال له ولفاطمة، رضي الله عنهما: "إذا أويتما إلى فراشكما، أو: إذا أخذتما مضجعكما - فكبرا ثلاثًا وثلاثين، وسبحا ثلاثًا وثلاثين، واحمدا ثلاثًا وثلاثين"

The Messenger of Allāh ﷺ said to me and to Fatima ﷺ, "When you go to bed, recite, takbīr (Allāhu Akbar)' thirty-three times and tasbīḥ (SubḥānAllāh) thirty-three times and taḥmīd (Alḥamdulillāh) thirty-three times."[52]

Idhā awaytumā ilā firāshikumā aw akhadhtumā madajaʿakumā, "When you go to your bed to sleep or you lay down to rest," *fakabbirā thalātha wa thalāthīn wa sabbiḥā thalātha wa thalāthīn wa aḥmidā thalātha wa thalāthīn,* "Make *takbīr* 33 times, *tasbīḥ* 33 times and *taḥmīd* 33 times: *'Allāhu Akbar,' 'SubḥānAllāh,' 'Alḥamdulillāh,'" mutaffaqun ʿalayh,* related by *Bukhārī* and *Muslim.*

Abū Hurayrah ﷺ narrated that the Prophet ﷺ said:

إِنَّ لِلَّهِ تِسْعَةً وَتِسْعِينَ اسْمًا مِائَةً غَيْرَ وَاحِدٍ مَنْ أَحْصَاهَا دَخَلَ الْجَنَّةَ "

Indeed Allāh has Ninety-Nine Names, one hundred less one.
Whoever counts them shall enter Paradise.[53]

Abū Hurayrah ﷺ narrated that the Prophet ﷺ said, "Allāh has 99 Allāh's Beautiful Names and Attributes; whoever counts them or memorize them or reads them will enter Paradise," and all *tasbīḥ* or *dhikrullāh* is done through these Beautiful Names and Attributes. It is said by many scholars, not many, but the majority of scholars say that the 99 Beautiful Names and Attributes are the better-known Names and easier on the tongue to address, but there are many, many other Names of Allāh ﷻ that you can make *dhikrullāh* with.

[52] Bukhārī and Muslim.

[53] Tirmidhī

And the importance of *dhikrullāh* is to make Allāh ﷻ happy, as He said:

أَنَا جَلِيْسُ مَنْ ذَكَرَنِي

I sit with the one who remembers me.[54]

So it has so many *fawāiḍ*, many benefits, too much benefits and we will count some of them. We mention one of them now:

Dhikrullāh yaṭrud ash-Shayṭān. Dhikrullāh will chase Shayṭān, Allāh ﷻ will throw him out from your heart when you are making *dhikrullāh.* He cannot enter a fortress. *Dhikrullāh* is our fortress in *dunyā,* it prevents Shayṭān from attacking, he can come to the wall, but he cannot enter. If you get heedless one moment he enters immediately, you have to be careful. *Wa yaqmaʿahu wa yaksuruh,* "and with *dhikrullāh* Allāh will put Shayṭān down and break him into pieces." So the first time you break him down and break him into pieces; the first time, by saying "*lā ilāha illa-Llāh*" or any of the *dhikr* that we mentioned already, it breaks him down and down.

Īmām at-Tirmidhi said in his Ṣaḥīḥ from ʿAbdAllāh ibn Masʿūd ؓ, one of the biggest *Ṣaḥābah,* that the Prophet ﷺ said:

لَقِيتُ إِبْرَاهِيمَ لَيْلَةَ أُسْرِيَ بِي فَقَالَ يَا مُحَمَّدُ أَقْرِئْ أُمَّتَكَ مِنِّي السَّلاَمَ وَأَخْبِرْهُمْ أَنَّ الْجَنَّةَ طَيِّبَةُ التُّرْبَةِ عَذْبَةُ الْمَاءِ وَأَنَّهَا قِيعَانٌ وَأَنَّ غِرَاسَهَا سُبْحَانَ اللهِ وَالْحَمْدُ لِلَّهِ وَلاَ إِلَهَ إِلاَّ اللهُ وَاللهُ أَكْبَرُ

I met Ibrāhīm ؑ on the night of my ascent, so he said, "O Muḥammad! Recite salām from me to your nation, and inform them that Paradise has pure soil and delicious water, and that it is a flat treeless plain, and that its seeds are: SubḥānAllāh (Glory is to Allāh), Alḥamdulillāh (all praise is due to Allāh), Lā ilāha illa-Llāh (none has the right to be worshipped but Allāh), and Allāhu Akbar (Allāh is the greatest."[55]

"When I went for *Isrā' wa 'l-Miʿrāj,* I saw Sayyīdinā Ibrāhīm ؑ." Allāh wanted him to see Sayyīdinā Ibrāhīm ؑ, *fa qāl yā Muḥammad aqri' ummataka minnī 's-salām,* that simple, that word, "O Muḥammad! Send, read to your *Ummah* my *salām.*" Sayyīdinā Ibrāhīm ؑ is asking the Prophet ﷺ, requesting to send his *salām* to *Ummat an-Nabī* ﷺ, *yā nāru kūnī bardan wa salāman ʿalā*

---

[54] Āḥmad , Bayhaqī

[55] Tirmidhī

Ibrāhīm, where Sayyīdinā Ibrāhīm ؑ tasted the peacefulness when Nimrod wanted to throw him in fire, and Jibrīl ؑ came and said, "Do you need any help?" and he replied, "The One Who sent you knows what I need."

And Allāh said:

$$\text{قُلْنَا يَا نَارُ كُونِي بَرْدًا وَسَلَامًا عَلَى إِبْرَاهِيمَ}$$

O fire! Be cool and peaceful on Ibrāhīm.[56]

If He had said "cool" only and stopped there without saying "peace", he would have frozen, but He said *bardan wa salāman*, "cold and peaceful", peaceful cold, as if he is in Paradise. He is sending that *salām* to *Ummat an-Nabī* ﷺ, that experience that he had hot/cold. "The fire is hot" means you are struggling with worse than Nimrod, that is Shayṭān! You are struggling with Shayṭān! So, "I am asking Allāh ﷻ to dress them as He dressed me, with that peacefulness and that coolness." That's why today we don't feel that heat within your heart because Sayyīdinā Ibrāhīm ؑ sent that *salām* to *Ummat an-Nabī* ﷺ. And when you say *salām*, what we have? It means Allāh...it means when you send *salām* it means you are sending peacefulness on people, *wa 'alaykum as-salām yā Ibrāhīm* ؑ. So he sent *salām* to *Ummat an-Nabī* ﷺ to everyone, with no exceptions! To everyone.

Be happy that Allāh created us from *Ummat an-Nabī* ﷺ! The grandfather of Sayyīdinā Muḥammad ﷺ sent *salāms* to all of you around the world, to every Muslim! *Wa akhbirhum anna 'l-jannah ṭayyibatu 't-turbah*, "And tell them that *Jannah* is very tasty, sweet and has a sweet, tasty soil." What kind of soil is that? Tasty and sweet, fertile with sweetness. *Wa anna ghirāsahā*, "and the plants of it," when you have nice fertile soil you plant in it, so it is all planted, "And tell them to plant more, those plants are '*subḥānAllāh w 'alḥamdulillāh wa lā ilāha illa-Llāh w 'Allāhu Akbar.*'" Those are the plants of Paradise! Every time you say, '*subḥānAllāh*,' one plant is planted there for you and your name is written on it.

Today there is in Canada a botanical garden and you pay them and they put a special flower in a color that you like, they mix all these genes and bring the color you like, like painting and they call it by your name.

---

[56] Sūrat al-Anbiyā, 21:69

They sell it under your name. So on every Heavenly plant that you plant by saying *"subḥānAllāh w 'alḥamdulillāh wa lā ilāha illa-Llāh w 'Allāhu Akbar,"* on every time you say *"subḥānAllāh,"* every time you say *"alḥamdulillāh,"* and every time you say *"Allāhu Akbar,"* one plant, one plant, one plant. If you say a hundred times after every prayer, you have 500 plants, times three, as three different types of plant in each *tasbīḥ*, those are 1500 plants every day and your name is written on each of them, and how can there be such a garden with your name written in it without you being present there? No, you will be present in your garden as this is your special garden, a garden of *dhikrullāh,* and by glorifying and thanking Allāh ﷻ and praising Him you will get that *barakah!*

Also narrated by Imam Tirmidhi, *ḥadīthun ḥasanun ṣaḥiḥ,* related from Jābir bin ʿAbdullāh ؓ that the Prophet ﷺ said:

مَنْ قَالَ سُبْحَانَ اللهِ الْعَظِيمِ وَبِحَمْدِهِ . غُرِسَتْ لَهُ نَخْلَةٌ فِي الْجَنَّةِ

Whoever says, "SubḥānAllāh al-ʿAẓīm wa bi-ḥamdihi (Glory is to Allāh, the Magnificent, and with His Praise)" a date-palm tree is planted for him in Paradise.[57]

"Every time you recite *'subḥānAllāh wa bi-ḥamdihi'* Allāh will plant for you one date palm in Paradise." Is it going to be like dates that we are eating here, or is it a special date? Dates of Earth, the Prophet ﷺ used to eat seven dates with one cup of milk every day at brunch time and it gave him power for the whole day; he ﷺ said that relieves people from head problems, brain problems and removes poison from the body. That is from the date tree on Earth, so do that.

But what about the date tree in Paradise? We leave you with this, and make *dhikrullāh* as much as you can and we will continue, *inshā-Allāh,* next time.

---

[57] Tirmidhī.

May Allāh forgive us and may Allāh bless us.

Wa min Allāhi 't-tawfīq, bi ḥurmati 'l-ḥabīb, bi ḥurmati 'l-Fātiḥah.
And with Allāh is success. For the sake of the Beloved, for his sake we recite the opening chapter of Holy Qur'ān.

Nine Miraculous Benefits of Dhikrullāh

Aʿūdhu billāhi min ash-Shayṭāni 'r-rajīm. Bismillāhi' r-Raḥmāni 'r-Raḥīm.
Nawaytu 'l-arbāʿīn, nawaytu 'l-ʿitikāf, nawaytu 'l-khalwah, nawaytu 'l-ʿuzlah,
nawaytu 'r-riyāḍa, nawaytu 's-sulūk, lillāhi Taʿalā fi hādhā 'l-masjid.
Atīʿūllāha wa atīʿū 'r-Rasūla wa ūli 'l-amri minkum. (4:59)

As-salāmu ʿalaykum wa raḥmatullāhi wa barakātuh. As-salāmu wājibun, to give *salām* is *mustaḥḥab,* is liked from the Prophet ﷺ and from Allāh ﷻ, and it is also a *Sunnah* of the Prophet ﷺ. And *salām* is to say to anyone...even when the ignorant people come to you, give them *salām* and don't dispute, give peace to everyone:

وَعِبَادُ الرَّحْمَنِ الَّذِينَ يَمْشُونَ عَلَى الْأَرْضِ هَوْنًا وَإِذَا خَاطَبَهُمُ الْجَاهِلُونَ قَالُوا سَلَامًا

The (true) servants of The Most Merciful are those who walk humbly on the Earth and who, when the ignorant people behave insolently towards them, say, "Peace be unto you."[58]

As-salāmu ʿalaykum wa raḥmatullāhi wa barakātuh! Salāms to all the viewers and those who are watching us at that moment here and to those who are here. We continue in this session about *dhikrullāh. Dhikrullāh* is the way we can save ourselves. It is said in *al-Musnad* in a *marfuʿ ḥadīth*:

أَكْثِرُوا ذِكْرَ اللهِ حَتَّى يَقُولُوا مَجْنُونٌ

Remember Allāh ﷻ so much that people start saying, "He has gone mad."[59]

Keep doing more and more *dhikr* until people say that you are a crazy one, because Allāh will be happy and people will be thinking you are doing too much *dhikrullāh* and, "O! You are a lazy person, you don't pay attention to *dunyā*," but Sayyīdinā Abū Bakr aṣ-Ṣiddīq ؓ was doing excessive *dhikrullāh* and still he was a big businessman, very rich. Sayyīdinā 'Umar ؓ was very rich—didn't he do *dhikrullāh*? They did *dhikrullāh.* Sayyīdinā

---

[58] Sūrat al-Furqān, 25:63.
[59] Āḥmad , *Musnad.*

'Uthmān ❖ and Sayyīdinā 'Alī ❖ and all the Ṣaḥābah ❖, many of them were very rich and they did *dhikrullāh*.

So from the many *ḥadīth* we have mentioned about *dhikrullāh* and we explained them in details, now we see what are the benefits of *dhikrullāh*. There are so many benefits that a person can benefit from remembering Allāh ﷻ:

The First Benefit

أنه يطرد الشيطان و يقمعه ويكسره

Annahu yaṭrud ash-shayṭān, "He will chase away Shayṭān from your heart," and this is the goal of Islam. Allāh made it a test to see who will chase Shayṭān away and who will listen to Shayṭān. So first of all the benefit of *dhikrullāh* is to get rid of Shayṭān from your heart. The heart cannot contain anyone except Allāh's Light; Allāh's Light will be contained, and not fully contained by the heart of *adh-dhākir*, Allāh ﷻ sends His Light to the heart of the one who remembers Allāh ﷻ. So His Light is there and Shayṭān cannot come; you will prevent Shayṭān from entering as it will burn him. So the benefit is to throw away Shayṭān. You broke him and suppressed him; he will be broken and cannot raise his head, because you are in a situation where your heart is dedicated to Allāh alone.

They say Sayyīdinā Ya'qūb ﷺ lost his son Sayyīdinā Yūsuf ﷺ for many, many years. Why? Because Allāh ﷻ wants to tell him...because he used to love his son so much as if his son is his life and he was crying and crying about losing his son until he became blind. Allāh left him blind to teach him a lesson. Allāh can teach His prophets and test them to see how much they will be patient. He was believing that his son is still alive, but he cannot. He's a prophet; prophets cannot know? They know, but Allāh sometimes veils them; if He wants to make a test He veils them from seeing, except the Prophet Muḥammad ﷺ.

So Sayyīdinā Ya'qūb ﷺ was blind and he was crying continuously for his son and saying, "*Yā Rabbī*, my son!" and according to some narrations he kept looking for his son for 37 years. Finally when he became blind he realized that his heart cannot contain two. He heard an angelic voice from Heavens through Jibrīl ﷺ, "*Yā* Ya'qūb! Your heart does not belong to you, it belongs to Allāh and whatever belongs to Allāh cannot have anyone else inside." This is a sign to tell us that you cannot have two in your heart, you cannot have Shayṭān there. When Sayyidinā Yaʿqūb realized his mistake Allāh gave him back his son.

Sayyidinā Ibrāhīm was also in love with Sayyidinā Ismāʿīl and Allāh wanted to test him, "Go and slaughter Ismāʿīl! Go give him to Me as a sacrifice," because he was so in love with Sayyidinā Ismāʿīl that his heart was going to shift. *Awliyāullāh* say, "Love your shaykh, you love that *walī*, don't love two," because a windmill can get water to irrigate land, but it cannot irrigate two gardens, only one. So it is one. So the heart when it does *dhikr* can irrigate one place not two, one heart not two, as if you are irrigating two. So He said to him, "Go and slaughter your son, sacrifice your son for Me," to teach him a lesson that, "No one can control your heart except Me," and when Allāh owns the heart, the heart is shining with *dhikrullāh*.

What are angels doing in Paradise, are they sitting still? No, they are doing *dhikrullāh* in different ways: some ways we know and some no one knows, and they are doing some in the way the Prophet informed us and some ways are hidden. And Allāh is continuously creating more and more angels, non-stop. You cannot say that Allāh created and stopped, you cannot! He is *al-Khāliq*, one of His Beautiful Names, The Creator. So He is creating more angels and more angels and more *dhikrullāh* in different ways, in different ways, in different ways. In Paradise, why is there no Shayṭān there? Because there is *dhikrullāh* there.

Allāh said:

$$\text{وَأَشْرَقَتِ الْأَرْضُ بِنُورِ رَبِّهَا}$$

And the Earth will shine with the Light of its Lord.[60]

"When Allāh shone His Beauty on Earth He shone many beauties on Heavens," and shining His beauty in Heavens comes from the *dhikr* that the angels are doing. That is why Shayṭān cannot be there. When Allāh kicked Iblees out of Paradise he came back and entered in the form of a snake, that's why anyone who has the character of Iblees is like a snake, as the character of a snake is to bite you. Be careful! If they bite us we lose. So

---

[60] Sūrat az-Zumar, 39:69.

dhikrullāh has many benefits and the first is to chase Shayṭān away, to break him and suppress him.

The. Second Benefit

أنه يرضى الرحمن عز وجل

It makes Allāh happy with you.

It makes Allāh satisfied with the *dhākir*, with the one making *dhikr*. Allāh likes for His *'abd* to mention Him. What does the *ḥadīth* say?

أَنَا جَلِيسُ مَنْ ذَكَرَنِي

I sit with him who remembers Me.[61]

"I am with the one who remembers Me." Allāh likes that, He likes us to remember Him, He likes His servant to show love to Him, to show they are dependent on Him, to show they are in need for Him, to show that nothing can be done without Him, to show that their lives are in His Hand, to show that the only one who takes difficulties from them is Him, to show that we are in need for Him in *dunyā* and we are in need for Him in *Ākhirah*, there is no other way. Allāh will be happy, *annahu yurḍi 'r-Raḥmān*. What is better benefit than this benefit?

Everyone can say that they like to make his shaykh happy, coming to the shaykh and giving gifts, is it not? You don't come empty-handed, you give gifts, and even any gift: expensive gift or reasonable gift or cheap gift, but you give a gift, you come with a gift. To Allāh ﷻ how can you come with nothing? You must come with a precious gift and He is saying, "The precious gift is to remember Me, to mention My Names, My Beautiful Names and Attributes that I will dress you with it."

You don't come to your family empty-handed. The children run to the door to see what you have, what you are bringing with you today. Chocolates? Allāh has chocolates? He has rivers in Paradise of everything, rivers that are mentioned in the Holy Qur'an and rivers we don't know: rivers of honey, rivers of milk, rivers of wine, rivers of everything, as in

[61] Āḥmad , Bayhaqī.

Ākhirah it is allowed. He is preparing for the Muslims, for the *mu'mins*. You are happy? Smiling? Allāh made wine in *Ākhirah*!

فِيهَا أَنْهَارٌ مِّن مَّاء غَيْرِ آسِنٍ وَأَنْهَارٌ مِن لَّبَنٍ لَّمْ يَتَغَيَّرْ طَعْمُهُ وَأَنْهَارٌ مِّنْ خَمْرٍ لَّذَّةٍ لِّلشَّارِبِينَ وَأَنْهَارٌ مِّنْ عَسَلٍ مُّصَفًّى وَلَهُمْ فِيهَا مِن كُلِّ الثَّمَرَاتِ وَمَغْفِرَةٌ مِّن رَّبِّهِمْ

In it are rivers of water incorruptible, rivers of milk of which the taste never changes, rivers of wine, a joy to those who drink, and rivers of honey pure and clear, in which they will have from all (kinds of) fruits and forgiveness from their Lord.
(Surah Muḥammad, 47:15)

He counted just now in the *āyah* of Holy Qur'an rivers of milk, rivers of honey, rivers of wine, *ladhdhatin li 'sh-shāribīn,* non-intoxicating. Allāh gave you these kinds of rivers which in *dunyā* are *harām*, as Allāh wants to check if you listen or not. "If you listen I give you in *Ākhirah*, you can taste." Why is He giving? Because He wants you to be happy, because you are innocent. He gives you milk, and milk is sign of innocence. Muslims, *mu'mins* are innocent in their belief, they don't make *shirk* to Allāh ﷻ, they mention Him: *Allāhu 'l-ladhī lā ilāha illā Hūwa,* there is no one except Him, *ar-Raḥmān, ar-Raḥīm,* 99 Names. We come with a little bit and He gives from His Oceans that never end and all of that by *dhikrullāh*, and we have mentioned many different types of *dhikrullāh*. So, *annahu yurḍi 'r-Raḥmān 'azza wa jall,* and Allāh will be happy with you when you make *dhikr*.

The Third Benefit

أنه يزيل الهم والغم عن القلب

Annahu yazīlu 'l-hamm wa 'l-ghamm 'ani 'l-qalb.

When you are upset or sad or angry, because most people get angry and get sad and worried, and everyone has a difficulty, everyone wants his children to be successful, everyone wants to be good in *dunyā*, but never do they come and ask to be good in *Ākhirah*. We don't ask, we only ask for *dunyā*, we forget to ask Allāh for *Ākhirah*. So, *dhikrullāh* takes away *al-hamm* and *al-ghamm*, sadness and worry; it takes it away from you, erasing it from the heart and making the heart happy and satisfied from *dhikrullāh*.

So it is easy: as you go to work, also there is work to do well in *dunyā*, to give you *rizq*, to give you success, to give you a good position, and to have a job, you have to do *dhikrullāh,* you have to remember Allāh, because He will do it for you. You cannot take your difficulties, you cannot say, "I applied for a job to seven universities and I got accepted by one." Who made that university to accept you? Allāh! You didn't do it by yourself, don't think yourself you are something. Allāh gave you that. Allāh gave you fame, Allāh gave you high position. So do *dhikrullāh* as much as you can.

The Fourth Benefit

أنه يجلب للقلب الفرح والسرور والبسط

It brings to the heart happiness and joy.

The Fifth Benefit

أنه يقوي القلب والبدن

It will give strength to the heart and to the body.

Every cell that you have is doing hidden *dhikr,* but we cannot hear. How?

وَإِن مِّن شَيْءٍ إِلاَّ يُسَبِّحُ بِحَمْدَهِ وَلَـكِن لاَّ تَفْقَهُونَ تَسْبِيحَهُمْ

There is not a thing but celebrates His Praises, and yet
you don't understand how they declare His Glory![62]

"Everything in this universe and in Heavens and from what Allāh created is doing *dhikrullāh." Tasbīḥ* is what? *Dhikr.* O those people who say, "Don't do *dhikr* in *jamaʿah,"* or "Don't do in a loud voice, or silently," Allāh is saying in the Holy Qur'ān, "Everything," *wa in min shay'in,* "Everything in this universe, in Heavens, in everything that Allāh created they are doing *dhikrullāh." Wa in min shay'in illā yusabbiḥu bi-ḥamdihi,* "Everything is glorifying and praising Him." And what is that? It is *dhikr, dhikrullāh.*

The Sixth Benefit

أنه ينور الوجه والقلب

[62] Sūrat al-'Isrā, 17:44.

It will illuminate the face and the heart.

You will become like a spotlight. It is like a hive of bees and the queen is there: with the queen everyone gets honey, with *dhikrullāh* you get honey, as it makes your face enlightened, illuminated, shining with no need for light to shine on your face. Allāh sends you Light from His Endless Light so you shine, and it is not necessary that you see light coming out, but you will be attracted. That light that is hidden in your face can attract your heart to that person and that's why he becomes a trap to attract people to that heart of the *walī*, because He makes his face shine like a spotlight. What do you see when you have spotlight? You see so many butterflies, running, running, and all these kind of beautiful butterflies with different colors, big ones and small ones. They like the light because they get energy from the light, their life comes from the light. So Allāh will make you a butterfly shining with different colors, like a rainbow of colors and people will immediately be attracted when they see you, when you do *dhikrullāh*.

I am not counting myself among them, I am using always...people ask me, "Why are you using books?" because I like to use books that are not from *Āhlu 's-Sunnah wa 'l-Jama'ah*, they are from Salafi books, in order to say to them, "You write it in your books, but you deny it when you speak to people." And this book is from Ibn Qayyim al-Jawziyya, the student of Ibn Taymīyya.

So *Āhlu 's-Sunnah wa 'l-Jama'ah*, of course they accept all these things—*dhikrullāh*, Intercession, *Mawlid*, all the love to Allāh and to His Prophet ﷺ—but Salafis are very literal, claiming, "No this, no that, it's *bida'*, it's *shirk*!" Yet this is from your own origin, from your own books! This is from the book *Al-Wābil aṣ-Ṣayyib min al-Kalam aṭ-Ṭayyib* by Ibn Qayyim al-Jawziyya. It is their book, not from our book. We take some from their book, not from our book, so they cannot deny it. They might say, "O! Our teacher made a mistake."

The Seventh Benefit

أنه يجلب الرزق

It will attract rizq.

People ask for *rizq,* provision. You do *dhikrullāh* you get *rizq*: *annahu yajlib ar-rizq,* "It will attract provision." That is why *awlīyāullāh* give you daily *awrād* and in it is all *dhikrullāh.* Don't say, "I didn't hear this and didn't hear that," you cannot hear everything; not even all the *Ṣaḥābah* ﷸ heard the same thing from the Prophet ﷺ. What this *Ṣaḥābī* ﷸ heard is different from what that *Ṣaḥābī* ﷸ heard. The Prophet ﷺ used to speak to groups, people coming and people going and he was speaking, so some of the *Ṣaḥābah* ﷸ didn't hear that *ḥadīth* or this *ḥadīth,* but they don't deny it and they do what the Prophet ﷺ has said. So it brings *rizq* for you. When you say, "*Yā Razzāq*!" is that not *dhikr*? Yes it is, and when you say it excessively what is the problem with that? *Yā Razzāq*! *Yā Razzāq*! *Yā Fattāḥ*! *Yā Fattāḥ iftaḥ lanā khayra 'l-bāb,* "O The Opener! Open for us the best of doors!" What's wrong with that? It brings *rizq* for you.

The Eighth Benefit

أنه يكسو الذاكر المهابة والحلاوة والنضرة

It will dress the one making dhikr with beauty, with sweetness and with delicious taste.

Look at the mirror and say, as the Prophet ﷺ used to say, "*Alḥamdulillāhi 'Lladhī aḥsana khuluqī kamā aḥsana khalqī,* Praise be to Allāh, Who has perfected my body, perfected my behavior, my manners as He perfected my body," thanking Allāh ﷻ that He gave you this body, this face. Smile! (*Shukr, yā Rabbī*!) Yes. *Shukran yā Allāh, alḥamdulillāh.* Allāh will be happy, He will dress you with *mahāba,* majestic power. He will dress you with that and when people look at you they will say, "O! *Mashā-Allāh,* this person carries something special," and add on it *ḥalāwa,* "sweetness," so you become a sweet person and they like to eat you! (Laughter.) Because you are *dhākirAllāh,* you are making *dhikr,* people will love you and care for you and come to you to get from you a smile, and it will be enough and they will be happy with that.

The Ninth Benefit

أنه يورثه المحبة التي هي روح الإسلام وقطب رحى الدين ومدار السعادة والنجاة وقدجعلالله لكل شيء سببا وجعل سبب المحبة دوام الذكرفمن أرادأن ينال محبة اللهعزو جل فليلهج بذكره فإنه الدرس والمذاكرة كما أنه باب العلم الذكرباب ا محبة وشارعها الأعظم وصراطها الأ قوم

He will give you love, He will build the love, spirit of Islam, in you.

There are people who have no love in their heart, they have tyranny in their heart, with hate, jealousy, malice. They don't like people to be better than them as they want to be the best and everyone else zero. When you make *dhikr,* Allāh will give you *maḥabbah,* love. What do you think, love of Whom? Love of Allāh ﷻ and love of the Prophet ﷺ!

He ordered all His Creation to love Sayyīdinā Muḥammad ﷺ and He will give you that power to love, because we are rude. It is very difficult to love except ourselves, and Allāh wants us to love Him and love His Prophet ﷺ and to love Islam. The *rūḥ al-Islām,* the spirit of Islam is love, there is nothing else. So the *dhākir,* Allāh will give him the spirit of Islam not only to be a Muslim, but He will give him the secret of Islam, which means He will give him merit, give him that love as a gift so that Islam will flourish in him.

Wa quṭbuhu rāḥa 'd-dīn, Allāh will give you a grinder to grind everything that you dislike and take it away from you and give you what is fruitful for you in your life.

Wa qad jaʿalā 'Llāhu li kulli shay'in sababan wa jaʿalā sababa 'l-maḥabbata dawām adh-dhikr, Allāh made cause and effect for everything in this life: you do this you get this, and love cannot be but by *dhikrullāh.* So do *dhikrullāh* and you will get love: love to Allāh and love to the Prophet ﷺ.

So as we mentioned yesterday, do *dhikr: SubḥānAllāh wa 'l-ḥamdulillāh wa lā ilāha illa-Llāh w 'Allāhu Akbar,* and in another narration it says to add, *wa lā ḥawla wa lā quwatta illa billāhi 'l-ʿAlīyyu 'l-ʿAẓīm. SubḥānAllāh wa bi-ḥamdihi, astaghfirullāhi 'l-ʿAẓīm wa atūbu ilayh, tawbatan ʿabdan ẓālīmān li nafsihi, lā yamliku li nafsihi ḥayātan wa lā mawtan wa lā nushūra,* "repentance of a servant who is an oppressor to himself, who doesn't hold the power of life for himself, nor death, nor of resurrection."

Subḥān-Allāh! Beautiful, eloquent words behind each other that you cannot translate. They have the Holy Qur'ān...they say it is a 'translation,' but we must not fall into this mistake as you cannot translate Allāh's Words with created words. Words are created, but the Arabic words of the Holy Qur'ān are not created as it is Allāh's Ancient Words, and any other languages are created. So you cannot translate the Holy Qur'an which is Uncreated Words with created words, but they came with another word, "commentaries." It means that no one really knows the meanings of Allāh's Holy Words as you cannot translate it. Even in Arabic language these words carry secrets. When you read Holy Qur'an it is *dhikrullāh*. When you read Holy Qur'an, every letter you read from every word has infinite knowledge and you cannot limit it. It is oceans of knowledge into which Allāh has put *tā'wīl* of Holy Qur'an:

وَمَا يَعْلَمُ تَأْوِيلَهُ إِلاَّ اللهُ وَالرَّاسِخُونَ فِي الْعِلْمِ يَقُولُونَ آمَنَّا بِهِ كُلٌّ مِّنْ عِندِ رَبِّنَا

No one knows the interpretation of the Holy Qur'ān except Allāh ﷻ. And those who are firmly grounded in knowledge say, "We believe in the Book; the whole of it is from our Lord."[63]

No one knows its interpretation except Allāh! He is the Creator and *rāsikhūna fi 'l-ʿilmi,* "Those who are firmly established in religion say, *'āmannā bihi kullun min ʿinda rabbinā,* everything is from Allāh.'" So Allāh gives them from time to time in their hearts and inspiration with a commentary, a *tā'wīl,* a commentary that they didn't know before. It comes like secrets, slowly, slowly, slowly, slowly.

May Allāh ﷻ bequeath to us *dhikrullāh, yuwārithunā,* dress us with what no eye has seen, what a heart never imagined, what no eye has seen, what no ear has heard and what no heart has understood or thought about!

---

[63] Sūrat Āli 'Imrān, 3:7.

مَا لاَ عَيْنٌ رَأَتْ، وَلاَ أُذُنٌ سَمِعَتْ، وَلاَ خَطَرَ عَلَى قَلْبِ

What no eye has ever seen no ear has heard nor has ever occurred to the human heart.[64]

Inshā-Allāh we will continue next time, and there are so many benefits; there are 60 mentioned here, but there are thousands and thousands of benefits from *dhikrullāh.* Do *dhikrullāh* and you will be saved, you will be lucky, and for those who do not do *dhikrullāh* may Allāh guide them to do *dhikrullāh.* And also may Allāh guide us, because we are heedless!

فَلَا تُزَكُّوا أَنفُسَكُمْ

Don't praise yourself.
(Sūrat an-Najm, 53:32)[65]

Don't praise yourselves. We say, "We are heedless, *yā Rabbī*! Don't judge us according to our heedlessness, judge us according to Your *Raḥmāh.*"

May Allāh forgive us and may Allāh bless us.

Wa min Allāhi 't-tawfiq, bi ḥurmati 'l-ḥabīb, bi ḥurmati 'l-Fātiḥah.
And with Allāh is success. For the sake of the Beloved, for his sake we recite the opening chapter of Holy Qur'ān.

[64] *Ṣaḥiḥ Muslim.*
[65] *Ṣaḥiḥ Muslim.*

Dhikrullāh Represents You in the Divine Presence

Aʿūdhu billāhi min ash-Shayṭāni 'r-rajīm. Bismillāhi' r-Raḥmāni 'r-Raḥīm.
Nawaytu 'l-arbāʿīn, nawaytu 'l-ʿitikāf, nawaytu 'l-khalwah, nawaytu 'l-ʿuzlah,
nawaytu 'r-riyāḍa, nawaytu 's-sulūk, lillāhi Taʿalā fī hādhā 'l-masjid.
Atīʿūllāha wa atīʿū 'r-Rasūla wa ūli 'l-amri minkum. (4:59)

As-salāmu ʿalaykum wa raḥmatullāhi wa barakātuh. O Muslims! Brothers and sisters, wherever you are, may Allāh bless you in this morning. As we said before, *dhikrullāh* is the most important aspect of Islam or principle of Islam because every *ʿamal* we do is *dhikrullāh.* Like we pray, it is *dhikrullāh; tawḥīd,* saying, *"Ash-hadu an lā ilāha illa-Llāh wa ash-hadu anna Muḥammadu 'r-Rasūlullāh,"* is *dhikrullāh; zakāt* is *dhikrullāh; ṣadaqa* is *dhikrullāh.*

When you give *zakāt* or *ṣadaqa,* charity, it makes people thank Allāh and so you get the reward of what they are saying, which is more valuable than what you gave, but giving is the cause for them to say, *"Shukran, yā Allāh!"* because they are in need and your charity came to them and they are very happy. And we have experience in this issue; when you distribute to areas where there are wars, disasters or epidemics in Africa, you give these provisions to them, food in boxes, and they praise Allāh and pray for the person who gave them, so you get a reward and they get a reward and it is *dhikrullāh.* Also *Hajj* is *dhikrullāh.* So every *ʿamal* that is good *ʿamal,* if the *ʿamal* is for Allāh ﷻ it is considered *dhikrullāh,* and every *ʿamal* that is an obligation on us is considered *dhikrullāh.*

Your Dhikr Remembers You at the ʿArsh

Imam Āḥmad mentioned in his *Musnad* that Prophet ﷺ said:

إِنَّ مِمَّا تَذْكُرُونَ مِنْ جَلاَلِ اللهِ التَّسْبِيحَ وَالتَّهْلِيلَ وَالتَّحْمِيدَ يَنْعَطِفْنَ حَوْلَ الْعَرْشِ لَهُنَّ دَوِيٌّ
كَدَوِيِّ النَّحْلِ تُذَكِّرُ بِصَاحِبِهَا أَمَا يُحِبُّ أَحَدُكُمْ أَنْ يَكُونَ لَهُ - أَوْ لاَ يَزَالَ لَهُ - مَنْ يُذَكِّرُ بِهِ

The Messenger of Allāh ﷺ said, "What you mention of Allāh's Glory, of tasbīḥ (subḥānAllāh), tahlīl (Allāhu Akbar) and taḥmīd (alḥamdulillāh), revolve around the Throne buzzing like bees, remembering the reciter.

Wouldn't any one of you like to have or continue to have something that remembers him (in the Presence of Allāh)?[66]

"Whatever you are remembering of Allāh ﷻ, whatever you are saying, praising Allāh by *taḥmīd, takbīr, tamjīd, tahlīl,* whatever you choose," and there are so many ways of *adhkār, awrād,* so many ways of remembrance that Prophet ﷺ has mentioned, and we have mentioned many of them before, this might be the last session on *dhikrullāh,* so whatever we mentioned of *tasbīḥ, taḥmīd, takbīr, tahlīl, tamjīd, tawḥīd, ʿazhamatullāh ʿazza wa jalla,* as Prophet ﷺ said all of them come together, they are alive. They are alive! When you mention Allāh's Words they are alive. Our words are dead, but Allāh's Words from Holy Qur'an and Holy Ḥadīth are alive. So they come together, *yanʿatifna,* and they arrange themselves into something like bees in the hive, how they come together and they come together all of them *ḥawl al-ʿarsh,* around the Throne, *al-ʿArsh.*

وَسِعَ كُرْسِيُّهُ السَّمَاوَاتِ وَالأَرْضَ

And His Throne extends over the Heavens and the Earth.[67]

The Throne is different from *Kursīyy, ʿArsh* is different. *"Kursīyy"* in Arabic is The Chair that you cannot describe, except Allāh described it in Holy Qur'ān as *wasiʿa kursīyyuhu 's-samāwāti wa 'l-ʿarḍ,* "His Chair contained Heavens and Earth," the whole universe is contained in the Chair, the Chair is bigger than that, so imagine then His Throne, what do you think about His Throne, *al-ʿArsh*? How big is it? The Chair takes into it everything created, but it does not take Allāh into it. Everything Allāh created is contained in the Chair, so what then do you think about the Throne? Allāh ﷻ overpowered the Throne, *Allāh istawa ʿalā al-ʿarsh:*

الرَّحْمَنُ عَلَى الْعَرْشِ اسْتَوَى

The Most Gracious is firmly established on the Throne (of authority).[68]

---

[66] *Sunan Ibn Mājah.*
[67] Sūrah al-Baqarah, 2:255.
[68] Sūrat ṬāḤā, 20:5.

Allāh "overtook" the Throne; the Throne cannot overtake Allāh where Allāh sits on it, like someone sitting on a throne! If you explain it like that, you went out of Islam, because Allāh cannot be contained, not by the Throne, not by the Chair! Allāh took over the Throne, *istawā* the Throne, *istawā ʿalā 'l-ʿarsh, istawā* is not sitting. This is an essential understanding from *tawḥīd,* that Allāh did not "take over" the Throne, not sitting nor standing, but the *ʿArsh* was already contained by this *istiwa* of Allāh ﷻ.

So the *tasbīḥ, tamjīd, taḥmīd, tahlīl,* this *dhikr* will be circumambulating the Throne and they all come together, *yanʿatifna ḥawl al-ʿarsh,* connect together and *lahunna dawīyyu ka-dawīyyu 'n-nahl,* and they have a sound like bees, *an-nahl,* like the sound of bees at the hive and you are afraid to approach them, you are worried to approach them as they might sting you quickly, so you cannot approach them. So these *tasābīḥ,* nothing can approach them as they circumambulate the Throne and the angels can hear their *lahunna dawīyyu,* buzzing and humming, their sound like buzzing and humming of bees. They are making their *tasbīḥ* there and they will rise up by angels when you are reciting and they let them free around the Throne.

Lahunna dawīyyu ka-dawīyyu 'n-nahli tudhakkaru bi ṣāḥibihā. What are they busy with? When you are busy here on Earth with your *tamjīd, tasbīḥ, takbīr, tahlīl, tamjīd,* then they are busy reciting that and at the same time they are mentioning through their circumambulation of the Throne the name of the individual who has made that *tasbīḥ* on Earth. And, *alā yuḥhibbu āḥadukum an yakūna lahu aw lā yazāla lahu man yudhakkaru bih,* "Do you not like to recite and be mentioned in the Presence in Heavens, and being your words..." because they are live words circumambulating the Throne. And in another *athar,* saying:

وقد جاء اثر معناه أن العبد المطيع الذاكر لله تعالى إذا أصابته شدة أو سأل الله تعالى حاجة قالت الملائكة يا رب صوت معروف من عبد معروف والغافل المعرض عن الله عز وجل إذا دعاه وسأله قالت الملائكة يارب صوت منكر من عبد منكر

If the devout, obedient servant who is always remembering Allāh is suddenly in difficulty and asks Allāh help in his need, the angels say, "O Lord! The well-known voice of a well-known servant.'"

For example, he became ill and suddenly needs an operation, that is a difficulty, or who was wealthy and suddenly got bankrupted, that is a difficulty or a family member suddenly died, or anything that is a difficulty, and he is one of the ones who remembers Allāh ﷻ, who is doing *dhikrullāh* so much, so you cannot say, "O! We do *dhikrullāh* so why are we in difficulty?" No, Allāh sent difficulty to raise you up!

Allāh Sends Difficulty to Raise Your Station

The Prophet ﷺ, with his endless superiority over all human beings, Allāh gave him difficulties in his life. Who is the Best of Creation? Who is the one whose name you mention and you go to Paradise? When you mention "Muḥammad" ﷺ, that word alone, when you mention Muḥammad the Prophet, and many people's names are Muḥammad, they enter Paradise without account.

The Prophet ﷺ said:

أفضل الأسماء ما عبد وما حمد

The best names are the ones which indicate servanthood or praise of Allāh.

The best of names are *mā ʿubbid wa mā ḥummid*, those which begin with "*ʿabd*," and those that praise Allāh, and also Muḥammad." You go to Paradise with no account (if you have those names). So when you change your names, change to "*ʿAbd ar-Raḥmān*" or any of the Beautiful Names and Attributes, and also "Muḥammad."

So when you make *dhikrullāh* and you encounter a problem, you ask Allāh, "*Yā Rabbī*! Take that difficulty away," and your tongue is pure because you are always busy with *dhikrullāh* and with what we said, *SubḥānAllāh w 'alḥamdulillāh wa lā ilāha illa-Llāh w 'Allāhu Akbar wa lā ḥawla wa lā quwatta illa billāhi 'l-ʿAlīyyu 'l-ʿAẓīm*. Now what happened? When you say any *tasbīḥ* that Prophet ﷺ has mentioned to us, every *ʿamal* is being raised to the Divine Presence by the angels! The angels take your *duʿā* to the Heavens because you are a *dhākir*, someone who is always remembering his Creator.

How much lovely is it when your young son calls you and runs to you? So how much lovely is it when the *ʿabd* runs to his Lord? Does Allāh like that or not? Yes! And run to Him by thanking Him and praising Him. How much will Allāh dress him with different Manifestations of Allāh's Beautiful Names and Attributes? Allāh is generous, not like us, not like His servants. Allāh will give with no account. Take! If He gives you from His Treasures,

His Treasures never end. He is the Creator of Treasures. If He gives you one treasure, what is the problem? If He gives you ten treasures, if He keeps giving you to infinity, is there any problem? Does He have a shortage of rewards? No, no! Look at what Greatness Allāh gave us through his Prophet ﷺ, the Best of Creation!

So the angels will raise your pure *'amal* since your tongue is pure, because it is busy in *dhikrullāh*. Because if you don't do *dhikrullāh* your tongue will go somewhere else, maybe it gets busy in *ghība* and *namīma*, in backbiting and spreading false rumors and accusations, speaking on this one, on that one, and your tongue goes so much stretched! Grandshaykh, may Allāh bless his soul, used to say that the tongue of human beings can be stretched all the way to backbite Sayyīdinā Ādam ؉, not just enough to backbite those around him, but he will go to the deceased ones too, all the way to Sayyīdinā 'Ādam ؉! So if your tongue is not busy with *dhikrullāh*, then it is going to be busy with everything that Allāh doesn't like.

Allāh likes *tamjīd, tahlīl, takbīr, tasbīḥ* and Allāh likes *ṣalawāt* of the Prophet ﷺ and Allāh likes any poetry on love of the Prophet ﷺ, because Prophet ﷺ did approve poetry in a decent language, but Allāh does not like *ghība* and *namīma*. *Ghība* is to speak behind the back of your brother and *namīma* to create a story that is not true and then they spread it like a sickness, it's a virus between people. They used to say viruses are between human beings, but now they say there are viruses between computers. What is that virus? And it is contagious. That computer has a virus in it? *Allāhu Akbar*. So don't let your tongue to have a virus.

Angels Praise Who Makes Dhikrullāh and Deny Who Doesn't

Keep your *tasbīḥ* and angels will raise your *du'ā* to relieve your difficulty. And they say, *Yā Rabbī ṣawtun ma'rūf*, "*Yā Rabbī*! This voice is known here in the Divine Presence and we are familiar with that voice." *'Ajīb* – how strange! How did they know that voice? *Min 'abdin ma'rūf*, "from a servant that is known to us." As that servant is making *dhikrullāh* a lot and angels are always raising that *dhikrullāh* to the Throne and it is circumambulating the Throne like bees around their hive, because where do these words belong? *Tasbīḥ* of *subḥān-Allāh, alḥamdulillāh, lā ilāha illa-Llāh, Allāhu Akbar, ṣalawāt* on Prophet ﷺ, where do they have to go, where is the best place for them, where do they belong? They belong to Allāh ﷻ! So they go to the *'Arsh* and the angels say, "We know them, we heard this sound, we know this person," and they can identify everyone person-by-person by his *dhikrullāh!*

Look how important it is to do *dhikrullāh*, and some people come to you and say it is *"bid'a, kufr, shirk*, you make too much *ṣalawāt* on the Prophet ﷺ and that is *shirk, harām*!" They say that, although this is from their books that I am speaking. We use their books as it is evidence against what they are saying.

So they say, "*Yā Rabbī*! This sound is known to us and this servant is known to us," and they raise his *'amal* and offer it to Allāh ﷻ and for sure Allāh will relieve that servant of his problem. And the one who is *ghāfil* and is heedless of these benefits and turns away from Allāh ﷻ, and only when he is in difficulty then he calls on Allāh ﷻ and he asks Allāh ﷻ, the angels say, "*Yā Rabbī ṣawtun munkar*, "*Yā Rabbī*! That is an unknown voice." It is, *inna ankara 'l-aṣwāti la-ṣawtu 'l-hamīr*, "a disliked sound."

Bismillāhi 'r-Raḥmāni 'r-Raḥīm.

وَلَا تُصَعِّرْ خَدَّكَ لِلنَّاسِ وَلَا تَمْشِ فِي الْأَرْضِ مَرَحًا إِنَّ اللَّهَ لَا يُحِبُّ كُلَّ مُخْتَالٍ فَخُورٍ وَاقْصِدْ فِي مَشْيِكَ وَاغْضُضْ مِن صَوْتِكَ إِنَّ أَنكَرَ الْأَصْوَاتِ لَصَوْتُ الْحَمِيرِ

And swell not your cheek at men (from pride), nor walk in insolence through the Earth, for Allāh loves not any arrogant boaster, and be moderate in your pace and lower your voice, for surely the harshest of sounds without doubt is the braying of the donkey.[69]

"Don't walk with arrogance and pride. You are not going to penetrate through Earth to Heavens whatever you are doing, and remember the worst of voices is that of donkeys." It means you are a donkey, and a donkey does not know anything except, "Heehaa!" That's it, is there anything else? So that *'abd* all his life doesn't remember Allāh ﷻ; only when difficulty comes, then he remembers Allāh. *Ṭayyib*, why are you not doing your obligations and remembering Allāh ﷻ in your daily life, but only when you have a difficulty? And so angels say (his supplication is), "A strange and disliked voice from a strange and disliked servant; he is not familiar to us, he is not

[69] Sūrat Luqmān, 31:18-19.

humming and buzzing with us around the Throne, circumambulating the Throne, praising You, O Our Lord."

It is said in a *ḥadīth marfuʿ* from Muʿadh ﷺ meaning a ḥadīth attributed directly to the Prophet ﷺ that the Prophet ﷺ said:

مَا عَمِلَ ابْنُ آدَمَ عَمَلاً أَنْجَى لَهُ مِنْ عَذَابِ اَللَّهِ مِنْ ذِكْرِ اَللَّهِ

A man does nothing to rescue himself from Allāh's punishment better than remembering Allāh. [70]

The best that a servant of Allāh can do of *ʿamal*, "the best" means Prophet ﷺ put it on the highest level, "There is no deed better for a servant to do when it is accepted that takes you away from Allāh's Punishment, than *dhikrullāh*." When you make *dhikrullāh*, it is the best *ʿamal* you can do in your life. This is mentioned *ʿan Muʿadh marfuʿan*, which means a *ḥadīth* specifically attributed to the Prophet ﷺ, not a Companion or a Successor by the scholars of ḥadīth Imam Anas bin Mālik, Imam Abū ʿĪsā at-Tirmidhī and Imam aṭ-Ṭabarānī.

Dhikrullāh is a cause that makes angels request that you will be manifested with Allāh's *Sakīnah*, His Tranquility, to feel that peace in your heart when you do *dhikrullāh*. That is why it is recommended through many *shuyūkh* that when you do *awrād* to cover yourself with a white sheet, and to wear white clothes and a white *ʿamāmah*, turban, or white hat, and ladies wear a white scarf, wearing white and covering yourself with a white sheet, and doing *dhikrullāh*. Then that *dhikr* will immediately absorb through your clothes leaving a Heavenly smell! *Awlīyāullāh*, sometimes you are sitting and you smell a nice smell. That happens. Does that happen to anyone here? Raise your hands. That is the smell of a *walīullāh* passing or an angel passing or a pious *mu'min jinn* passing. His clothes already absorbed that Heavenly smell by his making too much *dhikrullāh*, and his body and his clothes have absorbed that Heavenly smell. White is the best to absorb these smells and to attract angels. That is one of highest of ways of *dhikrullāh*.

So the Prophet ﷺ said, "*Dhikrullāh* is the cause to bring *sakīnah*, tranquility down into your heart, and mercy, *ar-Raḥmāh*. That mercy will

[70] Related by Ibn Abī Shaybah and aṭ-Ṭabarānī with a good chain of narrators.

come over you and *ḥufūfu 'l-malā'ikah,* the circumambulation of angels around you," or they touch you and you feel goose bumps, *ra'sha* or a shiver which has pleasure in it, ecstasy, by itself. That is a touch of an angel; it touched you while passing by you. This is *ḥufūfu 'l-malā'ikah,* when they come and touch you or rub you and then they go. That happens by *dhikrullāh,* as the Prophet ﷺ mentioned. So *dhikrullāh* has so many benefits and I will summarize some without explaining:

More Benefits of Dhikrullāh

1) *Yu'rithuhu 'l-maḥabbah,* it will bequeath to him love, give him Heavenly Love as an inheritance. That is *'irth,* to inherit from father or mother or someone. Heavens will inherit (bequeath) the Real Love into your heart when you do a lot of *dhikr,* then you get Allāh's Love:

ما يزال عبدي يتقرب إلي بالنوافل حتى أحبه فإذا أحببته كنت سمعه الذي يسمع به وبصره الذي يبصر به ويده التي يبطش بها ورجله التي يمشي بها وإن سألني لأعطينه ولئن استعاذني لأعيذنه وما ترددت عن شيء أنا فاعله ترددي عن نفس المؤمن يكره الموت وأنا أكره مساءته ولا يزال عبدي يتقرب إلي بالنوافل حتى أحبه، فإذا أحببته كنت سمعه الذي يسمع به وبصره الذي يبصر به، ويده التي يبطش بها ورجله التي يمشي بها،

My servant does not cease to approach Me through voluntary worship until I will love him. When I love him, I will become the ears with which he hears, the eyes with which he sees, the hand with which he acts, and the legs with which he walks (and other versions include, "and the tongue with which he speaks.").[71]

"My servant keeps approaching Me through voluntary worship until I love him," so that is *yu'rith maḥabbatullāh,* which means you will be blessed with Allāh's Love by showing him love, by approaching Him, and that is through voluntary worship and one of which is *dhikrullāh,* and it is the Spirit of Islam.

2) *Yu'rithuhu 'l-murāqabah,* it will bequeath you with meditations, contemplation, *murāqabah, tafakkur,* by thinking, by thought. You will be inheriting all this. The power of *murāqabah,* because many people say, "We do *murāqabah* and we cannot connect to the Prophet ﷺ or to *Ka'bah* or to *Ḥaram an-Nabawī* or with *mashaykh,*" and that is because of not doing

[71] Ḥadīth Qudsī , Bukhārī.

enough *dhikrullāh*. Do more *dhikrullāh* in the way I described, when you sit under a white sheet, wearing white and doing *dhikr* of *"lā ilāha illa-Llāh"* or "Allāh" and you will be dressed by *murāqabah,* it will open up.

3) *Yuʿrithuhu 'l-ʿinābah,* it will bequeath him with repentance to Allāh, to come back to Allāh ﷻ.

4) *Yuʿrithuhu 'l-qurba minhu,* you will inherit the *qurba,* to be near Allāh, to be approaching more and more.

5) *Yuʿrithuhu fat-ḥa 'l-abwāb,* it will inherit (bequeath) to him all Doors to Paradise to open for him.

6) *Yuʿrithuhu 'l-haybah,* He will dress you in the Beautiful Majestic Names.

7) *Yuʿrithuhu ḥayāt al-qalb,* it will bequeath you and dress you with a heart that is alive, the life of the heart, not to be dead heart.

8) *Yuʿrithuhu lisānu 'l-fasīḥ,* it will bequeath you to speak eloquently and to speak only religion and to speak the best for people and not cursing and shouting and lying and spreading what Allāh doesn't like.

9) *Yuʿrithuhu qūtu 'l-qūlūb,* It will bequeath you the food of the hearts.

10) *Yuʿrithuhu qūtu 'r-rūḥ,* it will bequeath him the food of the spirit.

And finally:

11) *Yuʿrithuhu jalā al-qalb,* He will inherit the polishing of the heart. Of all he inherits, the final is polishing the heart, and all of these are treasures cannot be compared to *dunyā* matters as these are all Heavenly matters. They are living and you don't know what you will get from doing that. So at the end they clear his heart from all kinds of rust that he has accumulated and darkness that he has veiled his heart with, and he extinguished the Light that Allāh gave into his heart when he was born, because everyone is born on innocence so that Light is there and you don't want that Light to be extinguished. So whatever you inherit is going to give you a way to polish your heart from the rust that went into it.

لأن أقول: سبحان الله، والحمد لله، ولا إله إلا الله، والله أكبر، أحب إلي مما طلعت عليه الشمس" (رواه مسلم).

Abū Hurayrah related from the Prophet: The uttering of the words "SubḥānAllāh w 'alḥamdulillāh wa lā ilāha illa-Llāh w'Allāhu Akbar" is dearer to me than anything over which the sun rises. (Muslim)

"That to say, 'SubḥānAllāh w 'alḥamdulillāh wa lā ilāha illa-Llāh w'Allāhu Akbar!' is more dear to my heart and so lovely to me, more than any time in my day or in my life or whatever the sun shines on." When the Sun comes with all its light and shines on it, all this is nothing compared to saying once, "SubḥānAllāh w 'alḥamdulillāh wa lā ilāha illa-Llāh w'Allāhu Akbar."

May Allāh forgive us and may Allāh bless us.

Wa min Allāhi 't-tawfīq, bi ḥurmati 'l-ḥabīb, bi ḥurmati 'l-Fātiḥah.
And with Allāh is success. For the sake of the Beloved, for his sake we recite the opening chapter of Holy Qur'ān.

Allāh's Light is in the Hearts of Believers

Aʿūdhu billāhi min ash-Shayṭāni 'r-rajīm. Bismillāhi' r-Raḥmāni 'r-Raḥīm.
Nawaytu 'l-arbāʿīn, nawaytu 'l-ʿitikāf, nawaytu 'l-khalwah, nawaytu 'l-ʿuzlah,
nawaytu 'r-riyāḍa, nawaytu 's-sulūk, lillāhi Taʿalā fī hādhā 'l-masjid.
Atīʿūllāha wa atīʿū 'r-Rasūla wa ūli 'l-amri minkum. (4:59)

As-salāmu ʿalaykum wa raḥmatullāhi wa barakātuh. Alḥamdulillāhi rabbī 'l-ʿalāmīn wa 'ṣ-ṣalāt wa 's-salām ʿalā ashrafi 'l-anbīyā wa 'l-mursalīn Sayyidinā wa nabbiyinā Muḥammadin wa ʿalā ālihi wa ṣaḥbihi ajmaʿīn.

Ayyuha 'l-mushāhidūn wa 'l-mustamiʿūn. O Believers! From wherever you are, *dhikrullāh* never ends, that's why we can go on and on explaining that and it has no beginning and no end. Allāh ﷻ wants His angels to make *dhikr*. They are always in *dhikrullāh,* they never stop, and every angel has a different *dhikr* and the *dhikr* he mentioned the first time is not same as the one he says the second time. Don't think they are like us, always repeating the same *dhikr*. No, it is the Greatness of Allāh ﷻ that no angel repeats the same *dhikr*. Every moment in his *dhikr*, the second *dhikr* is different from the first and third is different from the second, etc.

When you say, "*Allāhu Akbar*!" that means there is no limit to His Greatness, and since there is no limit there is endless *dhikrullāh* and you cannot compare their *dhikr* with our *dhikr*. Although He made the human beings to be honored, Allāh honored them with that honor, our *dhikr* is different from angels' *dhikr,* and He made us to say, if we say one *dhikr* once, angels will be with us saying it until the Day of Judgment! And for that reason, if the heart is ready and is not veiled it will shine, the hearts of Believers will shine with *dhikrullāh*.

The Many Redeeming Rewards of *Dhikrullāh*

It is related in *Bukhārī* and *Muslim* that Abū Hurayrah ؓ related from the Prophet ﷺ:

مَنْ قَالَ لاَ إِلَهَ إِلاَّ اللَّهُ، وَحْدَهُ لاَ شَرِيكَ لَهُ، لَهُ الْمُلْكُ وَلَهُ الْحَمْدُ، وَهُوَ عَلَى كُلِّ شَيْءٍ قَدِيرٌ. فِي يَوْمٍ مِائَةَ مَرَّةٍ، كَانَتْ لَهُ عَدْلَ عَشْرِ رِقَابٍ، وَكُتِبَ لَهُ مِائَةُ حَسَنَةٍ، وَمُحِيَتْ عَنْهُ مِائَةُ سَيِّئَةٍ، وَكَانَتْ لَهُ حِرْزًا مِنَ الشَّيْطَانِ يَوْمَهُ ذَلِكَ، حَتَّى يُمْسِيَ، وَلَمْ يَأْتِ أَحَدٌ بِأَفْضَلَ مِمَّا جَاءَ بِهِ إِلاَّ رَجُلٌ عَمِلَ أَكْثَرَ مِنْهُ

Whoever says, "Lā ilāha illa-Llāh waḥdahu lā sharika lahu 'l-mulk wa lahu 'l-ḥamd wa Hūwa ʿalā kulli shayin qadīr," one-hundred times will get the same reward given for freeing ten slaves and one-hundred good deeds will be written in his accounts and one-hundred sins will be deducted from his accounts and it will be a shield for him from Shayṭān on that day until night, and nobody will be able to do a better deed except the one who does more than he."[72]

So simple, so easy. We say it one time: *Lā ilāha illa-Llāh waḥdahu lā sharīk lahu 'l-mulku wa lahu 'l-ḥamd wa Hūwa ʿalā kulli shayin qadīr*. If you say it a hundred times a day, it is as if you have freed persons from Hellfire. "Freed people from Hellfire," means here from people who are going to be like slaves to someone and it is as if you freed them. If we want to take the interpretational meaning of it, not the literal meaning, it is as if you freed ten people from the hand of Shayṭān. And if you free one person, Allāh will free you from Hellfire, if you free one person from Shayṭān, or you free one person from a tyrant owner.

Wa kutiba lahu mi'yatu ḥasanatin wa muhīyat ʿanhu mi'yatu sayyiāt wa kānat lahu ḥirzan min ash-shayṭān yawmahu dhālika ḥattā yumsīyy. "And it will be written for him a hundred good deeds and erase a hundred sins from him and it will be like a protection from Shayṭān," and Shayṭān cannot approach you that whole day. "From the morning when you say it," like we said it just now in *Fajr* time, until the evening, its effect will stay there. Even if you do a sin, that sin will be erased by the power of that *tasbīḥ* that the Prophet ﷺ has mentioned in another hadith, "Whoever says, "*SubḥānAllāh wa bi-ḥamdihi*" a hundred times during the day, his sins are wiped away, even if they are like the foam of the sea.[73]

Wa man qāl, "And whoever says, '*SubḥānAllāh wa bi-ḥamdihi*' a hundred times per day, all his sins will be erased even if they are as many as the foam of the ocean!" Like the foam of the ocean, how much foam is there on the waves? It never stops. It means your forgiveness will continue, it never stops, even if you say it one time a day or a hundred times, all your sins will be erased.

---

[72] Abū Hurayrah in *Ṣaḥiḥ al-Bukhārī*.

[73] *Ṣaḥiḥ al-Bukhārī*.

وفي صحيح مسلم عن أبي هريرة قال : قال رسول الله صلى الله عليه و سلم: لأن أقول
سبحان الله والحمد لله ولا إله إلا الله والله أكبر أحب إلي مما طلعت عليه الشمس

It is related from Abū Hurayrah ؈ that the Prophet ﷺ said:

*For me to say, "Glory be to Allāh! All Praise is for Allāh! There is no god but Allāh!
Allāh is the Greatest!" is dearer to me than all that the sun rises upon.*[74]

"If I say that it will be better for me, that day will be the best in my life." So say, "SubḥānAllāh w 'alḥamdulillāh wa lā ilāha illa-Llāh w 'Allāhu Akbar."

اللَّهُمَّ إِنِّي أَصْبَحْتُ أُشْهِدُكَ وَأُشْهِدُ حَمَلَةَ عَرْشِكَ، وَمَلَائِكَتَكَ وَجَمِيعَ خَلْقِكَ،
أَنَّكَ أَنْتَ اللهُ لَا إِلَهَ إِلَّا أَنْتَ وَحْدَكَ لَا شَرِيكَ لَكَ، وَأَنَّ مُحَمَّداً عَبْدُكَ وَرَسُولُكَ

Allāhumma innī asbaḥtu ush-hiduka wa ush-hidu ḥamalata 'arshika, wa malā'ikataka wa jamī'a khalqika, annaka Anta 'Llāhu lā ilāha illa Anta waḥdaka lā sharīka laka, wa anna Muḥammadan 'abduka wa Rasūluka.

In the *ḥadīth* of Anas ؈ from the Prophet ﷺ:

*Whoever says in the morning and in the evening, "O Allāh! I have entered a new
morning and call upon You and upon the bearers of Your Throne, upon Your
angels and all Creation, to bear witness that surely You are Allāh, that there is none
worthy of worship but You alone, You have no partners
and Muḥammad is Your servant and Your messenger."*[75]

Whoever says that *dhikr*, Allāh will free one-quarter of you from Hellfire. If you say it twice, half of you will be free from Hellfire, three times, three-quarters, four times all of you, once in the morning and once in the evening. Is it easy or difficult? It is easy if we keep our tongue wet with *dhikrullāh*, it is difficult if we let Shayṭān in!

وحكي عن رجل من العباد أنه نزل برجل ضيفا فقام العابد ليله يصلي وذلك الرجل مستلق
على فراشه فلما أصبحا قال له العابد : سبقك الركب أو كما قال فقال : ليس الشأن فيمن
بات مسافرا وأصبح مع الركب الشأن فيمن بات على فراشه وأصبح قد قطع الركب

---

[74] Ṣaḥīḥ al-Muslim.
[75] Abū Dāwūd, al-Bukhārī in *al-Adab al-Mufrad*;Tirmidhī.

How to Remain Connected to Allāh

Ibn Qayyim relates a narration in Al-Wābil aṣ-Ṣayyib: *Wa ḥukīyā ʿan rajalun min al-ʿubād,* There were two people, and "one of the sincere, pious worshippers who does everything right" one day was coming to a village and he was the guest of someone who hosted him in his home, *fa qām al-ʿabidu laylahu yuṣallī,* and that visiting worshipper kept worshipping Allāh ﷻ all night and the man, the host, was sleeping all night, resting. When they woke up in morning, the worshipper said to the host, *sabaqak ar-rakab,* "The caravan (of worshippers) already went ahead of you, because you were sleeping and not worshipping." The man was worshipping and the host was sleeping. *faqāla laysa ash-shānu fīman bāta mūsāfiran wa aṣbaḥa maʿ ar-rakab ash-shān fīman bāta ʿalā firāshi wa aṣbaḥa qad qataʿ ar-rakab,* "The one who worshipped all night and was with the caravan is not like the one who lay down and he overpassed the caravan," because the one who was on his bed sleeping, his heart was with Allāh ﷻ and *alṣaqā ḥabbat qalbihi,* he glued his heart around the *ʿArsh,* so his heart was circumambulating around *ʿArshullāh,* and with the angels.

It means here that even that one who is a pious worshipper is not better than the one laying down, because the one laying down, his heart was with Allāh ﷻ. That is why when *awlīyāullāh* take rest, their heart is immediately connected, so though sleeping his heart was always working and the Prophet's heart was always with his Lord, his body was with people:

لي ساعة مع الرب وساعة مع الخلق

I have one side (or one hour) with my Lord and
one side (or one hour] with the people.

It means, "I have one hour with Allāh," meaning one face or image, "and one hour with the people." This means there are two images of the Prophet ﷺ: one always standing at Allāh's ﷻ Door, circumambulating the Throne and the other one with the people, teaching them and purifying them.

Dhikrullāh nūrun li 'dh-dhākir, "It is Light for the one making *dhikr,"* *wa nūrun lahu fi qabrihi,* "and it is a light for him in the grave, and it is a light for him on *aṣ-Ṣirāṭ al-Mustaqīm."* Graves will become enlightened with too much light in it, because that person in his life was doing *dhikrullāh,* so Allāh will shine Light his grave.

Allāh ﷻ said in Holy Qur'ān:

أَوَ مَن كَانَ مَيْتًا فَأَحْيَيْنَاهُ وَجَعَلْنَا لَهُ نُورًا يَمْشِي بِهِ فِي النَّاسِ كَمَن مَّثَلُهُ فِي الظُّلُمَاتِ لَيْسَ
بِخَارِجٍ مِّنْهَا كَذَلِكَ زُيِّنَ لِلْكَافِرِينَ مَا كَانُواْ يَعْمَلُونَ

Can he who was dead, to whom We gave life and a Light so he can walk among men be like him who is in the depths of darkness, from which he can never come out? Thus to those without faith their own deeds seem pleasing.[76]

"To the one who is dead, We bring him back to life and we make for him a Light," *nūran yamshī bihi,* "that he moves in it, that shows him the way." *Nūr* is guidance: when there is light you can see and be guided and when there is no light you are not guided. So Allāh is saying, "The one whose heart is already dead, we give him a light as he wants to do *dhikrullāh,"* and as soon as the servant begins to do *dhikrullāh,* Allāh gives a light and people run to him due to that spotlight. It is the light of *īmān* that Allāh is sending to their hearts. *Kaman mathaluhu fī ẓulumāti laysa bi khārijin minhā,* "Like the one whose heart is always dead has no light and is never going to come out of darkness." So the *mu'min* whose heart has been rejuvenated with the light of *īmān,* Allāh will put in his heart and He put His love and His knowledge and put *ma'rifat* in the heart of that person.

The second one is heedless; he doesn't ever turn to Allāh and he is *al-mu'riḍ 'an dhikrihi,* "He is turning away from *dhikrullāh,"* and that is dangerous! I say to myself and to you that it is dangerous to turn away from *dhikrullāh,* because Allāh will turn away from you. That is why the Prophet ﷺ always used to ask, *Yā Rabbī ij'al fī laḥmī nūran,* "O my Lord put the Light, *an-Nūr,* from His Beautiful Name *an-Nūr* in my body" and he used to ask for *Nūr* in his bones, in his nerves, in his head, in his face, in his ears, in his eyes, and to make the *Nūr* above him, below him, on his right, on his left, before him and behind him. *Allāhumma ij'al min fawqī nūran wa min taḥtī nūran wa 'an yamīnī nūran wa 'an yassārī nūran.*

[76] Sūrat al-An'am, 6:122.

So for us, that *nūr* is going dead. Look, the *nūr* of the charger is finished so we have to put another battery inside, and if we don't put a battery inside it will no longer work. If we don't recharge the battery in our hearts, that is a problem, in our hearts is the problem.

So also in lectures, in *ṣuḥbahs,* in advice, there are some examples like that, keep it in your mind. Don't say, "O the broadcasting was cut." No, it is a sign! Everything is a sign, that we spoke about Light that Allāh put in a heart that is dead and Allāh rejuvenates the heart and puts Light in it, then also the technology in daily life gives us an example! That is finished, it needs a battery and that means it needs to be rejuvenated just as the heart has to be revived in order to work another time.

Ibn Qayyim says:

فسأل ربه تبارك وتعالى أن يجعل النور في ذراته الظاهرة والباطنة وأن يجعله محيطا به من جميع جهاته وأن يجعل ذاته وجملته نورا

The Prophet ﷺ asked his Lord, to make the Light in his very atoms, both the physically-manifest and the inwardly-hidden, and to make him encompassed by light from every direction and to make his very essence as well as his body to be Light.

So, the Prophet ﷺ was always asking Allāh to make him Light: *Allāhumma 'jaʿalnī nūran,* "O Allāh, make me Light, *nūr,*" and the *nūr* is *dhikr*. The Prophet's heart, body or mind, all the cells in his body, which in human beings number three trillion cells, are all making *dhikr* in different ways, not in the same way.

ابْنَ مَسْعُودٍ قَالَ : " إِنَّ رَبَّكُمْ لَيْسَ عِنْدَهُ لَيْلٌ وَلَا نَهَارٌ ، نُورُ السَّمَوَاتِ مِنْ نُورِ وَجْهِهِ

Ibn Masʿūd ؓ, one of the greatest *Ṣaḥābīs,* said:

Laysa ʿinda rabbakum laylun wa lā nahār nūru 's-samāwāti min nūri wajhih, there is no day and night for the Lord, the Light of the Heavens and the whole Universe, is from the shining Light of His Face.[77]

[77] Related by ad-Dārimī from Ibn Masʿūd.

Allāh's Beautiful Name an-Nūr, is always there, as Allāh ﷻ said:

وَأَشْرَقَتِ الْأَرْضُ بِنُورِ رَبِّهَا

And the Earth will shine with the Light of its Lord.[78]

When that Light dresses the Earth, there will be no more day and night, at that time it will be one, it is His Light.

وَلَمَّا جَاءَ مُوسَىٰ لِمِيقَاتِنَا وَكَلَّمَهُ رَبُّهُ قَالَ رَبِّ أَرِنِي أَنظُرْ إِلَيْكَ قَالَ لَن تَرَانِي وَلَٰكِنِ انظُرْ إِلَى
الْجَبَلِ فَإِنِ اسْتَقَرَّ مَكَانَهُ فَسَوْفَ تَرَانِي فَلَمَّا تَجَلَّىٰ رَبُّهُ لِلْجَبَلِ جَعَلَهُ دَكًّا وَخَرَّ مُوسَىٰ صَعِقًا
فَلَمَّا أَفَاقَ قَالَ سُبْحَانَكَ تُبْتُ إِلَيْكَ وَأَنَا أَوَّلُ الْمُؤْمِنِينَ

When Moses came to the place appointed by Us, and his Lord addressed him, He said, "O my Lord! Show (Yourself) to me, that I may look upon You." Allah said, "By no means can you see Me (direct), but look upon the mount; if it abide in its place, then you shall see Me." When his Lord manifested His glory on the Mount, He made it as dust and Moses fell down in a swoon. When he recovered his senses, he said, "Glory be to You! To You I turn in repentance, and I am the first to believe."[80]

When Sayyīdinā Mūsā ؑ asked to see Allāh, He said, "Look at the mountain and if it stays in its place, you can see Me." Then Allāh sent one ray of His *Nūr* and the mountain shattered like powder from that Light, from the power that Allāh has put inside His Light! It made the mountain melt completely and there was no more mountain. The hearts of *awlīyāullāh* melt, and the hearts of prophets for sure will melt from the greatness that Allāh showers on them from His Light!

اللَّهُ نُورُ السَّمَاوَاتِ وَالْأَرْضِ

Allāh is the Light of the Heavens and Earth.[81]

There is nothing except Light and nothing is attainable, only the Light that is shining that you can see, but you cannot reach. The Prophet ﷺ

---

[78] Sūrat az-Zumar, 39:69.

[80] Sūrat al-Āʿrāf, 7:143.

[81] Sūrat an-Nūr, 24:35.

mentioned in many *aḥādīth* and in many *tafāsīr* of Holy Qur'ān that Allāh ﷻ will be seen in Paradise:

لاَّ تُدْرِكُهُ الأَبْصَارُ وَهُوَ يُدْرِكُ الأَبْصَارَ وَهُوَ اللَّطِيفُ الْخَبِيرُ

No vision can grasp Him, but His grasp is over all vision.
He is above all comprehension, yet is acquainted with all things.[82]

"You can see, but you cannot reach," you cannot be there, you can see from far the Light that Allāh will send to Paradise to appear and people can see their Creator; those who are:

فِي مَقْعَدِ صِدْقٍ عِندَ مَلِيكٍ مُّقْتَدِرٍ

Fī maqaʿdi ṣidqin ʿinda malīkin muqtadir.

In an Assembly of Truth, in the Presence of an Almighty King.[83]

They are there, with the Prophet ﷺ. They can see, but *lā tudrikuhu 'l-abṣār*, they cannot reach to know Him and to see Him from near at hand. You cannot be there. The example of that is the Sun: you can see its light during the daytime, but can you be there? No, although you see it from afar. So what you see is traces of the Reality, but if you reach the Sun there might be so many important realities happening there. From far away they say that the core of the Sun is burning at 50 million degrees Centigrade. What is 50 million degrees Centigrade? At 2,000 degrees iron and gold melt from the heat! The Sun is 50 million degrees Centigrade and it doesn't melt! If the Earth were 50 million degrees it would melt. Why does the Sun not melt? Are there different planets that Allāh created that don't melt?

The hearts of the Believers don't melt, like the light of the Sun. The heat the Sun produces is like the heat the heart produces, of *ʿishq*, of love to Allāh ﷻ! How will Allāh make that heart disappear? No, it's alive: in his grave he is alive, in his *dunyā* he is alive, in his *Ākhirah* he is alive!

O Muslims, Believers! Through *dhikrullāh*, Allāh ﷻ granted us many things we cannot understand. Ubay ibn K'ab related that where Allāh said:

---

[82] Sūrat al-Anʿam, 6:103.
[83] Sūrat al-Qamar, 54:55.

اللَّهُ نُورُ السَّمَاوَاتِ وَالْأَرْضِ مَثَلُ نُورِهِ كَمِشْكَاةٍ فِيهَا مِصْبَاحٌ الْمِصْبَاحُ فِي زُجَاجَةٍ الزُّجَاجَةُ كَأَنَّهَا كَوْكَبٌ دُرِّيٌّ يُوقَدُ مِن شَجَرَةٍ مُّبَارَكَةٍ زَيْتُونِةٍ لَّا شَرْقِيَّةٍ وَلَا غَرْبِيَّةٍ يَكَادُ زَيْتُهَا يُضِيءُ وَلَوْ لَمْ تَمْسَسْهُ نَارٌ نُّورٌ عَلَىٰ نُورٍ يَهْدِي اللَّهُ لِنُورِهِ مَن يَشَاءُ وَيَضْرِبُ اللَّهُ الْأَمْثَالَ لِلنَّاسِ وَاللَّهُ بِكُلِّ شَيْءٍ عَلِيمٌ

> *Allāh is the Light of the Heavens and the Earth. The parable of His Light is as if there were a Niche and within it a Lamp, the Lamp enclosed in Glass, the Glass as it were a Brilliant Star lit from a Blessed Tree, an olive, neither of the East nor of the West, whose oil is well luminous, though fire scarce touched it. Light upon Light! Allāh guides whom He will to His Light. Allāh sets forth parables for men and Allāh knows all things.[84]*

"Allāh is the Light of Heavens and Earth and the example of His Light is the heart of a Muslim!" *Allāhu nūru 's-samāwāti wa 'l-arḍ ka-mishkātin mathalu nūrihi fī qalbi muslim.* "Mishkāt" in the literal meaning is an opening in the wall (niche) where you put the lamp in the old times, *qubbah*, like a niche in the wall where you put the lamp and it shines and gives you light. He is comparing the heart of the Muslim to a niche in the wall, a niche in the body where the heart is; the lamp is as if within that niche, the body is like the niche and in it you hang the heart and the lamp is always shining.

Mathalu nūrihi fī qalbi muslim – "that example of that *nūr* is the light that Allāh has put in the heart, that clean heart, because he is a Muslim." You say, "*Lā ilāha illa-Llāh Muḥammadan rasūlullāh*," so you are Muslim. Allāh has put a heart that has light in it in your body. *wa Hūwa nūrahu anzalahu ilayhim fa aḥyāhum bihi wa ja'alahum yamshūna bihi bayn an-nās*, Allāh has made the heart of Muslims and particularly those whose light increases, increases, increases, those people become *awlīyāullāh* and their duty, their job is to go around the Earth meeting with people in order for that light to be reflecting it's reality on to other people so that they can see them.

That is why *sīyāḥa*, traveling, is the habit of prophets. They don't stay in one place, they move, *hijra*, they move from one place to another. Never was a *walī* buried in the place he was born, because he always goes somewhere else, because he is going to be a reflector of that light to the heart, like a spotlight to people in that area.

---

[84] Sūrat an-Nūr, 24:35.

Fa minhum man nūrahu k' ash-shams, "Some of them, the light in their hearts is like the Sun," *minhum man nūrahu ka 'l-qamr,* "some like the moon" and some like the stars, some like a lamp, some have very little light, there is some sincerity on that person, but not too much. And Allāh ﷻ, according to how much light is in you, He gives you light on *Ṣirāṭ al-Mustaqīm* , He gives you light to cross that Bridge over Hellfire to Paradise as you have to cross the Bridge of *Ṣirāṭ al-Mustaqīm.* It depends on how much light you have to see the way and pass quickly, or with no light you might fall down. May Allāh protect us from falling down as falling down is dangerous!

Majlis of *Dhikr* is the *Majlis* of Angels

Innamā majālis adh-dhikri majālis al-malā'ikah, "Certainly, the *majlis* of *dhikr* is the *majlis* of angels." As we said at the beginning, Allāh ﷻ made His angels to make *dhikr* and their *dhikr* is different each time, they don't repeat, and what He said to them?

إِنَّ اللهَ وَمَلَائِكَتَهُ يُصَلُّونَ عَلَى النَّبِيِّ يَا أَيُّهَا الَّذِينَ آمَنُوا صَلُّوا عَلَيْهِ وَسَلِّمُوا تَسْلِيمًا

Verily, Allāh and His angels send praise on the Prophet. O Believers! Pray upon him and greet him with a worthy salutation.[85]

"Allāh ordered His angels to make *ṣalawāt* on the Prophet ﷺ," so their *dhikr* is *ṣalawāt*, making *ṣalawāt* *ʿibādah,* a form of worship. Don't say, "Oh! I cannot do *ṣalawāt* on the Prophet ﷺ as that is *shirk.*" Allāh made angels to do *ṣalawāt* and He said, *majālis adh-dhikr majālis al-malā'ikah,* "The association of *dhikr* is the association of angels." Wherever there is *dhikr,* angels will come running to that place. *Fa laysa min majālisu 'dh-dhikr...Allāhu taʿalā fi,* "There is no place in *dunyā* for angels except the place where there is an association of *dhikr*, where people sit and remember Allāh ﷻ."

Ibn Taymiyya said, and I am quoting Ibn Taymiyya especially, not because I believe in his *ʿaqīdah,* no, but to tell those who follow him today they are free (to believe this). He said, "*Dhikrullāh* is for sure: *Inna naḥnu nazalnā 'dh-dhikr wa inna lahu la-ḥāfiẓūn.* "First, *dhikr* is to read Holy Qur'ān and second, to call on Him through Holy Qur'an and to call on Him through *Asmāu 'Llahi 'l-Ḥusnā,* His Beautiful Names, and on His *Ṣiffāt,* Attributes."

[85] Sūrat al-Aḥzāb, 33:56.

So it means that Ibn Taymiyya said you can call on Allāh through His Names, but when we call on Allāh by His Names, they object. Is not Allāh from His Names? The main Name that encompasses all the Beautiful Names and Attributes, is that His Name or not? The other Names, ar-Raḥmān, ar-Raḥīm, as-Salām, al-Quddūs, aṣ-Ṣabūr, with the Attributes, His Ṣiffāt, Attributes are also Names, the Names and Attributes of Allāh ﷻ. Ibn Taymiyya said, "You can ask Him through that," and that is why we say, "Yā Raḥmān," "Yā Raḥīm," "Yā Ḥafiẓ," "Yā Mujīb," "Yā Mu'izz," "Yā Laṭīf," "Yā Ghafūr," "Yā Sattār," "Yā Fattāḥ," "Yā Wadūd," "Yā Raḥmān," "Yā Raḥīm," as we are calling on Him through His Names!

So it is allowed to make *dhikrullāh* in gatherings and no one can (legitimately) say to you. "No, don't do it in gatherings!" That is what they say, "Do it by yourself." They say to you, "*Dhikr* is Holy Qur'an." Yes, we know that *dhikrullāh* is Holy Qur'an, but *dhikrullāh* is also as the teacher of the Salafi's, Ibn Taymiyya, said, remembering Allāh through Allāh's Beautiful Names and Attributes.

عَنْ أَبِي هُرَيْرَةَ قَالَ قَالَ رَسُولُ اللَّهِ صَلَّى اللَّهُ عَلَيْهِ وَسَلَّمَ إِنَّ لِلَّهِ مَلَائِكَةً يَطُوفُونَ فِي الطُّرُقِ يَلْتَمِسُونَ أَهْلَ الذِّكْرِ فَإِذَا وَجَدُوا قَوْمًا يَذْكُرُونَ اللَّهَ تَنَادَوْا هَلُمُّوا إِلَى حَاجَتِكُمْ قَالَ فَيَحُفُّونَهُمْ بِأَجْنِحَتِهِمْ إِلَى السَّمَاءِ الدُّنْيَا قَالَ فَيَسْأَلُهُمْ رَبُّهُمْ وَهُوَ أَعْلَمُ مِنْهُمْ مَا يَقُولُ عِبَادِي قَالُوا يَقُولُونَ يُسَبِّحُونَكَ وَيُكَبِّرُونَكَ وَيَحْمَدُونَكَ وَيُمَجِّدُونَكَ قَالَ فَيَقُولُ هَلْ رَأَوْنِي قَالَ فَيَقُولُونَ لَا وَاللَّهِ مَا رَأَوْكَ قَالَ فَيَقُولُ وَكَيْفَ لَوْ رَأَوْنِي قَالَ يَقُولُونَ لَوْ رَأَوْكَ كَانُوا أَشَدَّ لَكَ عِبَادَةً وَأَشَدَّ لَكَ تَمْجِيدًا وَتَحْمِيدًا وَأَكْثَرَ لَكَ تَسْبِيحًا قَالَ يَقُولُ فَمَا يَسْأَلُونِي قَالَ يَسْأَلُونَكَ الْجَنَّةَ قَالَ يَقُولُ وَهَلْ رَأَوْهَا قَالَ يَقُولُونَ لَا وَاللَّهِ يَا رَبِّ مَا رَأَوْهَا قَالَ يَقُولُ فَكَيْفَ لَوْ أَنَّهُمْ رَأَوْهَا قَالَ يَقُولُونَ لَوْ أَنَّهُمْ رَأَوْهَا كَانُوا أَشَدَّ عَلَيْهَا حِرْصًا وَأَشَدَّ لَهَا طَلَبًا وَأَعْظَمَ فِيهَا رَغْبَةً قَالَ فَمِمَّ يَتَعَوَّذُونَ قَالَ يَقُولُونَ مِنْ النَّارِ قَالَ يَقُولُ وَهَلْ رَأَوْهَا قَالَ يَقُولُونَ لَا وَاللَّهِ يَا رَبِّ مَا رَأَوْهَا قَالَ يَقُولُ فَكَيْفَ لَوْ رَأَوْهَا قَالَ يَقُولُونَ لَوْ رَأَوْهَا كَانُوا أَشَدَّ مِنْهَا فِرَارًا وَأَشَدَّ لَهَا مَخَافَةً قَالَ فَيَقُولُ فَأُشْهِدُكُمْ أَنِّي قَدْ غَفَرْتُ لَهُمْ قَالَ يَقُولُ مَلَكٌ مِنْ الْمَلَائِكَةِ فِيهِمْ فُلَانٌ لَيْسَ مِنْهُمْ إِنَّمَا جَاءَ لِحَاجَةٍ قَالَ هُمْ الْجُلَسَاءُ لَا يَشْقَى بِهِمْ جَلِيسُهُمْ

So what does the *ḥadīth* here say? From Abū Hurayrah ؓ, and this is a strong *ḥadīth* in *Bukhārī* and *Muslim*, so they cannot deny that. *Inna lillāhi malā'ikatan faḍlan 'an kutāb an-nās*, "Allāh has angels in *dunyā* in addition to the scribes who write what you do of good and bad, other than that Allāh has special angels," *yaṭūfūna fi 't-ṭuruq yaltamisūna Āhl adh-dhikr*, "who roam about in the streets looking for people of *dhikrullāh*." *Fa idhā wajadū qawmun yadhkurūn Allāh ta'alā tanādaw halummū ila ḥājatikum*, "When they find a group of people making *dhikrullāh* (through reading Holy Qur'an or through His Names and Attributes) and when they find them, do they not hear them?" How do they hear them? Through their voices! So it means there is loud *dhikr* and there is hidden, *khafī dhikr* that you do by yourself. In *jama'at* they do *dhikr jahrī*, loud *dhikr*, not silent.

And this *ḥadīth* is proof that angels hear and see them and join them. How do they know they are doing *dhikr* if they don't hear them? Like this gathering, and there are many like this around the world, they could be talking anything, but he said, "They come because they know of *majālis adh-dhikr* by hearing them," so for sure they must hear them, and they will touch them with their wings. This shows angels have wings. *Fa yaḥufūnahum bi ajniḥatihim,* "They will be with them through their wings, they touch them." This shows that angels have wings. "They will be encompassing around and around them in circles and they will come with their wings all the way up to the First Paradise." How far is it and how many of them? This is *majlis adh-dhikr* and there are many all over the world like that. The angels will come in every *majlis adh-dhikr* in circles over them, with layer upon layer, all the way to the First Heaven.

How many of them are there? This universe is so huge! Our galaxy is (comprised of) 80 billion stars according to physicists and our Solar System is not even the head of a pin compared to the other stars, the whole Solar System. There are stars bigger than the entire Solar System, and scientists say there are at least 6,000 galaxies bigger than our galaxy, and this is all in *ḥadd ad-dunyā,* the limits of this world, meaning in this universe. Prophet ﷺ is saying in an authentic *ḥadīth* that the angels are in circles up to *samā ad-dunyā,* meaning, they go all the way above this entire universe. How many of them are there? If there are 80 billion stars in one galaxy which we multiply by 6,000, it gives us a number we cannot pronounce or imagine. Angels go all the way up to *samā ad-dunyā,* that means there are more than 80 billion times 6,000 and there are stars that are more than two or three billion light years away, not in normal years.

O our viewers, *as-salāmu ʿalaykum! Dhikrullāh* is not easy and it opens doors for everyone. Allāh asked the angels who are encompassing the universe all the way to First Heaven, in order for us to learn, as Allāh already knows, He asks, "What are My servants doing?"

They say, *Yusabbiḥūnaka wa yukabbirūnaka wa yaḥmadūnaka,* "They are making *tasbīḥ, takbīr, tahlīl.* They praise You, they make *tahlīl* and they glorify You!"

Three words and that is *dhikrullāh.* How do you make *tasbīḥ, tahlīl* and *tamjīd*? Is it not through His Beautiful Names and Attributes? So why do they object? Also, the angels are telling Allāh ﷻ, so that means they heard them say that, which means they are saying it in a loud voice. Salafis object to (making *dhikr* in) a loud voice, we know that. *Āhlu 's-Sunnah wa 'l-Jamaʿah* want to teach us, we are humble for them and at their threshold, but Salafis, keep your belief to yourself! Don't teach us about silent *dhikr* or tell us to keep our voices down!

What about the *ḥadīth* of the Prophet ﷺ, where he said:

أَكْثِرُوا ذِكْرَ اللهِ حَتَّى يَقُولُوا مَجْنُونٌ

Remember Allāh ﷻ so much that people start saying, "He has gone mad."[86]

How can they say that you are crazy if they don't hear you? This means that you should do loud *dhikr*. We like to do it loud, we like to do it hidden, we like to do it in any way, so keep to your way and we will keep to ours!

Allāh ﷻ asks, "Did they see Me?" and they give an oath, "By Allāh, with Your Greatness, they did not see You." Prophet ﷺ said that Allāh said, "Kayfa law ra'awnī, how will be their situation if they see Me?" And they say, "If they saw You they would be more stronger worshippers to You yā Allāh, and more strong with belief to Praise You...lawa rā-awk kānū ashada laka ʿibadatan wa ashadd laka taḥmīdan wa tamjīdan wa aktharu laka tasbīḥan, they would be more eager to make Praise, and to Glorify You and to make tasbīḥ for You." They would be more eager to do all that. Allāh asks, "What are they asking from Me? What do they want?" And they say, "They are asking for Your Paradise."

For sure, to enter Paradise is through *raḥmatullāh,* they want Paradise. There is nothing less in Paradise, there is everything more than what you have in *dunyā.*

Allāh says, "Did they see My Paradise?" And they say, "Lā yā Rabbī, by Your Honor and Greatness, they did not see it."

Allāh says, "How will they be if I show them My Paradise?"

The Prophet ﷺ said that they say, *Law annahum rā-awhā kānū ash-hadu ʿalayhā ḥarṣan wa ash-hadu lahā ṭalaban wa ʿaẓam fihā raghbatan,* "If they saw

---

86 Āḥmad , *Musnad.*

Paradise they would be more eager to see it and to be in it and their desires to be in it would be increased."

Allāh asks them, "From what are they seeking safety?" and the angels reply, "They are asking to seek refuge in You from Hellfire."

Allāh says, "Did they see My Hellfire?" and the angels say, "Verily, by Allāh, by Your Honor, no!"

Allāh asks, "How will they be if they see it?" And they say, "They would be more eager to escape it as much as they can, and to be afraid from it as much as they can be afraid."

The Prophet ﷺ said that Allāh says, "Fa ush-hidukum, I make you My witness, O My angels!" [and how many are they? It could be He asks all the angels, and this is His Greatness.] "I make you witness, O My angels!" [Are there billions, millions or trillions? There are infinite number of angels!] "I make you witness that verily I have forgiven them. [It is finished, no sins!]"

There are many *majālis* such as this one around the world, especially in Mecca and Madīnah where the gathering is bigger, and in different countries. Allāh is forgiving everyone who is sitting and making *dhikrullāh* through His Beautiful Names and Attributes!

Out of these billions and infinite number of angels, Allāh makes one of the angels to speak in order to show His Mercy. That angel says, "O Allāh! There is one between them who is not from the people of *dhikrullāh*. He is an intruder to the dhikr and he came because he was asking for something from someone. He has something to do with someone and saw him sitting there, so he sits waiting for him." Allāh says, *hum al-julasā lā yashqā bihim jalīsahum*, "They are those whom if you sit with them in their gathering you will never find punishment. Forgive him!"

SubḥānAllāh, that is Allāh's Mercy! That one came not asking what the people are asking: they are asking Allāh ﷻ for Paradise, love of Allāh, Prophet ﷺ, angels and Islam. He is not asking for that, but because he sat with them and that Mercy is covering them, Allāh says, "Y'Allāh, go with them to Paradise!" There is evidence of this in the Holy Qur'ān:

من بركتهم على نفوسهم وعلى جليسهم فلهم نصيب من قوله { وَجَعَلَنِي مُبَارَكًا أَيْنَ مَا كُنتُ }

This is the baraka of the one who sits with them, he receives a reward by sitting with them that is a portion of what Allāh ﷻ granted Sayyīdinā ʿIsā where He said on Sayyīdinā ʿIsā's tongue in the Holy Qur'ān:

وَجَعَلَنِي مُبَارَكًا أَيْنَ مَا كُنتُ

Allāh had made me blessed wherever I be.[87]

It means any association where you are mentioning the name of the Prophet ﷺ will turn into a blessed association and everyone will go to Paradise. That is why the *mu'min* is *mubārak*, blessed and a source of blessings and the *fājir*, the corrupted person, is punished. The gathering of *dhikr* is the gathering of angels and the gathering of heedless people, *ghaflah*, is the gathering of *shayaṭīn*. Everyone follows their group. May Allāh keep us to be from the group of angels, the group of *dhikrullāh*.

May Allāh forgive us and may Allāh bless us.

Wa min Allāhi 't-tawfiq, bi ḥurmati 'l-ḥabīb, bi ḥurmati 'l-Fātiḥah.
And with Allāh is success. For the sake of the Beloved, for his sake we recite the opening chapter of Holy Qur'ān.

[87] Sūrah Maryam, 19:31.

All Worship was Decreed Because of Dhikrullāh

Aʿūdhu billāhi min ash-Shayṭāni 'r-rajīm. Bismillāhi' r-Raḥmāni 'r-Raḥīm.
Nawaytu 'l-arbāʿīn, nawaytu 'l-ʿitikāf, nawaytu 'l-khalwah, nawaytu 'l-ʿuzlah,
nawaytu 'r-riyāḍa, nawaytu 's-sulūk, lillāhi Taʿalā fī hādhā 'l-masjid.
Atīʿūllāha wa atīʿū 'r-Rasūla wa ūli 'l-amri minkum. (4:59)

As-salāmu ʿalaykum wa raḥmatullāhi taʿalā wa barakātuh. Wherever you are, may Allāh ﷻ bless all of you viewers and listeners, bless all of you with His endless mercy that He dressed His Prophet ﷺ.

"If Only They Had Come to You and Asked Allāh's Forgiveness"

Allāh said in Holy Qur'an:

وَلَوْ أَنَّهُمْ إِذ ظَّلَمُوٓاْ أَنفُسَهُمْ جَآؤُوكَ فَاسْتَغْفَرُواْ اللهَ وَاسْتَغْفَرَ لَهُمُ الرَّسُولُ لَوَجَدُواْ اللهَ تَوَّابًا رَّحِيمًا

If they had only, when they were unjust to themselves, come to you and asked Allāh's forgiveness, and the Messenger had asked forgiveness for them, they would have found Allāh indeed Oft-returning, Most Merciful.[88]

"If only when they were oppressors to themselves they came to you, *yā* Muḥammad, and did *dhikrullāh.*" *Istighfār* is *dhikrullāh,* asking Allāh ﷻ for repentance through *dhikrullāh* by saying, *"Astaghfirullāh, astaghfirullāh, astaghfirullāh,"* then the Prophet ﷺ will make *dhikrullāh* on their behalf. But there is an immense difference between our *istighfār* and *dhikr* and the Prophet's *istighfār* and *dhikr*. So "they come to you, *yā* Muḥammad ﷺ, asking for repentance, asking for Allāh ﷻ to forgive them," *w 'astaghfara lahumu 'r-rasūl,* and at that moment the Prophet ﷺ will ask *istighfār* on their behalf.

So when you make *istighfār,* the Prophet ﷺ makes *istighfār* for you. When the Prophet ﷺ makes *istighfār* on your behalf, what will Allāh say? *La-wajadū 'Llāha tawwāba 'r-Raḥīma,* so there is a condition here. *La-wajadū 'Llāh,* "For sure they will find Allāh Forgiving and Merciful!" but there is a condition: your *istighfār* is not enough as it has to be with the Prophet's

[88] Sūrat an-Nisa, 4:64.

istighfār, because he is The Best of Creation ﷺ. Still we are comparing him to Creation and the Prophet ﷺ cannot be compare to Creation; he is higher than all creations that Allāh ﷻ created! The Prophet ﷺ is His Messenger and Allāh created him from *Ṣiffat an-Nūr*, the Divine Attribute of Light.

رواه عبد الرزاق بسنده عن جابر بن عبد الله بلفظ قال قلت: يا رسول الله، بأبي أنت وأمي، أخبرني عن أول شيء خلقه الله قبل الأشياء. قال: يا جابر، إن الله تعالى خلق قبل الأشياء نور نبيك من نوره،...

When Jābir ؓ asked, "Let my father and mother be sacrificed for you, O Prophet of Allāh! What is the first thing that Allāh ﷻ created before anything?" the Prophet ﷺ said, "The first thing that Allāh ﷻ created is the Light of your Prophet from His Light, O Jābir."[89]

So the condition is the Prophet ﷺ has to do *dhikr* on your behalf, then at that time, *la-wajadū 'Llāha*, "for sure they will find Allāh Forgiving and Merciful." So how to apply this verse of Holy Qur'an? It means we have to call on the Prophet ﷺ, "*Yā Rasūlullāh*! Allāh made it a condition to come to your presence," and at that time going spiritually through yourself, your soul, to the presence of Prophet ﷺ, calling on him, "*Yā Rasūlullāh*! *Yā Raḥmatan li 'l-ʿalāmīn*!"

That is not *shirk*. Those who are narrow-minded say, "Don't say that, it is *shirk*!" because from the beginning they had hate toward the Prophet ﷺ and they don't appreciate the greatness of Sayyīdinā Muḥammad ﷺ. They think, "O! He gave the message and then left." No, our duty is *taʿẓīm an-Nabī* ﷺ, to honor him. Allāh ﷻ honored him! If Allāh ﷻ honored him, then we have to honor him according to our small capacity. Allāh honored him with an honor that has no beginning and no end, but our duty is still to honor the Prophet ﷺ by making *ṣalawāt*, by calling on him. The *Ṣaḥābah* ؓ used to call on the Prophet ﷺ, so why can't we call on him? The *Ṣaḥābah* used to go to the presence of Prophet ﷺ and make *istighfār*. Why is it not allowed for us and only allowed for them? No one can reach the level of the honorable *Ṣaḥābah* ؓ, but that is open for everyone. Allāh opened for the *Ṣaḥābah* ؓ to see the Prophet ﷺ and we are not able to see him, but we believe in him.

---

[89] *Muṣannaf ʿAbdu 'r-Razzāq.*

"They Never Saw Me, but They Believe in Me"

Ibn Abbās ؓ narrated in Ṣahih Bukhārī:

وعن بن عباس أنه قال لجلسائه يوما :أي الناس أعجب إيمانا؟ قالوا : الملائكة. قال: وكيف لا تؤمن الملائكة والأمر فوقهم يرونه؟ قالوا :الأنبياء. قال: وكيف لا يؤمن الأنبياء والأمر ينزل عليهم غدوة وعشية؟ قالوا: فنحن.قال: وكيف لا تؤمنون وأنتم ترون من رسول الله ما ترون؟ ثم قال: قال رسول الله :" أعجب الناس إيمانا قوم يأتون من بعدي يؤمنون بي ولم يروني. أولئك إخواني حقا ".

That is why the Prophet ﷺ said, when he asked the *Ṣaḥābah* ؓ, *"ayyi 'n-nāsu āʿjabu īmānan"*, or in another narration, *"Man ashaddu īmānan,* who has the strongest belief?" They said, "The angels." The Prophet ﷺ said, "How are angels not going to have strong *īmān* when they see what they are seeing in Paradise?" They said, "The prophets."And the Prophet ﷺ said, "How can they not have strong *īmān* when *waḥīyy* is coming on them? They see the truth, of course they are going to have strong *īmān*." And they said, "Then us, your Companions." And the Prophet ﷺ said, "How can you not have strong *īmān* when I am between you?" They said, "Who then, *yā Rasūlullāh*?" So the Prophet ﷺ said, *qawmun yātūna min baʿdī yu'minūna bī wa lam yarawnī. Ūlā'ika ikhwānī ḥaqqan,* "A group from the last *Ummah*, coming after me who believed in me without seeing me. They have the strongest *īmān*."

And so we didn't see the Prophet ﷺ and we believe in him, and we go to him. And he said, "Those have the strongest of *īmān*. You are seeing me, you have strong *īmān*; they didn't see me and still they have strong *īmān*." *Yā* Allāh! Keep our *īmān* strong! So to apply this verse, it is through your heart: send your heart to the presence of the Prophet ﷺ. As we mentioned in the previous session on *dhikrullāh,* one has to put his heart on his side and make his heart to do *dhikrullāh.* So when we are doing *dhikrullāh* we have to be focusing to be in that presence of Sayyīdinā Muḥammad ﷺ. He will give his on our behalf that repentance to Allāh's Greatness. What did Allāh say? *La-wajadū 'Llāha tawwāba 'r-Raḥīma.* He ﷺ offers that repentance, saying, *"Yā Rabbī*! This is what they can do and as by Your Order in the Holy Qur'ān, they have to come to me and this is what I can do, and You, O Allāh, can do what You want, You can judge."

And what Allāh said? *La-wajadū 'Llāha tawwāba 'r-Raḥīma,* "They are going to find Allāh Forgiving, Merciful," by *dhikrullāh,* as *istighfār* is *dhikrullāh,* but the condition is to be in the presence of Prophet ﷺ through your heart.

عَنْ أَبِي سَعِيدٍ الْخُدْرِيِّ، قَالَ خَرَجَ مُعَاوِيَةُ عَلَى حَلْقَةٍ فِي الْمَسْجِدِ فَقَالَ مَا أَجْلَسَكُمْ قَالُوا جَلَسْنَا نَذْكُرُ اللَّهَ . قَالَ آللَّهِ مَا أَجْلَسَكُمْ إِلاَّ ذَاكَ قَالُوا وَاللَّهِ مَا أَجْلَسَنَا إِلاَّ ذَاكَ . قَالَ أَمَا إِنِّي لَمْ أَسْتَحْلِفْكُمْ تُهْمَةً لَكُمْ وَمَا كَانَ أَحَدٌ بِمَنْزِلَتِي مِنْ رَسُولِ اللَّهِ صلى الله عليه وسلم أَقَلَّ عَنْهُ حَدِيثًا مِنِّي وَإِنَّ رَسُولَ اللَّهِ صلى الله عليه وسلم خَرَجَ عَلَى حَلْقَةٍ مِنْ أَصْحَابِهِ فَقَالَ " مَا أَجْلَسَكُمْ " . قَالُوا جَلَسْنَا نَذْكُرُ اللَّهَ وَنَحْمَدُهُ عَلَى مَا هَدَانَا لِلإِسْلاَمِ وَمَنَّ بِهِ عَلَيْنَا . قَالَ " آللَّهِ مَا أَجْلَسَكُمْ إِلاَّ ذَاكَ " . قَالُوا وَاللَّهِ مَا أَجْلَسَنَا إِلاَّ ذَاكَ . قَالَ " أَمَا إِنِّي لَمْ أَسْتَحْلِفْكُمْ تُهْمَةً لَكُمْ وَلَكِنَّهُ أَتَانِي جِبْرِيلُ فَأَخْبَرَنِي أَنَّ اللَّهَ عَزَّ وَجَلَّ يُبَاهِي بِكُمُ الْمَلاَئِكَةَ

Abū Saʿīd al-Khuḍrī ﷺ reported that Muʿāwīya ﷺ went to a circle in the mosque and said, "What makes you sit here?" They said, "We are sitting here in order to remember Allāh." He said, "I adjure you by Allāh (to tell me whether you are sitting here for this very purpose)?" They said, "By Allāh, we are sitting here for this very purpose." Thereupon, he said, "I have not demanded you to take an oath, because of any allegation against you and none of my rank in the eye of Allāh's Messenger ﷺ is the narrator of so few aḥādīth as I am. The fact is that Allāh's Messenger ﷺ went out to the circle of his Companions and said, "What makes you sit?" They said, "We are sitting here in order to remember Allāh and to praise Him, for He guided us to the path of Islam and He conferred favors upon us." Thereupon he adjured by Allāh and asked if that only was the purpose of their sitting there. They said, "By Allāh, we are not sitting here but for this very purpose," whereupon he (the Messenger) said, "I am not asking you to take an oath because of any allegation against you, but for the fact that Gabriel came to me and he informed me that Allāh, the Exalted and Glorious, was talking to the angels about your magnificence."[90]

It is mentioned that one day Muʿāwīya, one of the *Ṣaḥābah,* went to the *masjid* and saw a group of people sitting there, and he asked them, "What made you sit together?" They said, *jalasnā nadhkurullāh,* "We sat together making *dhikrullāh,* to remember Allāh." He said, "Are you sure you are sitting for that only? *Qāl Allāhi mā ajlasakum illa dhāk,* are you sure it is for Allāh, that you sat only for *dhikrullāh*?" They said, *w 'Allāhi mā ajlasanā illa dhāk,* "We give an oath by Allāh ﷻ that we didn't sit except for *dhikrullāh.*" I

[90] Sahih Muslim.

am not comparing our sitting for *dhikrullāh* like their sitting, they are *Ṣaḥābah* ﷺ, their sitting is highly elevated and no one can be like them, but as the Prophet ﷺ said:

من تشبه بقوم فهو منهم

Who imitates a group of people are from them.[91]

So they gave an oath that they sat only to do *dhikrullāh*. Now this group of people and many others around the world today, many people sit in groups for *dhikrullāh*. Are they doing anything other than that? Look here and this is an example, thousands and millions of people are sitting doing the same thing doing *dhikrullāh* or speaking or lecturing for Islam, or they come together for reciting Holy Qur'an or reciting *ḥadīth*, that is all *dhikrullāh*. And he said, "*W 'Allāhi* I didn't ask you this question to accuse you of not making *dhikrullāh*, but I heard the Prophet ﷺ one time asking a group of *Ṣaḥābah* ﷺ sitting together like you, *mā ajlasakum*, "Why are you sitting, what is the reason of your sitting together?" *Qālū jalasnā nadhkuru 'Llāh*, They said, "We are sitting to remember Allāh ﷻ and to recite His, Allāh's Beautiful Names and Attributes and to do the *dhikr* you have taught us," *wa nāḥmaduhu ʿalā mā hadāna li 'l-islāmi wa manna bihi ʿalayna bika*, "and to thank Allāh that He honored us with Islam, thanking Him, showing *shukran lillāh*."

لَئِن شَكَرْتُمْ لأَزِيدَنَّكُمْ

If you thank Me, I will give you more.[92]

"We were thanking Him, glorifying Him and praising Him for honoring us by guiding us to be in Islam, *wa manna ʿalayna bika*, and honored us to be with you and honored us because of you. We are very happy for that." And the Prophet ﷺ said, *Allāhi, mā ajlasakum illā dhāk*, "Allāh! (as when you see something big), did you not sit except for that?" And they said, *w 'Allāhi yā rasūlullāh, mā ajlasanā illā dhāk*, "We did not sit except for that, to thank Him for His Favors that He granted us Islam, and

---

[91] Abū Dāwūd.

[92] Sūrah Ibrāḥīm , 14:7.

offered us to be with you." The Prophet ﷺ said, *qāla amā innī lam astaḥlifkum tuhmatan lakum,* "Allāh is my witness, I am not asking you, accusing of something, *wa lākinnahu ātānī jibrīl,* but Jibrīl came to me and said..."

What did Jibrīl say to the Prophet ﷺ? People sitting in a gathering and making *dhikrullāh,* and Prophet ﷺ asked them for what purpose? They answered, "For thanking Allāh that they were guided to Islam and guided to be with the Prophet ﷺ." So what will Allāh compensate them with? *W 'Allāhi ātānī jibrīl fa akhbaranī anna 'Llāh tabāraka wa taʿalā yubāhī bikum li 'l-malā'ikah.* When you hear this you melt completely. What is the word, like you "dissolve", immediately melting; they melted. What did he say? *Inna 'Llāha yubāhī bikum li 'l-malā'ikah,* "Allāh ﷻ tells His angels He is so happy with what you are doing that He will show off to His angels: Look! These are My servants. I am so happy with what they are doing and proud of them."

When Allāh is happy what does that mean? *Fa hādhihi mubāhāt ʿan rabbīhim, dalīlun ʿan sharaf adh-dhikr.* This showing-off of Allāh to His angels of the happiness from His servants is proof of the honor of their *dhikr* and the greatness of *dhikrullāh,* and of how much Allāh appreciates the one remembering Him!

Allāh is with the One Who Remembers Him

أَنَا جَلِيْسُ مَنْ ذَكَرَنِي

I sit with him who remembers Me.[93]

"I am with the one who remembers Me, I am sitting with the one who remembers Me." That means Allāh will give *dunyā* and *Ākhirah* to the one who sits and remembers Him. And we say we have difficulties in *dunyā,* so how is Allāh giving to us in *dunyā* and *Ākhirah*? But the Prophet ﷺ had difficulties in *dunyā,* he was the one most abused by his people and his family. Yes, Allāh is rewarding you in *dunyā,* it will be written for you and you will find that reward in *Ākhirah* in order to be saved. Although you see difficulties you will be rewarded for these difficulties because you are *dhākir*, your tongue has *nūr*, your mouth has *nūr*, your ears have *nūr*, your

[93] Āḥmad, Bayhaqī.

eyes have *nūr*, your body has *nūr*, and we have explained that before; you have *nūr*, light in front, you have *nūr* on your right and *nūr* on your left, in the back, above and below, everything is *nūr*. The Prophet ﷺ used to say, *Allāhumma 'ja'alnī nūran*, "O Allāh, make me Light." May Allāh ﷻ make us light. (*Amīn.*)

That happiness from Allāh ﷻ towards His servants when they are doing *dhikr* shows the honor of *dhikrullāh*, and Allāh's Love to that, for someone to call Him, not to call anyone else. It is said that people get addicted to drugs, is it not? It is not a good example, but there are some people who lost their way and they go and do drugs. Now it is everywhere, and before it was in some countries, but now every country around the world, they sell it and do drugs. So when they become drug-addicted there are also people addicted to something else, they are addicted to *dhikrullāh*. *Anna mudminu 'dh-dhikr yadkhul al-jannah wa hūwa yaḍ-ḥak*, "The one who is addicted to do *dhikrullāh* will enter Paradise smiling and laughing," because he is addicted.

When someone is addicted to drugs he doesn't know what he is doing, he smiles from *dunyā* but the one who is addicted to *dhikrullāh*, is drunk with Allāh's love, and drunk with the Prophet's love, and drunk with *awlīyā's* love, and drunk with Holy Qur'an, and drunk with *īmān*, and with Islam, and with *ihsān*. He is drunk with everything that Allāh gave him as a *mu'min*, he is drunk in that; his mind is *dhikrullāh* and his food is *dhikrullāh*!

I know such people very well; one is my uncle, who didn't eat and he only drank tea. He lived to 85 years of age and had only tea with one sugar, and he was one of the biggest scholars of Islam, president of the Circle of the Scholars of the Middle East. His library was full of books and he sat in his library and used to sleep in his library. Five years ago, I met someone who was one of the linguist geniuses in Arabic, and there was a dispute about one word and what it means in reality, as the Holy Qur'an came on seven *qirā'ats*, different dialects and it changes the words and the Prophet ﷺ agreed on all of them. There are more than seven, it goes up to fourteen, but the main ones are seven.

Five years ago, I went back home and was invited by some important people and among them was the archbishop of the Orthodox Christians, the big famous one, Metron Khiḍr. It was the first time I was meeting him and they asked me to speak something and he asked me, "From which family are you?" And I mentioned it and he knew there was a relation between my family name and my uncle's family name. He asked me, "Is this man related to you?"

And I said, "Yes, he is my uncle," and he was from those who do *dhikrullāh* and who are among thousands of books, and he read them all!

He said, "I will tell you a story that happened with your uncle." He is also a linguist, that archbishop. He said, "I used to go visit your uncle always as I knew his high level, and one day I mentioned that word and he gave me an example of that meaning and I disagreed with him, but he insisted on that meaning. He said, 'Give me a proof from the old writings of what you are saying,' (and this came haphazardly, not prepared beforehand like in a discussion that my uncle would have prepared something to show him, so it would have been very difficult to get a proof, but when knowledgeable people speak they understand.) And he looked at me not happy, but because those who have *dhikrullāh* don't show anger he said to me, 'Go to the right side of the shelves, and on the fifth shelf there is a book there. Look behind that book. Go five or six books back and you will find a book. Pull it out and bring it to me.' I did that and brought the book to him, and he said, 'Open x page and on the 16th line you will find your answer,' and it was that."

That comes from what? Purity of the mind. He still remembered where he read it from among these thousands of books and it was the right answer!

And the archbishop said, "I was surprised; he was going to make me Muslim!"

He had purity of mind due to *dhikrullāh* and he didn't eat, only pouring tea after tea, like Pakistani *dūdh patī*! So those who are doing a lot of *dhikr*, Allāh will be happy with them and show them to His angels, "Look how happy I am with them."

Inna jamīʿa 'l-ʿamal innamā shurriʿat iqāmatan li dhikrillāhi taʿalā, "All *ʿamal*—prayers, fasting, *zakāt, Hajj, Shaḥādah, Maqām al-Ihsān*—everything you do has been ordained by Divine Law in order to remind you of Allāh ﷻ, so that is *dhikrullāh.*"

So, *inna jamīʿa 'l-ʿamal innamā shurriʿat iqāmatan li dhikrillāh,* these actions are only decreed for the sake of *dhikrullāh.* These constitutions and orders are there for the purpose of *dhikrullāh*. (Someone present sneezed and said, "*alḥamdulillāh*.") Saying "*alḥamdulillāh*" is *dhikrullāh*! So the one addicted to *dhikrullāh* will enter Paradise laughing because of no *ḥisāb*; he is not there, his mind is already with Allāh, not in *dunyā*, and he is not seeing anything else as he is already with Allāh, he is only loving Allāh and that one does not need to walk on *aṣ-Ṣirāṭ al-Mustaqīm* as he is already there directly. So *dhikrullāh* is a safety for us to enter Paradise.

اتْلُ مَا أُوحِيَ إِلَيْكَ مِنَ الْكِتَابِ وَأَقِمِ الصَّلَاةَ إِنَّ الصَّلَاةَ تَنْهَى عَنِ الْفَحْشَاء
وَالْمُنكَرِ وَلَذِكْرُ اللهِ أَكْبَرُ وَاللَّهُ يَعْلَمُ مَا تَصْنَعُونَ

Recite what is sent of the Book by inspiration to you and establish regular prayer, for prayer restrains from shameful and unjust deeds. And remembrance of Allāh is the greatest (thing in life) without doubt. And Allāh knows the (deeds) you do.[94]

"Read from the Revelation that we have sent to you, *yā* Muḥammad! Read from these *waḥīyy*, revelations, *utlū mā uḥīyya ilayk*, read what has been revealed to you from the Book; that is *dhikrullāh*, reading Holy Qur'an is *dhikrullāh*. *Wa aqimi 'ṣ-ṣalāt*, and establish the prayer, begin to pray; that is *dhikrullāh*." When you enter the prayer, what do you say? "*Allāhu Akbar*," and then what do you say? "*Subḥānak allāhumma wa bi ḥamdika wa tabāraka 'smuka wa taʿalā jadduka wa jalla thanāuka wa lā ilāha ghayruk*." So when you enter your prayer, it's *dhikrullāh*. You enter your prayer with what? First you say, "*Allāhu Akbar*!" meaning, "*Yā Rabbī*! The way I'm doing my prayer, I'm sorry as it is not to Your Honor. My ego, my self, my bad *ʿamal* is blended with my prayer and it doesn't befit You, so forgive me. You are *Allāhu Akbar*, You are The Greatest, no one can reach You, *yā* Rabbī! I didn't praise You as You deserve." And then according to the Hanafi School you say, "*Subḥānak allāhumma wa bi ḥamdika*," you are making *tasbīḥ* and you are making *ḥamd*, *wa bi ḥamdika wa tabāraka 'smuka*, "Your Name be blessed," *wa taʿalā jadduka wa lā ilāha ghayruk*.

In the Shafiʿī School, you say:

إِنِّي وَجَّهْتُ وَجْهِيَ لِلَّذِي فَطَرَ السَّمَاوَاتِ وَالأَرْضَ حَنِيفًا وَمَا أَنَاْ مِنَ الْمُشْرِكِينَ

[94] Sūrat al-ʿAnkabūt, 29:45.

"For me, I have set my face, firmly and truly, towards Him Who created the heavens and the earth, and never shall I give partners to Allāh."[95]

قُلْ إِنَّ صَلاَتِي وَنُسُكِي وَمَحْيَايَ وَمَمَاتِي لِلّهِ رَبِّ الْعَالَمِينَ لاَ شَرِيكَ لَهُ وَبِذَلِكَ أُمِرْتُ وَأَنَاْ أَوَّلُ الْمُسْلِمِينَ

Say, "Truly, my prayer and my service of sacrifice, my life and my death, are (all) for Allāh, the Cherisher of the Worlds in Whose divinity none has a share. For thus have I been bidden-and I shall (always) be foremost among those who surrender themselves unto Him."[96]

This also has the *Tawḥīd* in it, it has *Hajj* in it, *wajjahtu wajhīyya lilladhī faṭara 's-samāwāti wa 'l-'arḍ,* "I directed my face to the One Who created Heavens and Earth and I am not *mushrik,*" *wa mā anā min al-mushrikīn*, "I am not from the *mushriks* that associate someone with You." *Inna ṣalātī wa nusukī wa maḥyā-ī,* all my prayers, all my *nusuk* (the different rituals: you begin with *ṭawāf, sa'ī,* going to 'Arafāt, coming to Mina, Muzdalifah, and going back to Mecca, all these are *nusukī*), *wa maḥyā-ī wa mamātī,* "My life and my death is in Your Hand, *yā Rabbī,*" *wa anā min al-muslimīn,* "and I am from the Muslims." This is the *du'ā* of Sayyīdinā Ibrāhīm ﷺ.

The Prayer Begins with Dhikrullāh

So that is why He said, *aqimi 'ṣ-ṣalāt,* "Establish the prayer," which means "begin with *dhikrullāh*", and you begin it with *dhikrullāh* and then when you open it with *dhikrullāh,* with showing *Tawḥīd* or showing *du'ā,* as Imam Abū Ḥanīfa ؓ mentioned, you enter the prayer reciting *Sūrat al-Fātiḥah.* Now you are clean, your tongue is clean, your smell is clean, your breath is clean, your heart is clean to read *Sūrat al-Fātiḥah.* You cannot read Holy Qur'an unless you are clean as it is Allāh's Words, especially *Sūrat al-Fātiḥah* as it is the secret of the Holy Qur'ān. So you begin by reciting *Fātiḥatu 'l-Kitāb* and *inna ṣalātī,* and in this way that you are doing your prayer, reading the *Fātiḥah* and a *sūrah,* and then you go into *ruk'ū* and you say, *"Subḥāna rabbī al-'Aẓīm wa bi ḥamdih."* Some people say, *"Subḥāna rabbī al-'Aẓīm,"* but it is not enough. Also say, *"wa bi ḥamdih,"* and that is *dhikr*. Then you stand up and you say, *"Sami' Allāhu līmān ḥamīdah, rabbanā wa laka 'l-ḥamd ḥamdan*

---

[95] Sūrat al-An'am, 6:79.
[96] Sūrat al-An'am, 6:162-163.

kathīran ṭayyiban mubārakan fīhi, mil as-samāwāti wa mil al-arḍa wa milā mā shi'ta min shayyin baʿḍ," and that is *dhikrullāh*, that is *duʿā* there.

Now people are in a hurry and they cut that and they say only, *"Samiʿ Allāhu līmān hamīdah, rabbanā laka 'l-ḥamd,"* that is if they say it, and they go for *sajda*, but in any case that is *dhikrullāh* and that kind of *dhikr* is in the prayer:

إِنَّ الصَّلَاةَ تَنْهَى عَنِ الْفَحْشَاءِ وَالْمُنكَرِ وَلَذِكْرُ اللهِ أَكْبَرُ

For prayer restrains from shameful and unjust deeds and the Remembrance of Allāh is greatest (thing in life) without doubt.[97]

What is in this *āyah,* this prayer prevents you to fall into *tanhā ʿani 'l-faḥshāi wa 'l-munkar,* the trap of Shayṭān to be *fāsiq*, a corrupt person. Allāh said, *wa la-dhikrullāhi akbar,* "but still put it in your mind that greater than that is *dhikrullāh." Wa la-dhikrullāhi akbar.* Allāh wants to show His *Dhikr*, not your *dhikr*, but "O My *ʿabd*, whatever you have praised Me in that *ṣalāt*, My return praising of you is greater! When I mention you, it is more than your mention of Me."

اذْكُرُونِي أَذْكُرْكُمْ

Remember Me, I will remember you.[98]

You have to remember that He remembers us differently than when we remember Him. We remember Him small and He remembers us greatly, according to His Greatness. *Wa la-dhikrullāhi akbaru w 'Allāhu yaʿlamu mā taṣnaʿūn,* Allāh's remembrance is greater, because Allāh knows what you are doing. When He sees you doing something small, He gives you something big.

That is why Sayyida ʿĀyesha mentioned in a *ṣaḥiḥ ḥadīth* that the Prophet ﷺ said:

إِنَّمَا جُعِلَ الطَّوَافُ بِالْبَيْتِ وَبَيْنَ الصَّفَا وَالْمَرْوَةِ وَرَمْىُ الْجِمَارِ لِإِقَامَةِ ذِكْرِ اللهِ

---

[97] Sūrat al-ʿAnkabūt, 29:45.
[98] Sūrat al-Baqarah, 2:152.

Going around the House (the Ka'bah), running between Ṣafā and Marwa and stoning of the pillars are meant to establish the remembrance of Allāh.[99]

The *ṭawāf* of the House has been ordered and running between Ṣafā and Marwa; it has been ordered for every person who enters *Ḥaram Makkī* to circumambulate around *Ka'bah* if he is coming for *'Umrah*. If he lives in Mecca he doesn't have to make *ṭawāf*; if he lives outside of Mecca, in Jeddah for example, and he comes to Mecca, he has to do *Ṭawāf al-Qudūm*; you make *Ṭawāf az-Ziyārah*, if you enter you make *ṭawāf*, you don't do *sa'ī*. If you are in *'Umrah*, you have to do *sa'ī* between Ṣafā and Marwa and to throw the stones in *Hajj* and all the other rituals, all of them are to remind you of *dhikrullāh* because they are *dhikrullāh*, all of these *nusuk*, actions are from *dhikrullāh*. Even throwing stones at the devil is *dhikrullāh*; you are stoning Shayṭān, but you are saying, *Riḍan li 'r-Raḥmān, raghman li 'sh-shayṭān*, "Allāh to be happy with us and for Shayṭān to be down," to reject Shayṭān and for *Ḥaqq* to be up, so that is *dhikrullāh*. And running between Safā and Marwa, reading all kinds of *du'ā* that the Prophet ﷺ used to make, that is *dhikrullāh*. *Ṭawāf* around *Ka'bah* is *dhikrullāh* and going to Mina is *dhikrullāh* and going to Arafat is *dhikrullāh* and going to Muzdalifa is *dhikrullāh*; all the *sharā'i* that has been put, the principles of *Ḥajj* are all *dhikrullāh*. So in *ṣalāt* there is *dhikrullāh* and in *Hajj* there is *dhikrullāh* and in visiting the Prophet ﷺ in Madīnah there is *dhikrullāh*, in making *ṣalawāt* and praying there, and so all of Islam is built on remembering Allāh ﷻ!

عن عبد الله بن بسر رضي الله عنه أن رجلا قال: يا رسول الله إن شرائع الإسلام قد كثرت علي فأخبرني بشيء أتشبث به؟ قال لا يزال لسانك رطبا من ذكر الله" الترمذي.

A man came to the Prophet ﷺ and said, "O Rasūlullāh! The rules of Islam became heavy on me, so give me news of something which I can maintain." Prophet ﷺ said, "Make your tongue wet with dhikrullāh."[100]

A Bedouin came to the Prophet ﷺ and said, "The conditions and principles of Islam are too much for me, *yā Rasūlullāh*, give me something small for me to do, that I can do." If we want to do what the Prophet ﷺ was doing, there are so many things to recite. The Prophet ﷺ used to recite in

[99] Abū Dāwūd and Tirmidhī.
[100] Tirmidhī.

every step in his life, in every moment: when he wanted to go out, when he wanted to come in, when there was *adhān*, when you want to eat, drink, fast, pray, if you see a dream you don't like, etc., and you need to recite these, and I think many western people cannot memorize that as their language is not Arabic. So the Prophet ﷺ said, "Keep your tongue moist, wet with *dhikrullāh*." That is why we have to keep our tongue wet with *dhikrullāh*.

More on Dhikrullāh from Ibn Qayyim

Here I will quote a few from among many sayings of Ibn Qayyim about *dhikrullāh* in his book, al-Wābil aṣ-Ṣayyib:

> There are many methods of *dhikrullāh* you can use. *Dhikrullāh* can be done by heart and by tongue, *wa dhālika afḍal adh-dhikr*, that is the best of *dhikr*. You can do by heart alone. You can do by tongue alone. You can do by heart and tongue, and that is the best of them. If you mix both, then that is the best *dhikr* of what you are doing.
>
> أن ذكر الله عز و جل من أكبر العون على طاعته
>
> Certainly *dhikrullāh* is, for sure, the best pillar to support us to obey Allāh ﷻ.
>
> أن ذكر الله عز و جل يسهل الصعب وييسر العسير
>
> *Dhikrullāh* will make the difficult easy and remove the obstacles.
>
> أن ذكر الله عز و جل يذهب عن القلب مخاوفه كلها
>
> *Dhikrullāh* takes away from the heart all things that cause the heart to fear.
>
> أن الذكر يعطي الذاكر قوة
>
> *Dhikrullāh* gives you a strong memory.
>
> الذكر أفضل من الدعاء
>
> *Dhikrullāh* is higher than supplication.
>
> الذكر ثناء على الله عز و جل بجميل أوصافه وآلائه وأسمائه

Dhikrullāh is praising Allāh by His Attributes, His Names, and His Greatness.[101]

والدعاء سؤال العبد حاجته

The *duʿā* is the request of the servant for his needs.

So the big difference between *duʿā* and *dhikr* is *duʿā* is the request of the servant for his needs, which means you are asking for yourself, but *dhikrullāh* is praising Allāh for Himself.

May Allāh forgive us and may Allāh bless us.

Wa min Allāhi 't-tawfīq, bi ḥurmati 'l-ḥabīb, bi ḥurmati 'l-Fātiḥah.
And with Allāh is success. For the sake of the Beloved, for his sake we recite the opening chapter of Holy Qur'ān.

[101] Another example for those who say don't make *dhikr* with *Asmāullāh* Allāh's Beautiful Names and Attributes, confirming its permissibility in Sharīʿah.

Dhikr Surpasses Supplication

Aʿūdhu billāhi min ash-Shayṭāni 'r-rajīm. Bismillāhi' r-Raḥmāni 'r-Raḥīm.
Nawaytu 'l-arbāʿīn, nawaytu 'l-ʿitikāf, nawaytu 'l-khalwah, nawaytu 'l-ʿuzlah,
nawaytu 'r-riyāḍa, nawaytu 's-sulūk, lillāhi Taʿalā fī hādhā 'l-masjid.
Atīʿūllāha wa atīʿū 'r-Rasūla wa ūli 'l-amri minkum. (4:59)

Salām ʿalaykum wa raḥmatullāhi wa barakātuh. Wherever you are around the world, we are simple people and you are simple people; you are making *sajda*, we are making *sajda* to Allāh ﷻ, so we are the same.

Allāh ﷻ said:

وَذَكِّرْفَإِنَّ الذِّكْرَى تَنفَعُ الْمُؤْمِنِينَ

And remind, for indeed, the reminder benefits the Believers.[102]

I get benefit you get benefit. *Fa dhakkir*, remind about what? About the Creator and about Creation, through Creation you know the greatness of Allāh ﷻ. That's why Allāh mentioned in Holy Qur'an that it is important:

إِنَّ فِي خَلْقِ السَّمَاوَاتِ وَالأَرْضِ وَاخْتِلاَفِ اللَّيْلِ وَالنَّهَارِ لآيَاتٍ لِّأُوْلِي الألْبَابِ الَّذِينَ يَذْكُرُونَ اللّهَ قِيَامًا وَقُعُودًا وَعَلَىَ جُنُوبِهِمْ وَيَتَفَكَّرُونَ فِي خَلْقِ السَّمَاوَاتِ وَالأَرْضِ رَبَّنَا مَا خَلَقْتَ هَذا بَاطِلاً سُبْحَانَكَ فَقِنَا عَذَابَ النَّارِ

Behold! In the creation of Heaven and Earth, and in the alternation of night and day, there are indeed signs for men of understanding, those who remember Allāh (always, and in prayers) standing, sitting and lying down on their sides, and contemplating the creation of the Heavens and the Earth, (saying), "Our Lord! You have not created (all) this without purpose! Glory to You! Give us salvation from the torment of the Fire."[103]

Those who make *dhikr* in 24 hours, they are remembering Allāh standing, sitting and lying down, going to work or coming from work, or in the house; whatever they are doing they remember Allāh, but Allāh ﷻ

[102] Sūrat adh-Dhāriyat, 51:55.
[103] Sūrat Āli 'Imrān, 3:191-192.

added on that *wa yatafakkarūn*, "they have to reflect on the creation of Heavens and Earth."

We are asking, as Allāh said:

ادْعُونِي أَسْتَجِبْ لَكُمْ

Call on Me, I will answer you.[104]

We are asking Allāh to grant us that and dress us with that. In our life everyone is like a tree, like how you plant the tree. When you plant a seed, what happens? The shoot will come out and you can see it; the seed you cannot see, it is gone, you dig and there is no more seed, only you see what is coming up. Also human beings are like seeds, but composed of a different matter, with different qualifications. And after a while it becomes a child and the child does not stay a child, he or she will grow just like the seed doesn't stay a seed, it will grow into a tree and become the main trunk with many branches. Also human beings were a living species in the womb of the mother, from the father and mother, and Allāh ﷻ will create a child and cause that child to grow and it becomes like a tree with different branches.

You might have a dead tree, *yābisa*, that is dry, and you might have a living tree that is blossoming and gives fruits. These fruits come from obedience to Allāh and from *dhikrullāh*, as without *dhikrullāh* there is nothing. As a tree needs water every day or every week, also the human being needs water to keep it alive and that is *dhikrullāh.* So if you make *dhikr*, your heart, which is the main trunk of the body and keeps it alive, that *dhikr* makes it to be alive. If you don't make *dhikrullāh* you are killing and drying that heart, which becomes dark and where Shayṭān comes and enters.

The difference between *dhikr* of the heart and *dhikr* of the tongue is a great difference. The best *dhikrullāh* is *dhikr* of the *qalb*, heart, to make your heart work. As you know, in the emergency room operations sometimes the patient is brought in and the heart has stopped, so they use electric shock to make the heart muscles move. The heart also needs an electric shock. The power of *dhikrullāh* by tongue is less than the power of *dhikrullāh* by heart. So from *dhikrullāh* by tongue, you need to make an electric shock to make the *dhikrullāh* move the heart in order for the body to survive. You will be

[104] Sūrat al-Ghāfir, 40:60.

pumping light that *dhikrullāh* produces, the Heavenly Light that goes to every part of the body and makes *dhikr* of 'Allāh' in every cell. Say, "Allāh!"

قُلِ اللهُ ثُمَّ ذَرْهُمْ فِي خَوْضِهِمْ يَلْعَبُونَ

Say "Allāh," then leave them to plunge in vain discourse and trifling.[105]

O our Salafi brothers! Allāh said this in the Holy Qur'an, and you say one cannot do *dhikr* by saying "Allāh," that it is *ḥarām* and that you must do *dhikr* of *lā ilāha illa-Llāh*. O our friends, the Salafis! Allāh said this in the Holy Qur'ān, *Qūli 'Llāh thumma dharhum fī khawḍihim yalʿabūn.* "Say, 'Allāh,' *thumma dharhum fī khawḍihim yalʿabūn*, and don't bother with them, leave them in their ways, in their nonsense, playing! We don't need them, they are playing with toys."

But when you say "Allāh," you are not playing with toys, you are calling the Creator directly. Don't they say, "Don't make intercession, go to Allāh directly." Why then don't they make *dhikrullāh,* "Allāh, Allāh, Allāh." Allāh ﷻ said in the Holy Qur'ān, "*Yā* Muḥammad! Say 'Allāh' and don't bother with them. They are going to come to you bowing their heads to Allāh ﷻ, making *sajda*."

Dhikru 'l-qalb yuthmiru 'l-maʿrifah, the fruit of *dhikru 'l-qalb,* when the heart makes *dhikr,* is knowledge; knowledge will be coming into your heart.

Dhikrullāh Brought Yūnus out of the Belly of the Whale

Sayyīdinā Yūnus ﷺ said, *lā ilāha illa Anta Subḥānak! Innī kuntu min aẓ-ẓālimīn,* "There is no god but You! Glory to You! Certainly, I was one of the oppressors." If he didn't make *dhikr* in the belly of the whale, he would have been left there until Judgment Day, but he made the *dhikr* that Allāh loves the most, *Lā ilāha illa Anta Subḥānak! Innī kuntu min aẓ-ẓālimīn*! Except when he got upset with his people he left them; Allāh ﷻ sent him to his people and they didn't accept him and he got upset and left. Allāh gave him a lesson to teach him, "Don't pray against your people, don't ask Me to destroy them. You go and deliver your message." He got upset with them because they did not listen and he left his people, *ghāḍiban*, and was angry with his people. He went to the beach to observe Allāh's Greatness and a whale came

---

[105] Sūrat al-Anʿam, 6:91.

and swallowed him and he would have remained in the whale's belly until the Day of Judgment.

$$\text{فَلَوْلَا أَنَّهُ كَانَ مِنْ الْمُسَبِّحِينَ, لَلَبِثَ فِي بَطْنِهِ إِلَى يَوْمِ يُبْعَثُونَ.}$$

If he had not been of the *musabbiḥīn*, those who make *tasbīḥ*, the people of *dhikrullāh*, praising Allāh, thanking Allāh ﷻ, remembering Allāh ﷻ, Allāh would not have ordered the whale to spit him out and he would have stayed there. So *dhikrullāh* will take you out from your darkness into light when you are doing *dhikrullāh* either by tongue or by heart. Heart *dhikrullāh* is stronger, because it will dress you with knowledge and it is stronger that *dhikrullāh* by tongue. Allāh ﷻ brought him out from the whale and if we make *dhikrullāh* like Sayyīdinā Yūnus ؑ, "*Lā ilāha illa Anta Subḥānak! Innī kuntu mina 'ẓ-ẓālimīn*, You are the Creator, there is no god except Allāh ﷻ! Yā Rabbī! I am sorry, surely I was from the oppressors," not like the way we say it with our tongue, "I am an oppressor." When Sayyīdinā Yūnus was saying that from his heart, with full confidence that he was an oppressor, then Allāh ﷻ gave him back life.

Inside the whale, is there light? It is darkness, there is no light. He was in darkness when he said, "*Lā ilāha illa Anta Subḥānak*, You are the Creator, *yā Rabbī*, there is no god but You!" and speaking directly to Allāh. "*Anta*, You are the One, *yā* Allāh, the Creator, and I am Your weak servant, the oppressor!" When he declared that and began his *tasbīḥ* with that, then after a while Allāh ﷻ took him out of that darkness, and that *tasbīḥ* has light in it and that light showed him the way inside the whale and the whale spat him out. So Allāh ﷻ will make our heart move from darkness, take us from the darkness and spit us out into Heavenly Light, *nūr*. That *nūr* is beyond our mind. *Inshā-Allāh* if there is time we will mention it.

Dhikrullāh by heart will give us *maʿrifatullāh* and will instigate love of Allāh ﷻ and take you from sins and then take you to do *murāqabah*. When this Light is so strong in your heart, it will make the heart move, and when it moves it begins to see what is in the universe, like a child in the womb of the mother when it is moving. How is it moving? Who made it to move? You? No way, and if he didn't move to turn his head down, then he would die. So that means there is a system to do *murāqabah*, to make the heart move in the right direction, or else you need a C-section. What is that C-Section? It is to polish you to have a good character, that the Prophet ﷺ said, "I was sent to perfect and complete the manners of the *Ummah*."

What is better, *adh-dhikr* or *ad-duʿā*? Allāh said, *idūʿnī astajib lakum,* "Call on Me, I will answer you." It is said that *dhikrullāh* is to praise Allāh and *duʿā* is asking for one's self. There is a big difference! *Awlīyāullāh* submit, they don't ask for themselves, they only make *dhikrullāh. Dhikrullāh* is to look into one's heart and see there is no one except Allāh ﷻ.

ما وسعني أرضي ولا سمائي ولكن وسعني قلب عبدي المؤمن

Neither My Heavens nor My Earth contain Me, but the heart of My believing servant contains Me.[106]

It is said that neither the Heavens nor Earth contained Me but the heart of My believing servant contained Me." That is *nūr*. That *dhikrullāh* is *nūr*, and *Allāhu nūru 's-samāwāti wa 'l-ʿarḍ,* "Allāh is The Light, *Nūr* of the Heavens and Earth." That *nūr* comes from *dhikrullāh*, you are praising Allāh ﷻ. It is recommended every moment in your life to praise Allāh ﷻ. When you say, "O Allāh I am a weak servant, I cannot do more," then when you show that, Allāh will create angels to do *dhikrullāh,* to continue on your behalf, to make it as if you are in full worshipness the whole day and the whole night. But you have to start the car, turn the ignition, then the car works, then it moves. The ignition, the key is *dhikrullāh. Duʿā* is *suāl al-ʿabd*, the *duʿā* is asking of a servant to Allāh ﷻ.

Dhikrullāh is by ʿAsmā'ullāh wa 'l-Husna

It is mentioned that *dhikrullāh* is through Allāh's Beautiful Names and Attributes. The Prophet ﷺ said:

كلمتان خفيفتان على اللسان ثقيلتان فى الميزان حبيبتان إلى الرحمن سبحان الله و بحمده سبحان الله العظيم

There are two words that are very easy to say, yet very heavy on the Scale, most beloved to The Merciful, "SubḥānAllāh wa bi-ḥamdihi subḥānAllāhi 'l-ʿAẓīm."[107]

What do you want more than that? If you say that, Allāh will be happy with you! Two words, very light on the tongue and very heavy on the Scale.

---

[106] *Ḥadīth Qudsī, Al-Iḥyā* of Īmām al-Ghazali.
[107] Al-Bukhārī and Muslim.

That means they will push the sins away, these two words are so heavy they will push the Scale down and you will enter Paradise. *SubḥānAllāh wa bi-ḥamdihi subḥānAllāhi 'l-ʿAẓīm.* If you say them, Allāh ﷻ will give you Paradise, Allāh will open for you light in your heart, and open light for you in Heavens.

يَقُولُ الرَّبُّ عَزَّ وَجَلَّ مَنْ شَغَلَهُ ذِكْرِي عَنْ مَسْأَلَتِي أَعْطَيْتُهُ أَفْضَلَ مَا أُعْطِي السَّائِلِينَ

The Prophet ﷺ said, "The Lord, Blessed and Most High is He, said, 'Whoever is too busy remembering Me to ask Me, then I shall give him more than what I give to those who ask.'"

"If someone becomes busy with My remembrance, *man shaghalahu ʿan dhikrī akthar min mas'alatī,* more than he asks Me, I will give him more than anyone else, *afḍala mā ūʿtī 's-sā'ilīn,* I will give him more than what I give to those who ask! If you ask Me, I give you, and if you praise Me, I give you more."

So praise Allāh ﷻ with *ḥamd, taḥmīd, tamjīd, takbīr* and *tahlīl*, and don't be cheap!

عَنْ عَبْدِ اللَّهِ بْنِ بُرَيْدَةَ الأَسْلَمِيِّ، عَنْ أَبِيهِ، قَالَ سَمِعَ النَّبِيُّ صلى الله عليه وسلم رَجُلاً يَدْعُو وَهُوَ يَقُولُ اللَّهُمَّ إِنِّي أَسْأَلُكَ بِأَنِّي أَشْهَدُ أَنَّكَ أَنْتَ اللَّهُ لاَ إِلَهَ إِلاَّ أَنْتَ الأَحَدُ الصَّمَدُ الَّذِي لَمْ يَلِدْ وَلَمْ يُولَدْ وَلَمْ يَكُنْ لَهُ كُفُوًا أَحَدٌ . قَالَ فَقَالَ " وَالَّذِي نَفْسِي بِيَدِهِ لَقَدْ سَأَلَ اللَّهَ بِاسْمِهِ الأَعْظَمِ الَّذِي إِذَا دُعِيَ بِهِ أَجَابَ وَإِذَا سُئِلَ بِهِ أَعْطَى

The Prophet heard a man supplicating and he was saying, "O Allāh! Indeed, I ask you by my testifying that You are Allāh! There is none worthy of worship except You, The Unique, Self-Sufficient, The One Who begets not nor was He begotten, and there is none who is like Him." So the Prophet ﷺ said, "By The One in Whose Hand is my soul, he has asked Allāh by His Greatest Name, the one which if He is called upon by it, responds, and when He is asked by it, gives."[108]

It is mentioned in Sahih ibn Hibbān that the Prophet ﷺ heard a man making *duʿā* and he was saying, *Allāhumma innī as'aluka bi annī ash-hadu annaka Anta 'Llāh lā ilāha illa Anta al-Āḥadu 'ṣ-Ṣamad al-ladhī lam yalid wa lam yūlad wa lam yakun lahu kufūwan āḥad.* "O Allāh! I am asking You to be

---

[108] Tirmidhī, Sahih ibn Hibban.

witness that I say that You are the Creator and You are The Only One, *al-Āḥad,* Unique, and *aṣ-Ṣamad,* Who does not need anyone, is independent of all, The One that has no children, *lam yalid wa lam yūlad,* and has no partners." The Prophet ﷺ said, *w'alladhī nafsī bi yadihi,* "I give an oath," to show how much it is important. Without giving an oath, whatever the Prophet ﷺ said people believed, but to confirm to you what was revealed to me of this *du'ā* he said, *laqad sa'ala 'Llāhu bi 'smihi 'l-'Aẓam,* "He asked Allāh by His Greatest Name."

He asked Allāh when he read that, and I will read it another time and all of us will read it:

Allāhumma innī as'aluka bi annī ash-hadu annaka Anta 'Llāh
lā ilāha illa Anta al-Āḥadu 'ṣ-Ṣamad al-ladhī lam yalid wa lam yūlad
wa lam yakun lahu kufūwan āḥad.

We said it, *alḥamdulillāh,* so we will get the *barakah* of that *du'ā,* where the Prophet ﷺ said that man through that *du'ā* asked Allāh by means of His Greatest Name. All prophets were asking (seeking) in their life to ask Allāh by His Greatest Name. Allāh didn't give it and no one knows what is the Greatest Name of Allāh ﷻ. Some scholars and awlīyāullāh say it is in the beginning of the first two or three ayats in every sūrah, from the beginning to the end. *Ismullāhi 'l-'Aẓam,* The Greatest Name is in one of them although it is not recognized as He only gives to the Prophet ﷺ, and what Allāh wants him to know he knows. As the Prophet ﷺ said, *laqad sa'ala 'Llāhu bi 'smihi 'l-'aẓam,* "He asked Allāh by His Greatest Name," so he knew. "He asked Allāh by His Greatest Name, *wa idhā su'ila bihi a'ṭā,* that if anyone asked by it, it is answered." If anyone wants his *du'ā* to be answered immediately, it must be by *Ismullāh al-'Azham.* And we don't know where, but the Prophet ﷺ is mentioning through that *ḥadīth* that it is in those two lines, *Ismullāhi 'l-'Aẓam* is there.

Su'ila ba'du ahli 'l-'ilm, some scholars asked, *ayyuma anfa'ū li 'l-'abd at-tasbīḥ aw al-istighfār,* which is better for a servant of Allāh, to praise Allāh or to ask forgiveness of Allāh? Which is more beneficial, better for us? What is better, praise or *istighfār*? If you praise and don't make *istighfār,* in the mind of people you have to make *istighfār* first and then praise. That comes out easy. I made a sin and praised Allāh? No, I have to say *"astaghfirullāh"* and come clean. So which is higher? Praise or *istighfār*? I confused you, because the first was the right answer, to praise.

It is said if you have clean clothes, you need to put incense or *bakhūr* on top of them or perfumes. It is advisable to put it on clean clothes, and on dirty clothes what is the benefit to put perfume and incense? You need to put soap and water. So how then, if we are dirty by sins? *Istighfār* will clean us to be able to put perfume on the clothes you are going to wear. So for sure praise is higher, but *istighfār* is what cleans you and polishes you, and grants you cleanliness and presents you clean, and makes you able to receive the manifestations of Allāh's Beautiful Names and Attributes. Then you can put the perfume and incense; you don't put perfumes and incense on dirty clothes. So don't praise Allāh ﷻ without asking for forgiveness. Make *istighfār* and then praise Him.

Rabbanā ẓalamnā anfusanā, Allāh said that we should say:

$$قَالاَ رَبَّنَا ظَلَمْنَا أَنفُسَنَا وَإِن لَّمْ تَغْفِرْ لَنَا وَتَرْحَمْنَا لَنَكُونَنَّ مِنَ الْخَاسِرِينَ$$

> The two of them [Ādam and Eve] said, "O Allāh! We oppressed ourselves.
> If you don't forgive us and send Your Mercy, we will be losers."[109]

We must first say, So first is asking forgiveness, *istighfār*, then you will be rewarded by praising Him. "*Lā ilāha illa Anta Subḥānak! Innī kuntu min aẓ-ẓālimīn*, there is no Creator except You, I am an oppressor." Sayyīdinā Yūnus ؑ humbled himself and confessed his wrongdoing, so the whale spat him out. *Dhikrullāh* is better than *du'ā*, but *du'ā* is necessary to take you to a clean *dhikrullāh* when you do it, to be clean, not to be dirty.

Sayyīdinā Abū Bakr aṣ-Ṣiddīq ؓ asked the Prophet ﷺ to teach him a *du'ā* to recite in his prayers. This *ḥadīth* is mentioned in *Bukhārī* and *Muslim*. And the Prophet ﷺ said, "*Qūl*, say, *yā* Abū Bakr aṣ-Ṣiddīq, '*Allāhumma…*'" And look how he begins it:

$$أَنَّ أَبَا بَكْرٍ الصِّدِّيقَ ـ رضى الله عنه ـ قَالَ لِلنَّبِيِّ صلى الله عليه وسلم يَا رَسُولَ اللَّهِ عَلِّمْنِي دُعَاءً أَدْعُو بِهِ فِي صَلاَتِي. قَالَ " قُلِ اللَّهُمَّ إِنِّي ظَلَمْتُ نَفْسِي ظُلْمًا كَثِيرًا، وَلاَ يَغْفِرُ الذُّنُوبَ إِلاَّ أَنْتَ، فَاغْفِرْ لِي مِنْ عِنْدِكَ مَغْفِرَةً، إِنَّكَ أَنْتَ الْغَفُورُ الرَّحِيمُ$$

---

[109] Sūrat al-'Arāf, 7:23.

Abū Bakr aṣ-Ṣiddīq said to the Prophet ﷺ, "O Allāh's Messenger ﷺ! Teach me an invocation with which I may invoke Allāh in my prayers."

The Prophet ﷺ said, "Say, 'Allāhumma innī ẓalamtu nafsī ẓulman kathīran wa innahu lā yaghfiru 'dh-dhunūba illā Anta faghfir lī maghfiratan min ʿindika wa 'rḥamnī innaka Anta 'l-Ghafūru 'r-Raḥīm. O Allāh! I have wronged my soul exceedingly and none forgives the sins but You, so please bestow Your Forgiveness upon me. No doubt, You are the Oft-Forgiving, Most Merciful).'"[110]

You begin by blaming yourself: *Allāhumma innī ẓalamtu nafsī ẓulman kathīran.* If someone is entering to see a leader, first you will say, "Forgive me." So what do you think about Allāh ﷻ, when someone is entering the door of Allāh ﷻ, what would he say? He wants to show humility. The Prophet ﷺ is showing Sayyīdinā Abū Bakr aṣ-Ṣiddīq ؓ humility, to say, "*Allāhumma innī ẓalamtu nafsī ẓulman kabīra,* I have oppressed myself so much, *wa innahu lā yaghfiru 'dh-dhunūba illā Anta,* and there is none to forgive Me except You! *Faghfir lī maghfiratan min ʿindika wa 'rḥamnī,* so forgive me with a special forgiveness from You and *w 'arhamnī,* send Mercy on me, be Merciful."

That is for Sayyīdinā Abū Bakr aṣ-Ṣiddīq ؓ, who was the Companion of the Prophet ﷺ, whom he took:

إِذْ يَقُولُ لِصَاحِبِهِ لاَ تَحْزَنْ إِنَّ اللهَ مَعَنَا

And he said to his companion, "Have no fear for Allāh is with us."[111]

He was Companion of the Prophet ﷺ migrating from Mecca to Madīnah.

And then comes the praising, "*Innaka Anta 'l-Ghafūru 'r-Raḥīm,* You are The One Who Forgives and You are The One Who is Merciful." So this *ḥadīth* combined *tawassul* to Allāh ﷻ by *maghfirah,* praising Him by asking for forgiveness. So let us say the *dhikr* that the Prophet ﷺ taught Sayyīdinā Abū Bakr aṣ-Ṣiddīq ؓ and, *inshā-Allāh,* we will be saved by that *duʿā* in this life and the Next Life by the *barakah* of that *duʿā:*

---

[110] Bukhārī, Muslim.
[111] Sūrat at-Tawbah, 9:40.

Then there is the *du'ā* of Sayyīdinā Ādam ﷺ and Sayyīdatinā Hawā:

قَالاَ رَبَّنَا ظَلَمْنَا أَنفُسَنَا وَإِن لَّمْ تَغْفِرْ لَنَا وَتَرْحَمْنَا لَنَكُونَنَّ مِنَ الْخَاسِرِينَ

Bismillāhi' r-Raḥmāni 'r-Raḥīm. Rabbanā ẓalamnā anfusanā wa in lam taghfir lanā wa tarhamnā la-nakūnanna min al-khāsirīn.

They said, "Our Lord! We have wronged our own souls: If You forgive us not and bestow not upon us Your Mercy, we shall certainly be lost."[112]

May Allāh bless us and may Allāh grant us His love, and bless us with the *barakah* and love He granted to the Prophet ﷺ and to *awlīyāullāh!*

Grandshaykh said, "If I lose something, I am the thief because I let it be stolen."

May Allāh forgive us and may Allāh bless us.

Wa min Allāhi 't-tawfiq, bi ḥurmati 'l-ḥabīb, bi ḥurmati 'l-Fātiḥah.
And with Allāh is success. For the sake of the Beloved, for his sake we recite the opening chapter of Holy Qur'ān.

[112] Sūrat al-Ā'rāf, 7:23.

Evidence of Various Forms of Remembering Allāh

Aʿūdhu billāhi min ash-Shayṭāni 'r-rajīm. Bismillāhi' r-Raḥmāni 'r-Raḥīm. Nawaytu 'l-arbāʿīn, nawaytu 'l-ʿitikāf, nawaytu 'l-khalwah, nawaytu 'l-ʿuzlah, nawaytu 'r-riyāḍa, nawaytu 's-sulūk, lillāhi Taʿalā fī hādhā 'l-masjid. Atīʿūllāha wa atīʿū 'r-Rasūla wa ūli 'l-amri minkum. (4:59)

As-salāmu ʿalaykum wa raḥmatullāhi taʿalā wa barakātuh! Bismillāhi 'r-Raḥmāni 'r-Raḥīm. wa 'ṣ-ṣalātu wa 's-salāmu ʿalā ashrafi 'l-mursalīna Sayyīdinā wa Nabīyyina Muḥammadin wa ʿalā ālihi wa ṣaḥbihi ajmaʿīn.

Dunyā is passing and day after day we are leaving and everyone is leaving. Don't think that there is time for this *dunyā* except for the time that Allāh ﷻ has mentioned, as this *dunyā* has to come to an end. What does Allāh want from us? Someone who loves you likes you to call him and thank him.

All Creations Praise Allāh and Seek His Forgiveness

I was thinking just now and sending not a question, but *istidaʿ*, clarification, from *awlīyāullāh* to see if there would be a response and, of course, they reach you because you are in *Majlis adh-Dhikr*, a gathering of *dhikrullāh.* They will try to make us able to absorb as much as we can, so they give. That is why scholars, ʿulamā, are in need of *awlīyāullāh,* in order that they will connect them and support them with different clarifications. I was asking for a clarification of how many angels have been created, how many human beings and *jinn* have been created, how many devils, *shayāṭīn* have been created, and how many four and two-legged animals and those that crawl on their chest have been created? How many different languages do they speak and yet all of them meet on one point: *dhikrullāh!*

وَإِن مِّن شَيْءٍ إِلاَّ يُسَبِّحُ بِحَمْدَهِ وَلَـكِن لاَّ تَفْقَهُونَ تَسْبِيحَهُمْ

There is not a thing but celebrates His Praises, and yet you don't understand how they declare His Glory! [113]

[113] Sūrat al-'Isrā, 17:44.

Verily 'everything,' that is all things that are created and will be created in the future, meaning their appearances will come into existence in their forms in *dunyā*. Their souls were existing, but when their forms appear, they immediately begin to make *tasbīḥ*, as Allāh likes to be praised. Their duty is to glorify and praise Him in every moment of their life and to ask forgiveness. So, as we asked, is *dhikr* better or *du'ā*? We came to the conclusion in previous sessions that *dhikr* is better. So every one of them is making *tasbīḥ*. When ten people sit and make *tasbīḥ*, you can hear them from a hundred meters away, so what do you think when all creatures are making *tasbīḥ*? They are *muttaqati'īn*, intersecting in their different voices and different languages, all making *tasbīḥ* in their own languages.

How many are there? We have to take *'ibrah* to see how small, as we are an epsilon compared to infinity, and epsilon still exists, but compared to infinity it is nothing, it might be smaller than an atom. So all of them are making *tasbīḥ* to Allāh ﷻ. How many are making *tasbīḥ*? That is the question, the clarification. How many? Allāh ﷻ said:

لَقَدْ أَحْصَاهُمْ وَعَدَّهُمْ عَدًّا وَكُلُّهُمْ آتِيهِ يَوْمَ الْقِيَامَةِ فَرْدًا

He does take an account of them (all) and has numbered them (all) exactly, and all of them are coming to Him on the Day of Resurrection alone.[114]

Laqad aḥṣāhum wa 'addahum 'adda, Allāh ﷻ counted them one by one and added them all together, *aḥṣāhum* "totaled them." He knows the total of how many He created, how many He is now creating and how many He will create in the future. He already knows, He did it as He is The Creator! *Aḥṣāhum wa 'addahum,* He counted them one by one, *wa kullahum ātīhi yawma 'l-qīyāmati farda* and all of them are coming to Him one by one on the Day of Judgment. *Allāhu Akbar*! One by one: angels, *jinn,* human beings, devils, animals, trees, everything will come. They will come individually, not in groups. When each one of them comes individually, what will happen? It will be like thousands of people marching in a group, all of them coming towards judgment. *Allāhu Akbar*!

[114] Sūrat Maryam, 19:94,95.

That is why Allāh ﷻ mentioned in the Holy Qur'an :

وَالَّذِينَ إِذَا فَعَلُواْ فَاحِشَةً أَوْ ظَلَمُواْ أَنْفُسَهُمْ ذَكَرُواْ اللهَ فَاسْتَغْفَرُواْ لِذُنُوبِهِمْ وَمَن يَغْفِرُ الذُّنُوبَ إِلاَّ
اللهُ وَلَمْ يُصِرُّواْ عَلَى مَا فَعَلُواْ وَهُمْ يَعْلَمُونَ

And those who, having done something to be ashamed of or who wronged their own souls, earnestly bring Allāh to mind and ask for forgiveness for their sins-and who can forgive sins except Allāh-and who are never obstinate in knowingly persisting in (the wrong) they have done.[115]

What do those who commit a sin or oppress themselves by doing *maʿasiya,* sins, have to do? You committed a sin, you know yourself that you were trapped by Shayṭān and entered into that ocean of sins that never ends for human beings, then what must you do? Make *istighfār*! Allāh ﷻ said, *dhakarū'Llāha fastaghfarū li-dhunūbihim,* "They remembered Allāh," it means "When Allāh throws (the awareness) into their heart that they did a sin, they repent." What are all of these angels, human beings, *jinn,* devils, animals, fish, billions of them doing? They are making *dhikrullāh* and asking forgiveness. And who do you think is going to forgive people from their sins? Is there anyone else besides Allāh ﷻ? No way! There is someone who asks forgiveness on your behalf, but Allāh is The One Who Forgives. Prophet ﷺ asks forgiveness on our behalf, as mentioned in the following *āyah,* and then Allāh forgives them, as it is said in the Holy Qur'ān:

وَلَوْ أَنَّهُمْ إِذ ظَّلَمُواْ أَنفُسَهُمْ جَآؤُوكَ فَاسْتَغْفَرُواْ اللهَ وَاسْتَغْفَرَ لَهُمُ
الرَّسُولُ لَوَجَدُواْ اللهَ تَوَّابًا رَّحِيمًا

If they had only, when they were unjust to themselves, come to you and asked Allāh's forgiveness, and the Messenger had asked forgiveness for them, they would have found Allāh indeed Oft-returning, Most Merciful.[116]

Now we have established that every creature Allāh ﷻ has created, Heavenly or Earthly, remembers Allāh and asks forgiveness, and Allāh is The One Who Forgives. The infallible ones have no sins. Who are they? Prophet ﷺ, all prophets and angels are infallible. Prophet ﷺ is infallible, but with that, what did Abū Hurayrah ؓ say in a *ḥadīth* narrated by *Bukhārī*?

---

[115] Sūrat Āli-ʿImrān, 3:135.
[116] Sūrat an-Nisa, 4:64.

قَالَ أَبُو هُرَيْرَةَ سَمِعْتُ رَسُولَ اللَّهِ صلى الله عليه
وسلم يَقُولُ " وَاللَّهِ إِنِّي لأَسْتَغْفِرُ اللَّهَ وَأَتُوبُ إِلَيْهِ فِي الْيَوْمِ أَكْثَرَ مِنْ سَبْعِينَ مَرَّةً

I heard Allāh's Messenger ﷺ saying, "By Allāh! I ask for forgiveness from Allāh and turn to Him in repentance more than seventy times a day."[117]

This is from someone who is infallible, with no sins! Prophet ﷺ is *nūr*:

قَدْ جَاءكُم مِّنَ اللهِ نُورٌ وَكِتَابٌ مُّبِينٌ

Indeed, there has come to you from Allāh a Light (Prophet Muḥammad) and a plain Book (this Qur'an).[118]

Here "*nūr*" refers to Sayyīdinā Muḥammad ﷺ. Allāh has sent him a Light from His Light. When Allāh ﷻ created Creation, us and everything, He created them in emptiness, where you cannot see. It was in the Time of Souls, *Alastu bi-rabbīkum,* on the Day of Promises. We do not know when that was, but it is in His Knowledge and we were in complete non-existence. It was from a non-existing space, we cannot say "space" nor "area," but a complete non-existence, emptiness, dark and *ʿadm,* non-existence, from complete non-existence to existence. They appeared by Allāh's Will, but were still in darkness. Then Allāh ﷻ shed that Light and with it came *ḍīyā,* the emergence of light, illumination. Anyone on whom that Light hit became a Muslim and *mu'min.* Anyone on whom that Light did not hit is still not Muslim nor *mu'min,* he is still in darkness, and that is why his heart is dead.

We must be happy that that Light hit us! That Light of Creation that Allāh has sent on us is from the Light of the Best of Creation, what Allāh created first is the Light of Muḥammad ﷺ. That Light went over all those who were created and wherever that Light came down and touched, that person became a Muslim, a *muwāḥḥid,* monotheist, and a believer, *mu'min*! So say "*Lā ilāha illa-Llāh Muḥammadun Rasūlullāh!*" The Light of the *mu'min* and Muslim is there and doesn't go away, but when we do sins that Light gets covered with a veil, just like curtains cover the sunlight. Through *dhikrullāh,* that Light will appear again and shining!

---

[117] Bukhārī.

[118] Sūrat al-Mā'idah, 5:15.

Istighfār is Dhikrullāh

So to make *istighfār* is from *dhikrullāh*. Why do you have to ask for forgiveness? You remember that the Creator will judge you one day, so what do you do? You say *"astaghfirullāh,"* which is one of the best *dhikrullāh*. Say, *"Yā Rabbī, astaghfirullāh,"* and it will go directly to Allāh ﷻ! The Prophet ﷺ is saying it more than seventy times a day. How many times are we saying it? Sometimes we say and sometimes we forget. How many sins come in between the times we say it? May Allāh open our hearts.

It is mentioned by al-Agharrī 'l-Maznī ؓ that Prophet ﷺ said:

إِنَّهُ لَيُغَانُ عَلَى قَلْبِي وَإِنِّي لَأَسْتَغْفِرُ اللَّهَ فِي الْيَوْمِ مِائَةَ مَرَّةٍ

Sometimes I perceive a veil over my heart and I supplicate to Allāh
for forgiveness a hundred times in a day.[119]

In one narration, it is mentioned '70 times' and in another '100 times'. So you see that there is a difference, 70 or 100; this means Prophet ﷺ is giving us a choice. If you think you are a heavy-duty sinner, you need 100 and if not heavy-duty, if lightweight, then you need 70. Nevertheless, *awlīyāullāh* like their followers to increase their *dhikr*. Also, Prophet ﷺ mentioned the minimum, because if he says more it becomes mandatory on people to do it that many times. *Awlīyāullāh* know that there are obstacles and difficulties on people and so they recommend their followers to do *istighfār* 300 to 700 times a day in order to throw away these obstacles.

One *ḥadīth* sheds light on doing *dhikrullāh* in public, because our brothers say, "Don't make *dhikrullāh* in public; make *istighfār*," as they do it like *Āhlu 's-Sunnah wa 'l-Jamaʿah*, but they say, "do it hidden." However, this *ḥadīth* gives a different direction, as narrated by ʿAbdullāh ibn ʿUmar ؓ:

عَنِ ابْنِ عُمَرَ، قَالَ إِنْ كُنَّا لَنَعُدُّ لِرَسُولِ اللَّهِ صلى الله عليه وسلم فِي الْمَجْلِسِ الْوَاحِدِ مِائَةَ مَرَّةٍ " رَبِّ اغْفِرْ لِي وَتُبْ عَلَىَّ إِنَّكَ أَنْتَ التَّوَّابُ الرَّحِيمُ

We counted that the Messenger of Allāh ﷺ would say a hundred times
during a meeting, "My Lord, forgive me and pardon me,
for You are The Pardoning and Forgiving One."[120]

---

[119] Muslim.

"We used to count." How can they count if they cannot hear? And he didn't say *kuntu a'ud*, "I used to count," but he said *"kunnā la-na'uddu,"* meaning many people with the Prophet ﷺ and all of them counting how many times he is making that *istighfār* and *du'ā*. So this means that he is in *jama'ah* and making *dhikr* in a loud voice or else how could they have counted? He said, "In every gathering with the Prophet ﷺ we used to count a hundred times that the Prophet ﷺ used to say, '*Rabbī 'ghfir lī wa tub 'alayya innaka Anta 't-Tawwābu 'r-Raḥīm*, "My Lord, forgive me and pardon me, for You are The Pardoning and Forgiving One!"

Abū Hurayrah ؓ narrated that the Prophet ﷺ said:

إِنَّ الْمُؤْمِنَ إِذَا أَذْنَبَ كَانَتْ نُكْتَةٌ سَوْدَاءُ فِي قَلْبِهِ فَإِنْ تَابَ وَنَزَعَ وَاسْتَغْفَرَ صُقِلَ قَلْبُهُ فَإِنْ زَادَ زَادَتْ فَذَلِكَ الرَّانُ الَّذِي ذَكَرَهُ اللَّهُ فِي كِتَابِهِ {كَلاَّ بَلْ رَانَ عَلَى قُلُوبِهِمْ مَا كَانُوا يَكْسِبُونَ}

When the Believer commits sin, a black spot appears on his heart. If he repents and gives up that sin and seeks forgiveness, his heart will be polished, but if (the sin) increases, (the black spot) increases until it gains the ascendancy over his heart. That is the rān (stain) mentioned by Allāh Most High (83:14), "No! Rather, the stain has covered their hearts of that which they were earning."[121]

As we polish everything with a stain remover, Allāh gave *Ummat an-Nabī* ﷺ a Heavenly stain remover. By saying *"astaghfirullāh"* you can remove any darkness from the heart, it is so easy. Let us say, *"astaghfirullāh, astaghfirullāh, astaghfirullāh."* So *dhikrullāh* is to clean that black spot. Allāh said, "By *dhikrullāh* made them to win." It removes the sins and the best of *dhikrullāh* for sins is *istighfār*.

Anas ibn Mālik ؓ narrated that the Prophet ﷺ said:

كُلُّ بَنِي آدَمَ خَطَّاءٌ, وَخَيْرُ الْخَطَّائِينَ اَلتَّوَّابُونَ

All the sons of Ādam are sinners, but the best of sinners are those who repent often.[122]

---

[120] Abū Dāwūd.
[121] Tirmidhī.
[122] Tirmidhī.

Ibn ʿUmar ﷺ related from the Prophet ﷺ:

إِنَّ اللَّهَ يَقْبَلُ تَوْبَةَ الْعَبْدِ مَا لَمْ يُغَرْغِرْ

Indeed, Allāh accepts the repentance of a servant as long as (his soul does not reach his throat).[123]

If it reached the throat and above it is finished and there is no repentance. If the soul begins to go out from the feet and up the legs and then up to the throat, you can still repent and Allāh will forgive. Look at how much time He gave for forgiveness, but past the throat there is no more forgiveness. May Allāh forgive us from all our sins!

I will mention this *ḥadīth* from Abū Dawūd and Tirmidhī:

مَنْ قَالَ أَسْتَغْفِرُ اللهَ الْعَظِيمَ الَّذِي لاَ إِلَهَ إِلاَّ هُوَ الْحَىَّ الْقَيُّومَ وَأَتُوبُ إِلَيْهِ . غُفِرَ لَهُ وَإِنْ كَانَ فَرَّ مِنَ الزَّحْفِ

Whoever says, astaghfirullāh al-ʿAẓīm alladhī lā ilāha illā Hūwa 'l-Ḥayyu 'l-Qayyum wa atūbu ilayh, "I seek forgiveness from Allāh, The Magnificent, of Whom there is none worthy of worship but Him, The Living, The Self-Subsisting, and I repent to him," then Allāh will forgive him, even if he fled from battle.[124]

The Prophet ﷺ said:

عَنِ النَّبِيِّ صلى الله عليه وسلم " سَيِّدُ الاِسْتِغْفَارِ أَنْ تَقُولَ اللَّهُمَّ أَنْتَ رَبِّي، لاَ إِلَهَ إِلاَّ أَنْتَ، خَلَقْتَنِي وَأَنَا عَبْدُكَ، وَأَنَا عَلَى عَهْدِكَ وَوَعْدِكَ مَا اسْتَطَعْتُ، أَعُوذُ بِكَ مِنْ شَرِّ مَا صَنَعْتُ، أَبُوءُ لَكَ بِنِعْمَتِكَ عَلَيَّ وَأَبُوءُ لَكَ بِذَنْبِي، فَاغْفِرْ لِي، فَإِنَّهُ لاَ يَغْفِرُ الذُّنُوبَ إِلاَّ أَنْتَ ". قَالَ "وَمَنْ قَالَهَا مِنَ النَّهَارِ مُوقِنًا بِهَا، فَمَاتَ مِنْ يَوْمِهِ قَبْلَ أَنْ يُمْسِيَ، فَهُوَ مِنْ أَهْلِ الْجَنَّةِ، وَمَنْ قَالَهَا مِنَ اللَّيْلِ وَهْوَ مُوقِنٌ بِهَا، فَمَاتَ قَبْلَ أَنْ يُصْبِحَ، فَهُوَ مِنْ أَهْلِ الْجَنَّةِ

The most superior way of asking for forgiveness from Allāh is, "Allāhumma Anta Rabbī lā ilāha illā Anta! Khalaqtanī wa ana ʿabduka wa ana ʿalā ʿahdika wa waʿdika m 'astaṭaʿtu aʿūdhu bika min sharri mā ṣanaʿtu, abū'u laka bi-niʿmatika ʿalayya wa abū'u laka bi-dhanbī faghfir lī fa innahu lā yaghfiru 'dh-dhunūba illa Anta." The Prophet ﷺ added, "If somebody recites it during the day with firm faith in it and dies on the same day before the evening, he will be from the People of Paradise, and

---

[123] Tirmidhī.
[124] Tirmidhī.

if somebody recites it at night with firm faith in it and dies before the morning, he will be from the People of Paradise."[125]

That is *dhikrullāh* through *istighfār*.

We Uphold the Sunnah of Prophet's Many Adhkār

There are many other *adhkār* (expressions or ways of remembering Allāh). When you are sleeping and you wake up from seeing a dream that made you afraid and disturbed, there are special *adhkār* for that. Also, there are special *adhkār* for dreams you like and don't like, there are *adhkār* for exiting and entering the house. *SubḥānAllāh,* the Prophet ﷺ was doing them all for 63 years! At the age of forty, he got the Message and at age 63, he left *dunyā*. In 23 years, he was making these *adhkār* day and night, non-stop: at *Tahajjud, Fajr, Duḥā, Ẓuhr, ʿAṣr, Maghrib, ʿIshā* and after *ʿIshā*!

يَا أَيُّهَا الْمُزَّمِّلُ.قُمِ اللَّيْلَ إِلَّا قَلِيلًا.نِصْفَهُ أَوِ انقُصْ مِنْهُ قَلِيلًا.أَوْ زِدْ عَلَيْهِ وَرَتِّلِ الْقُرْآنَ تَرْتِيلًا.

O You, wrapped in garments! Stand (in prayer) by night, but not all night, of one-half thereof or less, or add to it (at will), and recite the Qur'an calmly and distinctly, with your mind attuned to its meaning.[126]

Mainly, Prophet ﷺ often stood all night in prayer. "*Qumi 'l-layla illa qalīla,*" it means sleep a little bit and wake up completely for the rest of the night. How many *aḥādīth* did Prophet ﷺ mention? Do you think that in 23 years with sleeping only two hours a day, always being with *Ṣaḥābah* ؓ and speaking with them, mentioning different *tafsīr* and *aḥādīth* on what they have to recite and do, that he only mentioned 3,000 or 4,000 *ḥadīth* that are from *Bukhārī*? No! *ʿulamā* say that there are more than 100,000 or 200,000 *ḥadīth*. Imam Āḥmad bin Ḥanbal ؓ and Imam Shafiʿī ؓ were memorizing 300,000 *aḥādīth,* from weak up to strong. Also Imam Abū Ḥanīfa ؓ, who is *Imam al-ʿAẓam,* and Imam Mālik ؓ were knowledgeable in many *aḥādīth,* not just 3,000 or 4,000.

So Prophet ﷺ has mentioned everything, *subḥānAllāh*. When you enter a *masjid* there are different *adhkār,* when you hear the *adhān* there are

---

125 Bukhārī.

126 Sūrat al-Muzzammil, 73:1-4.

different *adhkār*. There are also *adhkār* for when you pray between two *sajdas*. Some say, *"Subḥāna Rabbī al-ʿĀlā,"* but you should say, *"Subḥāna Rabbī al-ʿĀlā wa bi-ḥamdih,"* and, *"Subḥāna Rabbī al-ʿAẓīm wa bi-ḥamdih"* in *rukʿū*. It is forbidden by Prophet ﷺ to recite Holy Qur'an in *sajda* and *rukʿū*, only *tasbīḥ* and praising Allāh. So it must be *"Subḥāna Rabbī al-ʿAẓīm wa bi-ḥamdih"* and *"Subḥāna Rabbī al-ʿĀlā wa bi-ḥamdih."* Additionally, there are all different kinds of *duʿā* to recite during prayers and after.

SubḥānAllāh, there is not one thing that the Prophet ﷺ did without mentioning what to recite with all its details! So now think about how everything in Creation including us is doing *dhikrullāh, wa in min shay'in illa yusabbiḥū bi-ḥamdihi,* "There is not a thing but celebrates His Praises," but we don't hear it, not because we cannot receive that, but because we are deaf. What do you do if you cannot hear? You go to the doctor and if there is too much wax, he sucks it out, but if you are deaf completely due to so many sins, then how will you fix your hearing? Let us fix ourselves before it is too late. You must close your ears from anything that arouses your bad desires, as that will make wax to fill them and you will not be able to hear anything. *Istighfār* and *dhikrullāh* will make you to hear what cannot be heard and see what cannot be seen!

That is why we said, and we must think well (believe it), that everything is making *dhikrullāh.* This is the immense Greatness of Allāh ﷻ! We must open our minds to understand, as it is something beyond our mind. No one can contain all these creatures except Allāh. *Aḥṣāhum, wa ʿaddahum ʿadda wa kulluhum ātīhi yawma 'l-qiyāmati farda,* "He totaled them and counted them, and all of them are going to come to Him on the Day of Judgment individually." *SubḥānAllāh*! Everyone will be judged by *"kun fayakūn,"* it will be so quick! *SubḥānAllāh!* Allāh will say, *"Kun fayakūn,"* and the *ḥisāb* will happen. That is why it is said, *Allāh jaʿalā al-ḥayyāt haythu 'n-nūr wa 'l-mawt haythu 'ẓ-ẓulma.*

Allāh has made life where there is light and that is Heavenly Light in their hearts, their hearts are always in light, and those whom light did not come to them are living in darkness. Anyone who did not accept *tawḥīd, "Lā ilāha illa-Llāh Muḥammadun Rasūlullāh,"* is in darkness. Even if he owns the entire Earth, he is leaving it and going. Where is he going to go? To the grave full of darkness, while the grave of the *mu'min* will be Paradise. May Allāh make our graves to be Paradises! So that element of *nūr* is what is important as that Light is a jewel. Allāh ﷻ said:

كنت كنزا مخفياً فأحببت أن أعرف فخلقت الخلق

I was a Hidden Treasure (and) I wanted to be known, so I created Creation.[127]

He created Creation from that jewel, that *Nūr*:

Muḥammad is a man, but not like other men!
He is a gem and human beings are stones.[128]

Sayyīdinā Muḥammad ﷺ is a human being, but he is not like us: he is a jewel and everyone is a pebble a rock. So that jewel is what Allāh ﷻ has planted into the hearts of *mu'mins* and Muslims:

وإعلموا أن فيكم رسول الله

And know Allāh's Messenger is in you.[129]

His Light is there and that Light takes us to Allāh's Door, where that Light will be shed on you. May Allāh forgive us and all Muslims around the world and bring them to unite under the Rope of Allāh ﷻ!

May Allāh forgive us and may Allāh bless us.

Wa min Allāhi 't-tawfiq, bi ḥurmati 'l-ḥabīb, bi ḥurmati 'l-Fātiḥah.
And with Allāh is success. For the sake of the Beloved, for his sake we recite the opening chapter of Holy Qur'ān.

---

[127] Ḥadīth Qudsī .
[128] Shaykh Muḥammad al-Busayri, *Burdat ash-Sharīf.*
[129] Sūrat al-Hujurāt, 49:7.

Who is Touched by Allah's Light is Guided

Aʿūdhu billāhi min ash-Shayṭāni 'r-rajīm. Bismillāhi' r-Raḥmāni 'r-Raḥīm. Nawaytu 'l-arbāʿīn, nawaytu 'l-ʿitikāf, nawaytu 'l-khalwah, nawaytu 'l-ʿuzlah, nawaytu 'r-riyāḍa, nawaytu 's-sulūk, lillāhi Taʿalā fī hādhā 'l-masjid. Atīʿūllāha wa atīʿū 'r-Rasūla wa ūli 'l-amri minkum. (4:59)

Salām ʿalaykum wa raḥmatullāhi wa barakātuh. Another day, a new day, a new page. For us days are new, but for Allāh there is nothing except that He knows, there is nothing new. Everything is in His Hands, *Yad al-Qudrah,* the Hand of Power. He is The One Who can say, *kun fayakūn,* "'Be!' and it will be." And it is said, *wa amruhu bayna 'l-kāfi wa 'n-nūn,* that His Order, or His Will is not yet to say '*nūn,*' but when He says "*kun*!" everything appears as He wants it to appear.

We are simple creatures, but Allāh ﷻ honored us:

وَلَقَدْ كَرَّمْنَا بَنِي آدَمَ وَحَمَلْنَاهُمْ فِي الْبَرِّ وَالْبَحْرِ وَرَزَقْنَاهُم مِّنَ الطَّيِّبَاتِ وَفَضَّلْنَاهُمْ عَلَى كَثِيرٍ مِّمَّنْ خَلَقْنَا تَفْضِيلاً

We have honored the Children of Ādam, provided them with transport on land and sea, given them for sustenance things good and pure, and conferred on them special favors above a great part of Our Creation.[130]

Allāh honored us and He provided us with everything. '*Ṭayyibāt*' means not only good provision, but Allāh is *Ṭayyib, Yuḥibb at-Ṭayyib. Ṭayyib* is something ripe and tasteful, something whose sweetness you cannot express; it is delightful. So Allāh ﷻ honored us with what, because we are honored. Honored us because He honored His Prophet ﷺ. How did He honor him? There are many things with which Allāh honored the Prophet ﷺ, but one of the main honors is that Allāh created him from His Light. Allāh created that Light and said, "*Kūnī Muḥammad* (Be, Muḥammad!)."

رواه عبد الرزاق بسنده عن جابر بن عبد الله بلفظ قال قلت: يا رسول الله، بأبي أنت وأمي، أخبرني عن أول شيء خلقه الله قبل الأشياء. قال: يا جابر، إن الله تعالى خلق قبل الأشياء نور نبيك من نوره،...

[130] Sūrat al-Isrā', 17:70.

When Jābir ؓ asked, "Let my father and mother be sacrificed for you, oh Prophet of Allāh! What is the first thing that Allāh ﷻ created?" the Prophet ﷺ said, "The first thing that Allāh ﷻ created is the Light of your Prophet from His Light, O Jābir."[131]

Awwala ma khalaq-Allāhu nūra nabīyyika, yā Jābir. The first thing Allāh created was *Nūr an-Nabī*, the Light of the Prophet ﷺ from His Light. So Allāh honored us because of *Nūr an-Nabī*, not because you are beautiful, or handsome, or rich or you have a Rolex in your hand, no, but because there is something special that He didn't give anyone, where He said in Holy Qur'ān:

قَدْ جَاءكُم مِّنَ اللّهِ نُورٌ وَكِتَابٌ مُّبِينٌ

Indeed, there has come to you from Allāh a Light (Prophet Muḥammad) and a plain Book (this Qur'an).[132]

"Certainly, there has come to you Light and a Perspicuous Book." There was first nothing, *ẓulmah*, darkness, no light, you cannot see, and then Allāh ﷻ sent that Light, *nūr an-nabī* ﷺ, *bihi, bi nūr an-nabī bi qudratullāh 'azza wa jall, wa bi nūri 'n-nabī*, that Allāh ﷻ dressed him with His Greatness, that *nūr*, and as we said before, wherever He ﷻ sent it, those people became enlightened.

إِنَّ اللَّهَ عَزَّ وَجَلَّ خَلَقَ خَلْقَهُ فِي ظُلْمَةٍ فَأَلْقَى عَلَيْهِمْ مِنْ نُورِهِ فَمَنْ أَصَابَهُ مِنْ ذَلِكَ النُّورِ اهْتَدَى وَمَنْ أَخْطَأَهُ ضَلَّ فَلِذَلِكَ أَقُولُ جَفَّ الْقَلَمُ عَلَى عِلْمِ اللَّهِ

The Prophet ﷺ said, "Indeed Allāh, the Blessed and Exalted, created His Creation in darkness, then He cast His Light upon them, so whoever is touched by that Light he is guided and whoever is not he goes astray. It is for this reason that I say that the pens have dried with Allāh's knowledge."[133]

Inna 'Llāha ta'alā khalaqa khalqahu fī ẓulmah, "Surely, Allāh created His Creation in darkness, all of it, nothing was left out." You cannot see anything. You are there, He will bring you quickly. And what is the

---

[131] *Musannaf 'Abdu 'r-Razzaq*.
[132] Sūrat al-Mā'idah, 5:15.
[133] Ḥadīth of 'Abdullāh ibn 'Umar ؓ reported by Imām Aḥmad in his Musnad..

continuation of the *ḥadīth*? *Fa-alqā ʿalayhim min nūrihi,* "Then He threw on them His Light." That Light that He dressed, that is the Light of the Prophet ﷺ. *Fa man aṣābahu min dhālika 'n-nūr ahtadā,* "Whoever reached the Light was guided." Allāh ﷻ said:

إِنَّكَ لَا تَهْدِي مَنْ أَحْبَبْتَ وَلَكِنَّ اللَّهَ يَهْدِي مَن يَشَاء

Surely you cannot guide whom you love, but Allāh guides whom He pleases.[134]

Be happy because Allāh chose you, He chose us all, so be thankful Allāh guided us or else we will be lost! *Wa man akhṭāhu ḍalla,* "And the one whom the Light missed was misguided, deviated, lost completely." *Aqūlu, jaff al-qalam bi ʿilmi 'Llāhi taʿalā.* The Prophet ﷺ said, "The Heavenly Pen has written everything, those who are guided and those who are not misguided, and the ink has dried, no more writing." And on the Day of *Alastu bi-rabbīkum,* that is finished, when some said yes and some said no to Allāh's question, "Am I not your Lord?" It is finished, no more ink in it. So the answer is written and *jaff al-qalam,* the ink became dry.

This is one of main, *aṣl,* the origin or the source of all *aḥādīth* related to *īmān,* which means to believe in the Unseen, *āmantu billāh,* "I believe in Allāh," and Allāh is Unseen; *wa malāʾikatihi,* and in His angels, also Unseen; *wa kutubihi,* and in His books, which can be seen; *wa rusūlihi,* in His prophets, who can be seen, but those at the first, the Level of *Īmān,* are Unseen; and you have to believe in the Unseen.

So that *nūr* that Allāh sent and it guided everyone, through that *nūr,* because the *malāʾikah* are from that *nūr* as it touched them completely and they are infallible, they are ascending and descending with the *ʿamal* of Banī Ādam ؑ, with what we do. If the *ʿamal* are good, the angels will rise all the way past the Seven Heavens and present that *ʿamal* to Allāh ﷻ, and Allāh ﷻ welcomes that one because he was remembering Allāh in *dunyā*! That is why *dhikrullāh* is very important: those whom that Light touched are doing *dhikrullāh*! They miss that Light, they are yearning for that Light, so Allāh ordered angels to bring their *ʿamal* up, to open the First Heaven if deserved, and to open the Second Heaven if it deserves, and the Third Heaven, and Fourth and further, all the way to the Seventh Heaven, until *maqʿadi 'ṣ-ṣidq.*

---

[134] Sūrat al-Qasas, 28:56.

And those whose *'amal* are not good, as soon as the angels carry their *'amal* reaching the First Heaven, *samā ad-dunyā,* the Heavens that are connected with *dunyā,* if not deserving then they don't raise up.

So our *'amal* is going all the way up to Heavens, past all these galaxies of this universe, all six-thousand of them. If the *'amal* is good, it raises past all that and reaches the First Heaven, and if no good it is sent back, thrown in their face and returned to *dunyā,* the place of *ẓulmah.* And there is no *nūr* here as *nūr* is only in the hearts of the Believers, or else a 'dead heart' is a *dunyā* heart that doesn't know, it doesn't think and they have no mind, and no religion even, they are secular, Atheists. They don't think. What do we say? Don't try to humiliate them as it is not our judgement, it is Allāh's Judgment, or else we will be humiliated, so we must leave their judgment to Allāh ﷻ. We are concerned with our homes; this Muslim world is our home and we are concerned with those who are Muslim. For non-Muslims, Allāh is Great and Allāh knows how He will judge them.

لَكُمْ دِينُكُمْ وَلِيَ دِينِ

To you is your religion and to ours, our religion.[135]

You have your religion, I have my religion, I follow the way that Prophet ﷺ has shown us, they follow something we don't accept and we feel okay with it and if they feel okay with it, bravo, welcome, and Allāh is The Judge. So that *Nūr* is the *Nūr* that Allāh ﷻ gave to the Prophet ﷺ and from that *Nūr* the Prophet ﷺ gave to the *Ummah.* It became stronger because it is coming from Allāh ﷻ on the Prophet ﷺ and from the Prophet ﷺ on us, so that means from the worshipness of the Prophet ﷺ we must be happy!

O Muslims! Through his *Nūr,* the worshipness of Prophet ﷺ will be manifested on his *Ummah,* because when he was born he ﷺ was saying, *"Ummatī, ummatī."* He was worried about his *Ummah*: in *dunyā* he was worried about his *Ummah,* in *Ākhirah* he is worried for his *Ummah,* and that means everything that Allāh gave him he will give to his *Ummah* to make them happy. He ﷺ will go into *sajda* in Allāh's Presence three times, as we mentioned the *ḥadīth* of Imam *Bukhārī* ؓ many times in Adab al-Mufrad,

[135] Sūrat al-Kāfirūn, 109:6.

asking Allāh to give *shafaʿah* to the *Ummah* every time and according to that *ḥadīth,* until everyone will go to Paradise.

Muḥammad bin Ṣāliḥ al-Harbī writes in his book, *Fawā'iḍ adh-dhikr at-tīb min al-wābil aṣ-Ṣayyib*:

واستنارت به الوجوه، وحييت به الأرواح، وأذعنت به الجوارح للطاعات طوعاً واختياراً، فازدادت به القلوب حياة إلى حياتها

With that Nūr, all faces were enlightened and souls were rejuvenated, and with that Nūr Allāh ﷻ makes all to accept, to obey.

That is why we say, *"Atīʿūllāha wa atīʿū 'r-Rasūla wa ūli 'l-amri minkum."* That is the Muslim motto: to obey Allāh and to obey the Prophet ﷺ and to obey your spiritual scholars or your heart to guide you. And with that, the hearts were increased with that *Nūr* until it gave it more and more life.

Muḥammad al-Harbī continues:

ثم دلّها ذلك النور إلى نور آخر، هو أعظم منها وأجلّ، وهو نور الصفات العليا، الذي يضمحل فيه كل نور سواه، فشاهدته ببصائر الإيمان مشاهدة نسبتها إلى القلب نسبة المرئيات إلى العين ذلك لاستيلاء اليقين عليها وانكشاف حقائق الإيمان لها،حتى كأنها تنظر إلى عرش الرحمن-تبارك وتعالى

Then that Light has guided us to another Light, which is more important than the first Light as it is the Light of Allāh's Beautiful Names and Attributes, and an-Nūr is one of Allāh's Beautiful Names. With that one Beautiful Name, Allāh guides us to all His Ṣifāt and all His Beautiful Names and Attributes, and may that Light that comes on His servant make his ʿamal beautiful and clean with nothing on it, with not a single particle of dust on it, and it will be raised to the Presence of Allāh ﷻ until He, as if that Light turned everything we are doing into a purifying process to be clean, as if that Light of yours is viewing the ʿArsh ar-Raḥmān, looking at Allāh's Throne!

Religion is Based on Advice and to Accept Advice is Sunnah

All of that is coming through remembrance of Allāh ﷻ! And what do you have to do for Allāh to be happy with you? The best thing that Allāh will be happy with you is for you to remember Him through His Beautiful Names and Attributes and to call people to Him and advise them. That is why the Prophet ﷺ insisted on advising each other; if you know more than your brother advise him, don't keep (knowledge) to yourself. And that is why it is said in a *ḥadīth*:

إِنَّ الدِّينَ النَّصِيحَةُ إِنَّ الدِّينَ النَّصِيحَةُ إِنَّ الدِّينَ النَّصِيحَةُ " . قَالُوا لِمَنْ يَا رَسُولَ اللهِ قَالَ " لِلَّهِ وَكِتَابِهِ وَرَسُولِهِ وَأَئِمَّةِ الْمُؤْمِنِينَ وَعَامَّتِهِمْ وَأَئِمَّةِ الْمُسْلِمِينَ وَعَامَّتِهِمْ " .

The Prophet ﷺ said, "Religion is advice! Religion is advice! Religion is advice!" They said, "To whom should it be directed, O Messenger of Allāh?" He said, "To Allāh, to His Book, to His Messenger, to the leaders of the Believers and to the general Muslims.[136]

What is best in religion? The focus of religion is *an-naṣīḥa*, advice. And what he ﷺ said? "*Ad-dīnu naṣīḥa*," and then said again, "*ad-dīnu naṣīḥa*" and again, "*ad-dīnu naṣīḥa*," and that is to confirm that religion is advice.

It means don't be stubborn, accept advice, don't be proud! There are too many people who are proud in their thinking; they do not accept anything, they are too proud to listen. And Prophet ﷺ said, "Religion is advice," which means put your head down when someone advises you in your religion.

إِنَّ الدِّينَ عِندَ اللهِ الإِسْلاَمُ

The religion in Allāh's view is Islam (submission to His Will).[137]

So accept. And they asked, "*Yā Rasūlullāh*! To whom do we have to give advice?" and the Prophet ﷺ said, "Advise people of Allāh's Book and of His Words, words which are not created." They are not like created words, everyone's words are created; there is a big difference between what is created and what is not created, and something uncreated relates to Allāh ﷻ. Holy Qur'an is uncreated and anyone that says it is created leaves Islam. It is Allāh's Words containing all kinds of secrets and all kind of powers and that is why the interpretation never ends. Go to my library which is a few books, perhaps a thousand books, and you see how many *tafsīrs* are there. That is what I have and what others have are thousands of *tafsīrs*. If you want to open a college to teach Islam, to get a license you must have at least

---

[136] Ḥadīth of Tamīm ad-Dāree reported by Abū Dāwūd.
[137] Sūrat Āli-ʿImrān, 3:19.

50,000 titles on Islam in your library and many *tafsīr* of Holy Qur'an and every *tafsīr* of Holy Qur'ān is different, and the same for *ḥadīth*.

Words of Allāh never end, so the advice is to people through Holy Qur'an and for Allāh and His Book, and for His Prophet, and for the *A'immat al-Muslimīn*, the leaders of Muslims, and then for *wa amātahum*, everyone included! So *naṣīḥa* comes from *dhikrullāh*, when you remember Allāh and how He gave you a nice way of living in *dunyā* and gave your heart full of light, so you want to share that with someone else, Prophet ﷺ is saying to share that with someone so everyone can learn.

عَنْ جَرِيرِ بْنِ عَبْدِ اللَّهِ , قَالَ " : أَتَيْتُ رَسُولَ اللَّهِ صَلَّى اللَّهُ عَلَيْهِ وَسَلَّمَ أُبَايِعُهُ , فَاشْتَرَطَ عَلَيَّ النُّصْحَ لِكُلِّ مُسْلِمٍ ، فَإِنِّي لَكُمْ نَاصِحٌ

When I (Jarīr) gave the pledge of allegiance to Allāh's Messenger ﷺ, he stipulated that I should give good advice to every Muslim.[138]

Uba'yūk 'ala 'l-Islam, "I came to the Prophet ﷺ and I (Jarīr) said, *aba'yāīu'hu 'alā 'l-islām*, 'O Prophet of Allāh ﷺ! I want to take *baya'*, to accept Islam.' *Fa ashataraṭ 'alayya*, He ﷺ accepted, but he put a condition on me, 'You want to take *baya'*, okay, I will give you *baya'*, but on one condition.'" Why? Because the Prophet ﷺ *ittaqū firāsati 'l-mu'min fa innahu yundhuru bi nūrillāh*, "He looks with the Light that Allāh ﷻ gave him," and through that Light the Prophet ﷺ knows the future! *F'ashataraṭ 'alayya an-nuṣ-ḥa li kulli Muslim.* He ﷺ put the condition to advise every Muslim because he was intelligent, he knows, and Prophet ﷺ wanted to use the power of Jarīr ؓ to affect his entire tribe, so he said, "Okay, I will give you *baya'*," although Prophet ﷺ will give *baya'* without giving a condition; if anyone accepts Islam he ﷺ will say yes for him, but because Prophet ﷺ knew Jarīr is powerful, he is intelligent, he ﷺ said, "I am giving you *baya'* on the condition that you advise others what you have learned from me." *Wa rabbu hadhi 'l-masjid innī lakum la-nāṣiḥ*, and Jarīr ؓ gave an oath, "By the Lord of this mosque, yā Rasūlullāh, of your mosque," *fa innī lakum la-nāṣiḥun*, "I am going to advise whoever wants to be advised."

This is an advice, as in Islam religion is advice, *"ad-dīnu naṣīḥa,"* that is an advice.

---

[138] Bukhārī.

Faith is to Love for Your Brother what You Love for Yourself

Anas ibn Mālik ؓ narrated that the Prophet ﷺ said:

لَا يُؤْمِنُ أَحَدُكُمْ حَتَّى يُحِبَّ لِأَخِيهِ مَا يُحِبُّ لِنَفْسِهِ

None of you (truly) believes until he loves for his brother that which he loves for himself.[139]

"Not one of you truly believes, *ḥattā yuḥibbu li akhīhi ma yuḥibbu li nafsihi*, until he loves for his brother what he loves for himself." You cannot simply say, "I love you," as what is the meaning? But when you do an action for the benefit of your brother, what you do for yourself, then you did something good as you want him to be good, so you do it for him by action, not by tongue, not just by saying, "I love you." Then you are a *mu'min*. He (a *murīd*) makes juices. He told me, "I love you," and after he told me "I love you," he brought cases of juice. Showing love and respect to each other shows *īmān* in their hearts, as Prophet ﷺ said, narrated by *Muslim* and *Bukhārī*. So we have to love for our brother what we love for ourselves.

The Prophet ﷺ said:

مَنْ نَفَّسَ عَنْ مُسْلِمٍ كُرْبَةً مِنْ كُرَبِ الدُّنْيَا نَفَّسَ اللَّهُ عَنْهُ كُرْبَةً مِنْ كُرَبِ يَوْمِ الْقِيَامَةِ وَمَنْ يَسَّرَ عَلَى مُعْسِرٍ فِي الدُّنْيَا يَسَّرَ اللَّهُ عَلَيْهِ فِي الدُّنْيَا وَالآخِرَةِ وَمَنْ سَتَرَ عَلَى مُسْلِمٍ فِي الدُّنْيَا سَتَرَ اللَّهُ عَلَيْهِ فِي الدُّنْيَا وَالآخِرَةِ وَاللَّهُ فِي عَوْنِ الْعَبْدِ مَا كَانَ الْعَبْدُ فِي عَوْنِ أَخِيهِ

Whoever relieves a Muslim of a burden from the burdens of the world, Allāh will relieve him of a burden from the burdens on the Day of Judgement. And whoever helps ease a difficulty in the world, Allāh will grant him ease from a difficulty in the world and in the Hereafter. And whoever covers (the faults of) a Muslim, Allāh will cover (his faults) for him in the world and the Hereafter. And Allāh is engaged in helping the worshipper as long as the worshipper is engaged in helping his brother.[140]

"Who helps his brother overcome a problem or a difficulty, Allāh will help him overcome a difficulty on Judgment Day," so if you know there is a

---

[139] Bukhārī and Muslim.
[140] Tirmidhī.

brother that has a problem, help him and Allāh will help you on Judgment Day.

Anas ibn Mālik ؓ narrated that the Prophet ﷺ said:

انْصُرْ أَخَاكَ ظَالِمًا أَوْ مَظْلُومًا

Help your brother, whether he is an oppressor or he is an oppressed one.[141]

Support your brother whether he is *ẓālimān*, oppressor, or *maẓlūman*, oppressed. If you see your brother is oppressed, many will hug him in support as he is oppressed, but that is not enough; it is a sign of respect and love, to hug the one who is oppressed and you listen to what he is saying and try to make him feel happy.

عَنْ أَبِي هُرَيْرَةَ , قَالَ : قَالَ رَسُولُ اللَّهِ صَلَّى اللَّهُ عَلَيْهِ وَسَلَّمَ: "انْصُرْ أَخَاكَ ظَالِمًا أَوْ مَظْلُومًا" , قَالُوا : "يَا رَسُولَ اللَّهِ هَذَا نَنْصُرُهُ مَظْلُومًا فَكَيْفَ نَنْصُرُهُ ظَالِمًا" قَالَ :" تَكُفُّونَهُ عَنِ الظُّلْمِ"

They asked, "O Allāh's Messenger ﷺ! It is all right to help him if he is oppressed, but how should we help him if he is an oppressor?" The Prophet ﷺ said, "By preventing him from oppressing others."[142]

So the Ṣaḥābah ؓ heard that ḥadīth and said, "We understand how to help the oppressed, but how to help him when he is an oppressor?" Because he said in that ḥadīth, *anṣur akhāka ẓālimān aw maẓlūman*, "Support your brother oppressor or oppressed." "Oppressed we understand, but the oppressor?" Anyone has an answer? [Stop him from oppressing.] *Allāhu Akbar!* Try to advise him to leave that kind of stubbornness in his mind of oppression, advise him to leave that bad habit. It is said, *takuffūnahu 'ani 'ẓ-ẓulm*. "To prevent him from going and being more of an oppressor to someone else by any means that you think about it." And all this comes under *naṣīḥa*, advising, it comes under remembering Allāh *adh-dhākir*, as the one remembering Allāh ﷻ will remember all human beings. Who

---

[141] Bukhārī.
[142] Bukhārī.

remembers and loves the Prophet ﷺ will remember all human beings! That is from *dhikrullāh*.

Overwhelming Benefits of Ṣadaqa

Abū Mūsā ؓ narrated that the Prophet ﷺ said:

عَلَى كُلِّ مُسْلِمٍ صَدَقَةٌ، قَالُوا: فَإِنْ لَمْ يَجِدْ؟ قَالَ: فَيَعْتَمِلُ بِيَدَيْهِ، فَيَنْفَعُ نَفْسَهُ، وَيَتَصَدَّقُ، قَالُوا: فَإِنْ لَمْ يَسْتَطِعْ، أَوْ لَمْ يَفْعَلْ؟ قَالَ: فَيُعِينُ ذَا الْحَاجَةِ الْمَلْهُوفَ، قَالُوا: فَإِنْ لَمْ يَفْعَلْ؟ قَالَ: فَيَأْمُرُ بِالْخَيْرِ، أَوْ يَأْمُرُ بِالْمَعْرُوفِ، قَالُوا: فَإِنْ لَمْ يَفْعَلْ؟ قَالَ: فَيُمْسِكُ عَنِ الشَّرِّ، فَإِنَّهُ لَهُ صَدَقَةٌ.

"Every Muslim must give ṣadaqa." They said, "And if he does not find anything (to give)?" He replied, "Then he should work his hands, benefit himself and then give ṣadaqa." They asked, "And if he is unable to or does not do it?" He replied, "Then he should help someone with a great need." They said, "And if he does not do it?" He replied, "Then he should command the good or command the correct." They said, "And if he does not do that?" They said, "He should refrain from evil. That is ṣadaqa for him."[143]

'Alā kulli muslimīn ṣadaqa, "For every Muslim there must be charity; every Muslim has to make charity." And they asked, *ara'ayta in lam yajid*, "What if he doesn't find anything to give charity?" *Qāla fa ya'tamilu bi yadayhi fa yanfa'u nafsahu wa yataṣaddaq*. And the Prophet ﷺ said, "Let him go and do an action with his hands," not to sit and wait, going and asking people, "Give me." No, go do something as you will benefit yourself and from that income give ṣadaqa, because your health needs ṣadaqa, your body needs ṣadaqa, your wealth needs ṣadaqa, your *'amal* needs ṣadaqa, your mind needs ṣadaqa, everything you do needs ṣadaqa, as without ṣadaqa nothing can be done!

الصدقة ترد البلاء وتزيد فى العمر

Sadaqah removes sickness and calamities and prolongs life.

Charity throws away affliction and stretches life, when he says, *Aṣ-ṣadaqatu tarudd al-balā*, "throw away affliction," not "one" affliction, but all

---

[143] Bukhārī.

kinds of afflictions that people have and different people have different kinds of problems, *ṣadaqa* will take away all these problems!

Like this story: Allāh sent Malak al-Mawt ﷺ, the Angel of Death, to take the soul of an old lady who was lonely and alone and didn't have anything, but she was a strong believer in Allāh ﷻ and His Prophet ﷺ. Every day she baked three loaves of bread and ate one in the morning, one in the evening, and at noon every day a needy person knocked on her door and collected his bread. That is her food, no curry, no spices, no *ladū*, but three breads: one in the morning, one in the evening and one at noon time for a needy person. So that day, which coincides with the day her soul was to be taken, she cooked as usual three breads. She wanted to eat in the morning and someone knocked on the door before she ate it and said, "Can you give me *ṣadaqa* from what Allāh gave you?" So she gave him the first morning bread, and then at noon time the usual one came and knocked at the door and took the second. So she didn't have except one, which she was going to eat in the evening. She waited until the evening, but when she came to eat another one came knocking at the door asking for *ṣadaqa* and she gave him the third loaf of bread.

At that time, the Angel of Death ﷺ came to take her soul. He wanted to take it from the toes; first of all, the soul goes from there upwards. He came to take her soul, then one bread came and covered them. It defended her, not allowing, "No, she gave *ṣadaqa,* so you cannot take from the toes." When he tried to take her soul from the belly, another bread came and covered the belly. When he tried to take her soul from the mouth, another bread came and covered the mouth. The Angel of Death ﷺ was then confused about what he should do and he heard a Voice, "I stretched her life because of that *ṣadaqa*." So that is an example of *ṣadaqa* that takes away affliction and stretches your life.

So go and work with your hands, cut the grass, don't be lazy! In the time of Hārūn ar-Rashīd, Hārūn ar-Rashīd was a successful king of Baghdad, very rich. He built a large dormitory and it was for lazy people, *ṭufaylīyyūn,* those who live on others, they cannot do anything, they want to be lazy, not doing anything, living, so one after one filling this place. And Hārūn ar-Rashid was king, he built that place not for everyone, but for those who cannot work, but it was filling up until the whole village was full of these people and they were eating, drinking, not doing anything, happy, lazy.

The Prophet ﷺ didn't allow laziness! In that *ḥadīth* it says to go and do something with your hands, you will benefit and you will give *ṣadaqa* from it; even if you earn one *rupee*, never mind, but show zeal, enthusiasm to do some work, to do something, not to sit and say, "I am waiting for my father and mother to give to me." No, go and work!

So those lazy ones were going inside, too many of them, then one enemy sent a message, "We are invading Baghdad!" He saw he didn't have enough soldiers as all of them were in the village of lazy people.

So his vizier said, "Why are you worried?"

He said, "All of them lazy and we don't have an army. I need people!"

The vizier said, "Don't worry, you want them all?"

He said, "Yes."

"It's okay, I will get them for you."

And so he went and put fire in the building, and the fire began to eat the wood and people were running away, and as they ran away they were taken to the army, until two were left and the fire was coming from the right and the man on the right side told the one on the left, "Move! The fire is approaching me!"

And the one on the left side told the one on the right, "Move your way, also the fire is approaching me!"

Then the vizier said, "These are correct, they are not lazy, they are really sick and they cannot move."

Two out of the whole village were really sick people. So our character is like that: we don't like to do anything. Some people like to do for *dunyā* with very much effort, but for *Ākhirah* they are shaky.

So the Prophet ﷺ said, "No, go and work, do something so people will benefit from you and you will benefit by giving *ṣadaqa*."

And Abū Mūsā ؓ said, "What if he cannot do anything?"

Then the Prophet ﷺ said, *yuʿīnu dha 'l-ḥājati 'l-malḥūf*, "Help the one in need by moving him or doing something for him."

Abū Mūsā ؓ said, "If he cannot do that, then what?"

The Prophet ﷺ said, *yā'muru bi 'l-khayr aw yā'muru bi 'l-maʿrūf,* "Call people to what is good and prohibit for them what is bad. Teach them so people can understand and give them an advice."

Abū Mūsā ؓ said, *ara'ayta in lam yafʿal dhālik,* "If he cannot even do that?"

The Prophet ﷺ said, *yumsiku ʿani 'sh-sharri fa-innahu lahu ṣadaqatun,* "To stop doing an evil action is considered *ṣadaqa,*" which means if someone stops doing a sin that he commits often, Allāh will consider that as *ṣadaqa.*

Look how much *raḥmāt* Allāh has sent to us through the Prophet ﷺ! Islam is full of *raḥmāt* and Islam is full of advice; you can advise your brothers and sisters.

That *ḥadīth* is *mutaffaqun ʿalayh,* "agreed upon," meaning it is related by *Bukhārī* and *Muslim.* May Allāh give us support in order that our *ʿamal* will be changed from imitational *ʿamal* or bad *ʿamal* to good *ʿamal* with the *barakah* of the Prophet ﷺ!

May Allāh forgive us and may Allāh bless us.

Wa min Allāhi 't-tawfiq, bi ḥurmati 'l-ḥabīb, bi ḥurmati 'l-Fātiḥah.
And with Allāh is success. For the sake of the Beloved, for his sake we recite the opening chapter of Holy Qur'ān.

Dhikr is the Head of Shukr

A'ūdhu billāhi min ash-Shayṭāni 'r-rajīm. Bismillāhi' r-Raḥmāni 'r-Raḥīm. Nawaytu 'l-arbā'īn, nawaytu 'l-'itikāf, nawaytu 'l-khalwah, nawaytu 'l-'uzlah, nawaytu 'r-riyāḍa, nawaytu 's-sulūk, lillāhi Ta'alā fī hādhā 'l-masjid. Atī'ūllāha wa atī'ū 'r-Rasūla wa ūli 'l-amri minkum. (4:59)

As-salām 'alaykum wa raḥmatullāhi wa barakātuh. Salām to all viewers wherever they are, and to those who are here, may Allāh ﷻ give us from His endless blessings. We mentioned before in this series since the beginning of *Ramaḍān* about the *ḥadīth* of the Prophet ﷺ, which is very important

الدين نصيحة

Religion is advice.[144]

Are you Muslims? [Yes.] I hope so, because the Prophet ﷺ said:

أخوف ما أخاف على أمتي الشرك الخفي

What I fear most for my Ummah is hidden shirk.

There is outside (external) *shirk* and we know you don't do it, but the hidden *shirk* is what is dangerous, when you listen to your ego and bad desires and don't listen to what Allāh ﷻ wants. So there is always a struggle here, "Should I do this or I don't do this? Do it for love of Allāh or listen to Shayṭān?" So it is a struggle and the Prophet ﷺ was worried for his *Ummah*, and there is obvious *shirk* where people are not worshipping Allāh ﷻ or they associate something with Allāh ﷻ, where they claim Allāh has a child or a son, or they call a plant or tree a god, but Prophet ﷺ was worried for us, wanting us not to have this hidden *shirk*, when people are not humbling themselves.

We are Muslims, *alḥamdulillāh*, Allāh created us Muslims, not because we are clever as we didn't do anything; we opened our eyes and we saw our parents praying and fasting, so we learned praying and fasting. So we

---

[144] Abū Dāwūd.

didn't do anything, but we just followed their footsteps all the way to Prophet ﷺ. That is what Allāh ﷻ likes, as He says in Holy Qur'ān:

قُلْ إِن كُنتُمْ تُحِبُّونَ اللهَ فَاتَّبِعُونِي يُحْبِبْكُمُ اللهُ وَيَغْفِرْ لَكُمْ ذُنُوبَكُمْ وَاللهُ غَفُورٌ رَّحِيمٌ

Say (O Muḥammad), "If you (really) love Allāh, then follow me! Allāh will love you and forgive your sins, and Allāh is Oft-Forgiving, Most Merciful.[145]

Do you love Allāh? Yes, by tongue, but *inshā-Allāh* also by heart. If it is by heart, then you have to follow the footsteps of the Prophet ﷺ. Are we following the footsteps of Prophet ﷺ? We hope we are, *inshā-Allāh*. Follow Muḥammad and Allāh loves you, that is so simple! The *Ṣaḥābah* ﷺ followed the Prophet ﷺ and Allāh made them stars in dark skies. The Prophet ﷺ said:

أصحابي كالنجوم بأيهم اقتديتم اهتديتم

My Companions are like stars (on a dark night); whichever of them you follow, you will be guided.[146]

To follow one of them is enough, even follow only one *ḥadīth* and it is enough, you will be taken to Paradise! So, *ad-dīnu naṣīḥa*, religion is good advice, and good advice is equal to religion. It is so simple. What is religion? It is based on one issue, in prayers we do it, in fasting we do it, in charity we do it, and in making *Hajj* we do it, in making *Shahādah* we do it, and all of that is *dhikrullāh*. Do you want Allāh ﷻ to be with you, as He said in Holy Ḥadīth and the Prophet ﷺ related to us:

أَنَا جَلِيسُ مَنْ ذَكَرَنِي

I sit with him who remembers Me.[147]

It is so easy. What do we have to do? Remember Allāh through the footsteps of the Prophet ﷺ, and there is a highway you must follow, don't exit! There are so many exits from the highway, with Shayṭān building all these bridges there to take you off the highway from the very beginning, so

---

[145] Sūrat Āli-'Imrān, 3:31.
[146] 'Abd ibn Ḥumayd, ad-Daraqutnī, ibn 'Adīyy, ibn 'Abd al-Barr with unsound chains but the meaning is sound.
[147] Āḥmad , Bayhaqī.

don't exit, keep on the highway and you will find so many nice places to rest and enjoy from Allāh's Favors on you, the gardens that Allāh gave to mu'mins, ḥilak adh-dhikr, the circles of dhikr.

قال رسول الله صلى الله عليه وسلم: (إذا مررتم برياض الجنة فارتعو) قالو وما رياض الجنة ؟قال حلق الذكر

> The Prophet ﷺ said to the Ṣaḥābah ؤ, "If you pass by the Gardens of Jannah, sit there and graze." They asked, "What are the Gardens of Paradise?" The Prophet ﷺ replied, "The circles of dhikr."[148]

"When you pass by the gardens of Paradise then sit with them." And they asked, "What are the gardens of Paradise?" The Prophet ﷺ said, "The circles of dhikrullāh," like this association, that is dhikrullāh. Dhikrullāh is not only recitation of different Beautiful Names and Attributes, but also to recite Holy Qur'an, reading ḥadīth, sitting in a naṣīḥa, as advice is from dhikrullāh. We related so many aḥādīth in the last ten lectures about dhikrullāh and to show us the importance of dhikrullāh the Prophet ﷺ said:

أَلاَ أُنَبِّئُكُمْ بِخَيْرِ أَعْمَالِكُمْ وَأَرْضَاهَا عِنْدَ مَلِيكِكُمْ وَأَرْفَعِهَا فِي دَرَجَاتِكُمْ وَخَيْرٍ لَكُمْ مِنْ إِعْطَاءِ الذَّهَبِ وَالْوَرِقِ وَمِنْ أَنْ تَلْقَوْا عَدُوَّكُمْ فَتَضْرِبُوا أَعْنَاقَهُمْ وَيَضْرِبُوا أَعْنَاقَكُمْ ". قَالُوا وَمَا ذَاكَ يَا رَسُولَ اللَّهِ قَالَ " ذِكْرُ اللَّهِ

> Shall I not tell you of the best of your deeds, the most pleasing to your Lord, those that raise you most in status, that are better than your gold and silver or meeting your enemy (in battle) and you strike their necks and they strike your necks?" They said, " What is that, O Messenger of Allāh?" He said, "Remembering Allāh (dhikrullāh)."[149]

Do you want me to tell you of your best deeds?

الدين نصيحة

Religion is advice.[150]

---

[148] Tirmidhī.
[149] Ibn Mājah.
[150] Abū Dāwūd.

Ad-dīnu naṣīḥa, "Religion is advice," and *naṣīḥa* is *ad-dīn,* and *ad-dīn* is *dhikr,* and therefore, *dhikr* is *naṣīḥa*! It is a simple formula. So the Prophet ﷺ wanted to tell them advice on *dhikrullāh.* It is easy, when you put it as easy then it is easy. So how much you are in this circle of *dhikrullāh*? What are you doing here? *Farta'ū,* when you find a circle of *dhikrullāh* then graze in it, literally, sit and enjoy good spiritual food as you cannot find that kind of food somewhere else. Not in the meaning that there are none others like that, but it means there are none like that nearby, but you might find around the globe thousands of gatherings like that, people are sitting and remembering Allāh. So the Prophet ﷺ said, "Do you want me to tell you of the best of your *'amal*?" "Of course," what more do they want than that? *Wa azkāhā 'inda malīkikum,* and the most delightful, very sweet and nice, and *zakī,* it is the most delightful in front of your King, the Creator, Allāh?" "*Wa arfa'a fī darajātikum,* it is most effective in taking you up in levels," *wa khayran lakum,* "the best for you, more than something important?"

So the Prophet ﷺ with all this introduction brought all this to tell you the importance of *dhikrullāh* in Allāh's Presence. It is the highest in levels, the sweetest and the best of your *'amal, infāqu 'dh-dhahab wa 'l-waraq,* it is better than spending gold and silver and paper money, as much as you can carry, and however rich you are, like there are billionaires today and trillionaires, you are richer than all of that if you spend time in *dhikrullāh,* and Allāh will give you more than that! *Wa khayrun lakum min an talqu 'adūwwakum fataḍribū 'anāqahum wa yaḍribū 'anāqakum,* and it is better for you, for every Muslim who remembers Allāh ﷻ, than to go to the battlefield and fight the enemy where you are striking their necks with your swords and they are striking your necks; with all that danger, doing *dhikrullāh* is better for you and to stand in front of that is nothing!

Qālū balā yā Rasūlullāh, "Yes, of course we are waiting to hear what is better," and he said, "*Dhikrullāh,* that is better than all those." Narrated by Tirmidhī, Ibn Mājah and Ḥākim, this is a *ṣaḥiḥ ḥadīth.* It means when you thank Allāh ﷻ you thank Him with the highest level possible by making *dhikrullāh,* thanking Him for His favors by *dhikrullāh.*

And I will introduce something here that will give us an idea, and you might say, "O, why mention that?" but this is *ḥadīth* and *lā ḥayāt fi 'd-dīn,* there is no shyness in religion. So to give you an idea, and we mentioned that the Prophet ﷺ said *dhikrullāh* is better than spending gold and silver in

Allāh's Way and better than jihad, and we mentioned *ḥadīth* that the Prophet ﷺ said to remember Allāh until they say you are crazy.

أَكْثِرُوا ذِكْرَ اللَّهِ حَتَّى يَقُولُوا مَجْنُونٌ

Remember Allāh ﷻ so much that people start saying, "He has gone mad."[151]

So *shukr* is the head of *dhikrullāh*. And I will introduce this *ḥadīth* to show how *shukr* goes from the bottom level to the highest. What is one of the best *niʿmah* that Allāh gave us, one of the best? Don't say no and don't smile! Whenever he (a *murīd*) eats, he rubs on his tummy and says, *yā lahā niʿmat*, "What a great favor Allāh gave human beings." Of course you eat *niʿmat*, but also if it stays too long inside your stomach, it becomes a poison. So Allāh gave you another *niʿmat*. I said don't smile! It is a *niʿmat* that you have to say, "Thank you, Allāh." *Yā lahā niʿmat*. If people only knew its value, *qadr*.

وكان بعض السلف يقول الحمد لله الذي اذاقني لذته وابقى في منفعة واذهب عني مضرته

Some of the predecessors used to say: Alḥamdulillāh that Allāh has granted us the pleasure of that food, that Allāh gave us nice food," abqā fiyya manfiʿatan, "He gave me the niʿmat of eating and kept it in my body the benefit of it, the vitamins."

How does the body know the vitamins and keep them? What kind of software is there? Is it correct, people watching on TV, what kind of knowledge that doctors cannot understand, that you eat the best of food and take the minerals and vitamins from the food and the rest goes out? Who does that? What kind of mechanism? There is a doctor of internal medicine here. And they continue, *wa adhhaba ʿannī maḍarratahu*, "Thank Allāh, that he takes out what is harmful."

There is a story of a king who liked to have someone with him to make jokes (a jester) after a lot of problems and depression during the day, so he had such a person and that man knew this *ḥadīth* of the Prophet ﷺ, because they studied *ḥadīth*.

---

[151] Āḥmad, Musnad.

He (the jester) said to him, "O my king! The best food of all you eat is the food you take out from your stomach. This is the biggest *niʿmat* that Allāh gave to you."

The king said, "How dare you say to the king like that!"

He (the jester) said, "King or not king, Allāh doesn't know as everyone is a servant! The best *niʿmat* is to get the food out of your stomach."

So the king put him in prison, as how dare he spoke to him that way!

He (the jester) said, "You have to celebrate that."

Lā ḥayāt fi 'd-dīn, There is no shyness in religion! We have to know these things. And so that king did not agree and put him in prison. Allāh knows what that man read on him as he was a hidden one, and the king was not able to go to the bathroom and was getting bigger and more bloated, and they advised the king, "We think this is from that man," so they brought that man.

He said, "O king! Did you believe what I told you?"

The king said, "Yes, now I believe it," and then the man rubbed his belly and immediately all came out.

That is a *niʿmat,* so *shukrullāh.* I mentioned this to know that the lowest favor is to go and change *wuḍū* when you have to go bathroom. So that is the lowest, but still you have to thank Allāh for it, and *adh-dhikru rāsu 'sh-shukr, dhikr* is the head of *shukr.* It is so simple: if someone is not making *dhikrullāh,* he is not thanking Allāh. Whatever you are, if you are a king or not, if you don't make *dhikrullāh* then you are not thanking Him and when you thank Him, you are doing *dhikrullāh.*

"If You Remember Me, You Have Thanked Me"

Sayyīdinā Mūsā ﷺ said, as mentioned by Bayhaqī:

أن موسى عليه السلام قال : رب قد أنعمت علي كثيراً فدلني على أن أشكرك كثيراً ، قال : "اذكرني كثيراً فإذا ذكرتني كثيراً فقد شكرتني كثيراً وإذا نسيتني فقد كفرتني "

"O Allāh! You gave me a lot of favors. I thank you for it and show me the way to thank You a lot. Fa dullunī ʿalā an ashkuraka kathīra, guide me to thank You a lot. I know a little bit how to thank you, but show me how to thank You a lot."

Allāh said, "Do you want to thank Me a lot?"

Sayyīdinā Mūsā ﷺ said, "Yes, of course, that is my intention."

Allāh replied, "*Udhkurnī kathīran*, Remember Me excessively and *fa idhā dhakartanī kathīran faqad shakartanī kathīran*, if you remember Me excessively you have thanked Me excessively, so *dhikr* equals *shukr*. And, *idhā nasītanī, faqad kafartanī*, if you forget Me then you have entered something dangerous," which here is not *kufr*, not believing in Allāh; sometimes in Arabic you use the same word but is has a different meaning, so here *kafartanī* means, "You denied Me, you did something wrong, a sin." So Allāh ﷻ said, "If you don't remember Me excessively, it means you denied Me excessively."

Bayhaqī narrates that ʿAbdullāh ibn Salām said that Sayyīdinā Mūsā ﷺ said:

قال موسى عليه السلام : يا رب ما الشكر الذي ينبغي لك فأوحى الله تعالى إليه : أن لا يزال لسانك رطباً من ذكري ، قال : يا رب إني أكون على حال أجلك أن أذكرك فيها ، قال : وما هي ؟ قال : أكون جنباً أو على الغائط أو إذا بلت ، فقال : وإن كان ، قال : يا رب ، فما أقول ؟ قال : تقول سبحانك وبحمدك وجنبني الأذى وسبحانك وبحمدك فقني الأذى

"What kind of shukr do you want me to remember You with?" And Sayyīdinā Mūsā ﷺ was inspired, "Fa awḥā 'Llāhu taʿalā ilayhi anna lā yazālu lisānaka raṭban min dhikrī, make your tongue always wet by remembering Me; don't let your tongue get dry," which means "keep it from moving (still), so keep it loose by having My dhikr on the tongue always."

Sayyīdinā Mūsā ﷺ said, "Sometimes I am in a situation and I like to remember You, and at that time I am not clean, I need a shower (as after maturity sometimes you need a shower). I am not clean, I have no wuḍū. What do I have to do? Qāla yā rabbī innī akūnu ʿalā ḥālin ujilluka an adhkuruka fihā, I like at that time to thank You and remember You and make Your dhikr. Qāla wa mā hīya? qāla akūnu junuban aw ʿalā 'l-ghāiṭa aw idhā bālta, but either I need a shower or I need to go to bathroom or go to the small bathroom, so can I use it?" And Allāh ﷻ said, "Wa in kān, even so, you are allowed to do dhikrullāh, no problem."

Although we are under obligation, I cannot say obligation, but a recommendation to be in *wuḍū* all the time, when you lose your *wuḍū* quickly make your *wuḍū*. Some people cannot make *wuḍū* all the time as it is difficult in certain places, but you can still do *dhikrullāh* it's no problem. Whatever you memorized, you can read it, there is no problem.

Sayyīdinā Mūsā ﷺ said, "*Qāla fa yā rabbī fa mā aqūl,* what do I have to say? I like to praise You and I like to remember You so what do I have to say, tell me something?"

Allāh ﷻ said, "*Qāla taqūl subḥānaka wa bi-ḥamdika wa janibnī al-adhā.* Say, 'O Allāh! Glory be to You and Your Praise, and thank You and protect me from any harm that comes to me, a harm from having a problem with my health. *Wa subḥānaka wa bi-ḥamdika faqinī al-adhā,* praise be to You and thank You and I am glorifying you that You protected from harm.'"

Sayyida ʿĀyesha ؓ said, and the *Ṣaḥābah* ؓ learned from the wives of the Prophet ﷺ all these female issues, Sayyida ʿĀyesha ؓ narrated:

عَنْ عَائِشَةَ، أَنَّ رَسُولَ اللَّهِ - صلى الله عليه وسلم - كَانَ يَذْكُرُ اللَّهَ عَلَى كُلِّ أَحْيَانِهِ

The Messenger of Allāh used to remember Allāh in all circumstances.[152]

Ibn Qayyim, in explaining this hadith says:

ولم تستثن حالة من حالة، وهذا يدل على أنه كان يذكر ربه تعالى في حال طهارته وجنابته وأما في حال التخلي، فلم يكن يشاهده أحد يحكي عنه، ولكن شرع لأمته من الأذكار قبل التخلي وبعده

Kāna yadhkurullāh ʿalā kulli aḥyānihi wa lam tastathni ḥālatin min ḥālah, "The Prophet ﷺ used to remember Allāh ﷻ in all cases," even when he was *junub,* meaning he needed a shower for ritual purification from *janāba* or when he did not have *wuḍū,* he continued doing *dhikrullāh* on his tongue and his heart never stopped doing *dhikrullāh." Ammā fi' t-takhalī 't-takhalī fa lam yakun yushāhiduhu āḥad,* "As for when he entered the bathroom, no one knows as no one was there; we don't know if he was doing *dhikr,*" but we think he stopped and then for sure only his tongue and heart stopped *dhikrullāh,* but other than that, his tongue was busy in *dhikrullāh. Wa lākinna sharraʿ li-ummatihi min al-adhkār qabl at-takhalī,* "He ﷺ gave you *dhikrullāh* that you can mention until the moment you enter the bathroom," so then imagine how important is *dhikrullāh*! So when you go to the bathroom, there

[152] Ibn Mājah.

is *dhikr* to mention: *innī aʿūdhū bika rabbī min al-khubūthi wa 'l-khabā'ith,* "I seek refuge in You, my Lord, from the evil of devils and their filth."

It is said that Allāh loves for His servant to do *dhikrullāh* even in markets, meaning any time of day or night, and wherever you may be, make *dhikrullāh* and do not stop.

يا معاذ، والله إني لأحبك، ثم أوصيك يا معاذ لا تدعن في دبر كل صلاة تقول: اللهم أعني على ذكرك وشكرك، وحسن عبادتك

Muʿadh told the Messenger of Allāh ﷺ held my hand and said, "O Muʿadh! Truly I love you! And I advise you O Muʿadh do not forget after every prayer to say, *'Allāhumma aʿinnī ʿalā dhikrika wa shukrika wa ḥusna ʿibādatik*" "O Allāh! Help me remember You, expressing gratitude to You and worship You in the best way."[153]

May Allāh grant us all this *barakah* that the Prophet ﷺ taught the *Ṣaḥābah* ﷺ!

Traits of a Believer

Abū Hurayrah ﷺ related that the Prophet ﷺ said:

الْمُؤْمِنُ مِرْآةُ الْمُؤْمِنِ وَالْمُؤْمِنُ أَخُو الْمُؤْمِنِ يَكُفُّ عَلَيْهِ ضَيْعَتَهُ وَيَحُوطُهُ مِنْ وَرَائِهِ

The Believer is the mirror of his brother. The Believer is the brother of a Believer: he protects him from ruin and guards his back.[154]

Al-mu'min mirāt al-mu'min, "The *mu'min* is the mirror of his brother." So you do *dhikrullāh* and he does also it, it's a mirror, a reflection, so you have to appear in the best form to your brother because you reflect yourself on him and he reflects himself on you and as you do *dhikrullāh* he does *dhikrullāh,* and you say, *"Shukr, yā Rabb,"*—I am sitting near you and I say, *"Shukran yā Rabb,"* what do you say? (*Shukran yā Rabb*), and that is like a reminder, an alarm, *fa dhakkir,* to remind people:

وَذَكِّرْ فَإِنَّ الذِّكْرَى تَنفَعُ الْمُؤْمِنِينَ

---

[153] Abū Dāwūd and An-Nasa'i.

[154] Bukhārī, al-Adab al-Mufrad.

Remind people that dhikrullāh is piety of the Believers.[155]

Don't say, "I already know it," because that is disregarding valuable advice. The Prophet ﷺ said, "The Believer is the brother of the Believer."

إن أحدكم مرآة أخيه ، فإن رأى به أذى فليمط عنه

And the Prophet ﷺ said, "One of you is the mirror of his brother, so if you see something wrong try to help him with that."[156]

That is part of the good manners and part of religion, where the Prophet ﷺ said:

انما بعثت لاتمم مكارم الاخلاق

I have been sent to perfect the best of conduct (your behavior and character).[157]

"I have been sent to complete the best of manners in you." What is best manner? *Dhikrullāh,* to remember Allāh, to remember all the Beautiful Names and Attributes that are the source of blessings for everyone! May Allāh ﷻ give us more and more from the *barakah* of the Prophet ﷺ. I will end with this and next time we will speak on love of *Āhl al-Bayt.*

Abū Bakr ؓ entered the *masjid* and the Prophet ﷺ was on the *minbar* giving *khuṭbah,* and Ḥasan ibn Sayyīdinā ʿAlī ؓ was by him on the *minbar. Wa Hūwa yukhbir ʿalā an-nāsi marratan wa ʿalayhi ukhrā.* When you are giving *khuṭbah* you don't want anyone to disturb and the *imām* doesn't want to be disturbed, but look at the love of *Āhl al-Bayt,* how the Prophet ﷺ was treating them. It is not like today where we don't mention their stories or their biographies and we say, "We are lovers of the Prophet ﷺ." We have to take the lesson of how they took *Shahādah fī sabīlillāh*! When they promised they kept their promise.

المؤمن إذا وعد وفى

A Believer keeps his promise.[158]

---

[155] Sūrat adh-Dhāriyāt, 51:55.
[156] Tirmidhī.
[157] Al-Bazzār.

Al-mu'minu idhā waʿda wafā. "When the Believer promises, he keeps it. Sayyīdinā al-Ḥusayn promised to support the people of Baghdad and they warned him not to go and he said, "I gave my word," and they killed him and killed his children in front of him and his whole family. And not only that, they cut them to pieces! How can they do that? And *Āhlu 's-Sunnah wa 'l-Jamaʿah* does not remember that incident to keep in their hearts how much the *Āhl al-Bayt* suffered for us to reach that level, for Islam to reach us.

قالَ أَبَا بَكْرَةَ لَقَدْ رَأَيْتُ رَسُولَ اللَّهِ صلى الله عليه وسلم عَلَى الْمِنْبَرِ وَالْحَسَنُ مَعَهُ وَهُوَ يُقْبِلُ عَلَى النَّاسِ مَرَّةً وَعَلَيْهِ مَرَّةً وَيَقُولُ " إِنَّ ابْنِي هَذَا سَيِّدٌ وَلَعَلَّ اللَّهَ أَنْ يُصْلِحَ بِهِ بَيْنَ فِئَتَيْنِ مِنَ الْمُسْلِمِينَ عَظِيمَتَيْنِ .

Abū Bakrah ؓ said, "I saw the Messenger of Allāh ﷺ on the *minbar* and al-Ḥasan was with him. He turned to the people sometimes and turn to him sometimes, and he ﷺ said, 'This son of mine is a leader (Sayyid) and it may be that Allāh ﷻ makes peace between two large groups of Muslims through him.'"

So Sayyīdinā al-Ḥasan ؓ was beside Prophet ﷺ on the steps of the *minbar*, and the Prophet ﷺ was directing his face to the people and giving *khuṭbah* and spoke one sentence, two sentences, then looked at Sayyīdinā al-Ḥasan and stroked him, making him to feel happy, showing the importance of love.

If you don't show love to your brothers and sisters, to your families, to your communities, then you are not following the *Sunnah* of the Prophet ﷺ! *In kuntum tuḥibbūna 'Llāha,* if you really love Allāh then follow Muḥammad ﷺ.

Then the Prophet ﷺ advised the people, then he looked at his grandson, then he said to the people, *"Wa yaqūl inna ibnī hadhā sayyidun,* this my grandson, my child is *sayyid,* master, leader. *Wa laʿal Allāha an yusliḥa bihi bayna fi'atayn min al-muslimīn ʿaẓīmatayn,* it is going to happen that through him, Allāh will bring about peace between two huge groups of people."

And that is what happened in order to avoid bloodshed: Sayyīdinā al-Ḥasan ؓ left the *Khilāfah,* he abdicated and gave it to Muʿāwīya. He was the

---

[158] Abū Dāwūd, Darqutnī, al-Ḥākim.

last to give *baya*ʿ, but he dropped it and didn't want the group of Sayyīdinā ʿAlī ؓ and Muʿāwīya to fight another time.

May Allāh forgive us and may Allāh bless us.

Wa min Allāhi 't-tawfiq, bi ḥurmati 'l-ḥabīb, bi ḥurmati 'l-Fātiḥah.
And with Allāh is success. For the sake of the Beloved, for his sake we recite the opening chapter of Holy Qur'ān.

From Darkness into Light

Aʿūdhu billāhi min ash-Shayṭāni 'r-rajīm. Bismillāhi' r-Raḥmāni 'r-Raḥīm.
Nawaytu 'l-arbāʿīn, nawaytu 'l-ʿitikāf, nawaytu 'l-khalwah, nawaytu 'l-ʿuzlah,
nawaytu 'r-riyāḍa, nawaytu 's-sulūk, lillāhi Taʿalā fī hādhā 'l-masjid.
Atīʿūllāha wa atīʿū 'r-Rasūla wa ūli 'l-amri minkum. (4:59)

As-salāmu ʿalaykum wa raḥmatullāhi wa barakātuh. Wherever you are, viewers and people who are here, may Allāh bless us all with this day, a blessed day, Monday. May Allāh keep us always remembering the birthday of the Prophet ﷺ, which was on Monday, the 12th of *Rabiʿ al-Āwwal,* and he ﷺ left Earth on the 12th of *Rabiʿ al-Āwwal* also.

O viewers, O Believers! If someone does something wrong, they call him to court and he tries to find a lawyer to defend him and lawyers are very well-established, they are very rich. Normal lawyers are cheaper, more established ones are expensive, so you will not end up between their hands except bankrupted as they ask a lot, but they can get you out of the problem. May Allāh not put us in this position, but every one of us wants to be saved from any difficulty or punishment. Some people are not and they go to prison for ten or twenty years or for a lifetime, as they lost. When the decision is taken it is taken, finished.

فَمَن يَعْمَلْ مِثْقَالَ ذَرَّةٍ خَيْرًا يَرَهُ وَمَن يَعْمَلْ مِثْقَالَ ذَرَّةٍ شَرًّا يَرَهُ

Whosoever has done an atom's weight of good shall see it
and whosoever has done an atom's weight of evil shall see it. [160]

"Who does one atom of goodness will see it and who does one atom of bad will see it." We don't want to go on the bad side or else we will be punished. We ask Allāh to forgive us!

Dhikrullāh Brings Favors, Heedlessness Brings Miseries

There is nothing like *dhikrullāh* that brings favors to human beings and there is nothing like heedlessness to bring misery to human beings.

---

[160] Sūrat az-Zalzalah, 99:7-8.

أنه جلاب للنعم، دافع للنقم بإذن الله

It (dhikr) attracts provision and repels afflictions.[161]

Dhikrullāh will attract the good things, it will attract the favors that Allāh favored you with and *dāfiʿun li 'n-niqam,* reject and push back all kinds of miseries (that result) from our heedlessness. So do we want to be saved, or not? So you bring a lawyer and pay money from your wealth to be saved and you pay as much as he wants until you are saved. What is Allāh ﷻ saying?

إِنَّ اللَّهَ يُدَافِعُ عَنِ الَّذِينَ آمَنُوا إِنَّ اللَّهَ لَا يُحِبُّ كُلَّ خَوَّانٍ كَفُورٍ

Certainly Allāh will defend those who believe. Indeed, Allāh does not like everyone treacherous and ungrateful.[162]

When you believe, Allāh will defend you and not ask you (to pay) money and not ask you something (in return), but He is asking for something, which is, *Bismillāhi 'r-Raḥmāni 'r-Raḥīm:*

يَا أَيُّهَا الَّذِينَ آمَنُوا اذْكُرُوا اللَّهَ ذِكْرًا كَثِيرًا وَسَبِّحُوهُ بُكْرَةً وَأَصِيلًا هُوَ الَّذِي يُصَلِّي عَلَيْكُمْ وَمَلَائِكَتُهُ لِيُخْرِجَكُم مِّنَ الظُّلُمَاتِ إِلَى النُّورِ وَكَانَ بِالْمُؤْمِنِينَ رَحِيمًا

O you who believe! Remember Allāh! Continue to mention Him without limit, before sunrise and before sunset. He is The One Who encourages, appreciates, and supports you all and replaces darkness and tyranny with Divine Light and is merciful to the Believers.[163]

Allāh ﷻ says, *inna-Llāha yudāfiʿu ʿani 'Lladhīna āmanū,* "He will defend the Believers," but He is saying, *yā ayyuha 'Lladhīna āmanū,* "O you who believe!" which means, "those who accept Holy Qur'ān, those who accept Prophet ﷺ, My Messenger, those who accept *Sunnat an-Nabī* ﷺ," *udhkurūllāha dhikran kathīra,* "this is what I want from you: to mention Me as much as you can." Allāh is saying *udhkurullāh,* "mention Him, make *dhikrullāh* continuously, don't stop." *Yā ayyuha 'Lladhīna āmanū 'dhkurūllāh.*

---

[161] Ibn Qayyim al-Jawzīyya, al-Wābil aṣ-Ṣayyib, "The 46th Benefit of Dhikr".
[162] Sūrat al-Ḥajj, 22:38.
[163] Sūrat al-Aḥzāb, 3:41-43.

He didn't say, "Remember Allāh for one-hundred years or five years or one hour," but *dhikhran kathīra,* "with no limits, excessively." Why? Because we said, *inna-Llāha yudāfiʿu ʿani 'Lladhīna āmanū,* "Allāh will defend you," so in this *āyah* He said, *udhkurūllāha dhikran kathīra wa sabbiḥūhu bukratan wa aṣīla,* "And remember Him day and night," *bukratan wa aṣīla,* "remember Allāh and praise Him from morning to evening by *dhikrullāh* then you will get," because you are described as *"Yā ayyuha 'Lladhīna āmanū,"* you are Believers, and *inna-Llāha yudāfiʿu ʿani 'Lladhīna āmanū,* "Allāh defends the Believers." Allāh will defend you on the Day of Judgment, Allāh will give all kinds of excuses to those who remember Him, although we are not remembering as it should be, but if you struggle and remember Him every time, every moment:

وَ لَئِن شَكَرْتُمْ لأَزِيدَنَّكُمْ

If you thank Me, I will give you more.[164]

"If you thank Me, I will give you more, through you saying *'Shukran yā Rabbī,'*" and what He said? *Hūwa 'Lladhī yuṣallī ʿalaykum,* He is, when you mention Him morning and evening, too much, excessively, then He is The One Who *yuṣallī ʿalaykum,* "Who praises you and defends you," He and His Angels! *Li yukhrijakum min aẓ-ẓulumāti ila 'n-nūr,* "to take you out from darkness to Light." And who is the Light?

قَدْ جَاءكُم مِّنَ اللهِ نُورٌ وَكِتَابٌ مُّبِينٌ

Indeed, there has come to you from Allāh a Light (Prophet Muḥammad) and a plain Book (this Qur'an).[165]

"There has come to you guidance, *nūr,*" which means Prophet ﷺ, "the Message, the Qur'ān came from Allāh ﷻ to you," because He loves us. He sent us that Light and that *hidāya,* guidance, and He sent *hidāya* how? Through the Prophet ﷺ. Allāh dressed him to be *Hādi al-Ummah,* He is the Guide of the *Ummah*:

---

[164] Sūrah Ibrāhīm, 14:7.
[165] Sūrat al-Mā'idah, 5:15.

قُلْ إِن كُنتُمْ تُحِبُّونَ اللَّهَ فَاتَّبِعُونِي يُحْبِبْكُمُ اللَّهُ وَيَغْفِرْ لَكُمْ ذُنُوبَكُمْ وَاللَّهُ غَفُورٌ رَّحِيمٌ

Say (O Muhammad), "If you (really) love Allāh, then follow me!"[166]

"If you really love Allāh, follow Muḥammad ﷺ," so Allāh gave him The Guidance; he guided the Ṣaḥābah ؓ and Allāh is defending and Allāh praising them and Allāh took them from darkness completely. Then *jāhilīyya* was the law of the jungle, the desert, with nothing but fighting between different tribes. Allāh brought them from darkness to Light and Allāh brought the Muslim *Ummah* from darkness to Light through the power of Sayyīdinā Muḥammad ﷺ!

Wa 'sh-shukru jallābun li 'n-niʿam, "*Dhikrullāh* brings you favors." There is no limit to the favors, *jallābun li 'n-niʿam* "brings you favors," and Allāh says, "*Idhkurūllāha dhikran kathīra wa sabbiḥūhu bukratan wa aṣīla. Hūwa 'Lladhī yuṣallī ʿalaykum wa malā'ikatahu li yukhrijakum min aẓ-ẓulumāti ila 'n-nūr.*" When He says "*dhikr* brings favors," here it means *dhikr* is important, for *dhikrullāh* to be excessive, not limited, but "*kathīran.*" Then *dhikrullāh* will bring you the favors of Allāh and the favor of angels to defend you, not only angels, Allāh will defend us!

Defend us from what? From our egos and from Shayṭān. Satan came to make Sayyīdinā Ādam ؑ to fall down, to commit the sin of eating from that Forbidden Tree, but Allāh forgave him because he is a *mu'min,* he is a prophet and he touched that tree for a wisdom (for us to learn). We leave the explanation, but with a wisdom and he asked Allāh ﷻ "*Tawbah,*" and He defended him against Shayṭān and Allāh told him, "Be careful of that one, that devil, he is My enemy. When I ordered him he didn't make *sajda,*" because he was an angel before and angels cannot refuse Allāh's Order, but because he refused Allāh cursed him, but still he asked Allāh ﷻ to keep him until the end of the days. Can't Allāh take him away and throw him in Hellfire? He accepted his *duʿā,* He said, "Okay, I will leave you, but I will defend My servant and I will test them and if they still remember Me I will defend them, I will take them out from your hands. I will take them from

---

[166] Sūrat Āli-ʿImrān, 3:31.

the darkness that you are showing them to Light, to Paradise. I tell them to leave *dunyā* and their concern is only for *Ākhirah*, for loving Me."

If Allāh wants to do that, who can say to Him, "Don't do it!" Allāh said it in *inna-Llāha yudāfiʿu ʿani 'Lladhīna āmanū*:

إِنَّ اللَّهَ يُدَافِعُ عَنِ الَّذِينَ آمَنُوا إِنَّ اللَّهَ لَا يُحِبُّ كُلَّ خَوَّانٍ كَفُورٍ

Certainly, Allāh will defend those who believe.
Indeed, Allāh does not like everyone treacherous and ungrateful. [167]

Allāh will forgive anyone by defending him and Allāh doesn't like those who betray Him by making *shirk*, not those who one day do *dhikr* and one day they don't—that is struggling—but those who left Him, those who don't say there is a Creator or that He has a partner. If He had a partner, they might fight with each other. You see partners everywhere, they fight with each other in the end, is it not? Who is going to take half of the universe, who is going to take the other half! Even son and father will fight. They want to make Allāh ﷻ like that? *Qūl Hūwa 'Llāhu Āḥad*!

قُلْ هُوَ اللَّهُ أَحَدٌ اللَّهُ الصَّمَدُ لَمْ يَلِدْ وَلَمْ يُولَد وَلَمْ يَكُن لَّهُ كُفُوًا أَحَدٌ

Say, "He is the One God, God the Eternal, the Uncaused Cause of All Being. He begets not nor is He begotten and there is nothing that could be compared to Him."[168]

Allāh is the Unique One with no resemblance. He doesn't need any sustenance from anyone, *Allāhu' ṣ-Ṣamad, lam yalid wa lam yūlad wa lam yakun lahu kufūwan Āḥad. SubḥānAllāh*! It is mentioned that when Allāh ﷻ created the angels to carry His Throne and His Throne was on the water:

وَكَانَ عَرْشُهُ عَلَى الْمَاء

And His Throne on the water.[169]

[167] Sūrat al-Ḥajj, 22:38.
[168] Sūrat al-Ikhlāṣ, 112:1-4.
[169] Sūrat Hūd, 11:7.

What that water is isn't our discussion now, but it was on water. He created angels to carry the *ʿArsh*. They said, "*Yā Rabbanā,* O our Lord! How can we carry Your Throne and on it is Your Greatness, *wa jalāluka,* and Your Majesty is on the *ʿArsh*?" It means not as a form, but as a manifestation, as Allāh sent His *tajallī*:

الرَّحْمَنُ عَلَى الْعَرْشِ اسْتَوَى

The Most Gracious is firmly established on the Throne.[170]

Allāh *istiwā,* "took over" the *ʿArsh;* He does not need to sit on it. Angels asked, "How can we carry Your Throne," and He said, "You know how you can carry My Throne, say this: '*Lā ḥawla wa lā quwatta illa billāhi 'l-ʿAlīyyu 'l-ʿAẓīm.*'" As soon as they said this they were able to carry the Throne, and Heavens will carry us when we say, "*Lā ḥawla wa lā quwatta illa billāhi 'l-ʿAlīyyu 'l-ʿAẓīm.*" Any difficulties will be taken from its root when you say, "*Lā ḥawla wa lā quwatta illa billāhi 'l-ʿAlīyyu 'l-ʿAẓīm,*" which means, "There is no way and no power except through Allāh ﷻ." So they were carrying the Throne and when Allāh wanted to show them His *ʿAẓama,* Greatness, He made them weak and they were falling and the *ʿArsh* pulled them up. It means, "Don't think you are something, I created you!"

The *ʿArsh* can carry them and by Allāh's order they can carry the *ʿArsh.* If they get tired, and that was an example (lesson) for them, when the *ʿArsh* was over water, *ḥamalatu 'l-ʿarsh,* the angels who carry the Throne asked, *rabbanā limā khalaqtanā,* "O our Lord! Why did you create us?" These type of angels are allowed to ask, and the answer came, *wa khalaqtukum li-taḥmila 'l-ʿarsh,* "I created you to carry My Throne." "You are created and that is an honor, and I created human beings."

وَلَقَدْ كَرَّمْنَا بَنِي آدَمَ

We have honored the Children of Ādam.[171]

It is an honor to us that Allāh created us or else you would not be here. He brought you from complete *ʿadm* (nothingness, emptiness) and you

[170] Sūrah ṬāḤā, 20:5.
[171] Sūrat al-'Isrā, 17:70.

appeared; if not, you would not know Him! By His Order everything appeared. They say (attribute the universe's creation to the), "Big Bang." Okay, let us go along with scientists and say the Big Bang happened and all these (creations), like glass you have an explosion and in it will shatter. When you shatter something in non-gravity zone, it keeps moving, it will not stop, like you push a ball in a vacuum where there is no gravity, no irritation, and you push it, it goes non-stop as there is no friction or irritation from the glass that you put it in; that energy never dies and it is existing always. So when this Big Bang blew up, all these particles exploded into a void, an empty vacuum, and it is moving with the speed of light with all these particles consisting of stars and planets.

Who stopped them in their places? How did they stop? There must be an equal opposing force to stop them in their places: if that stopping force is equal it will stop them in their places and if more it will push them back. That driving force was so precise that stopped them in their place. Who did that, scientists? Look at the constellations, *abrāj*, they are always in their places and never moved, they say for millions of years. Okay, we accept, but Who keeps them in their places, not moving even one fraction of a second? Allāh ﷻ!

Dhikrullāh Increases Divine Protection from Shayṭān

So cannot The One Who did that defend His servants from Shayṭān? But He is asking, "Give me a driving force. Your driving force is *dhikrullāh*." That is like bullets on the head of Shayṭān, because Shayṭān gets upset when you make *dhikrullāh* and he wants you to make *dhikr ash-shayṭān*, he wants you to be with him, with devils. *Tawbah yā Allāh, tawbah yā Rabb*! So Allāh says, "I will defend you, but only show Me an effort, come to Me a little bit and show Me more, then I will take you out of darkness and ignorance." We are in ignorance. Don't think only of technology and modern life; no, that is going, it is ignorance. We are not saying there is no technology; yes, there is, but how long is this Earth is going to remain?

Allāh ﷻ said in the Holy Qur'ān:

اقْتَرَبَتِ السَّاعَةُ وَانشَقَّ الْقَمَرُ

The Hour (of Judgment) is near and the Moon is cleft asunder (split).[172]

From that time of the Prophet ﷺ 1400 years ago, the moon split between the Prophet's fingers, Allāh said, "The Day of Resurrection is approaching, Signs of the Last Day are approaching, the Last Day is approaching! I will take you out of ignorance and teach you from Heavenly knowledge."

وَعَلَّمْنَاهُ مِن لَّدُنَّا عِلْمًا

Whom We had taught knowledge from Our Own Presence.[173]

"I will teach you and I will bless you in order that you will be able to get Heavenly *raḥmāh,* mercy, and knowledge." *Allāhu Akbar,* we are lucky! You think if you say, *"Lā ḥawla wa lā quwatta illa billāhi 'l-ʿAlīyyu 'l-ʿAẓīm,"* or *"SubḥānAllāh wal-ḥamdulillāh wa lā ilāha illa-Llāh wa 'Llāhu Akbar"* or any kind of *dhikrullāh,* that it will not take you? If you say it one time, as Allāh said, *idhkurūllāha dhikran kathīra,* "Remember Allāh excessively," then if you remember Him a little bit it is okay; He will *li yukhrijakum min aẓ-ẓulumāti ila 'n-nūr,* take you out of darkness of ignorance and pour into your heart from knowledge! But this knowledge will not be made apparent to you as you are not *āhlan li-dhālik,* ready for it, and it is not the right time as your heart is not completely polished. They don't throw diamonds to children, so they don't give it to you, but they send that *tajallī* on you and dress you with it without revealing it to you. So every time you make *dhikrullāh* you will be dressed with a different knowledge, because "*an-Nūr*" is also knowledge. "Take you out of darkness," means the veils of darkness are released one-by-one from your heart.

It is said that between us and the Prophet ﷺ are 70,000 veils that block us from seeing. Sometimes you see in dream and it is okay as that means the veils are less and less. And sometimes you see in a vision; that is for *awlīyāullāh,* which means they feel the presence as their hearts are more ready. So when you do *dhikrullāh* one time you get one medallion and when you do it two times you get two medallions, and so on. In a parade, if they put these medallions until the chest is full of them and that is in *dunyā,* what

[172] Sūrat al-Qamar, 54:1.
[173] Sūrat al-Kahf, 18:65.

about the medallions in *Ākhirah* that Allāh will put on your chest? He will do that just by *'idhkurullāha dhikran kathīra.* If you remember His favors through *shukrullāh,* thanking Allāh, remember that it is the head of wisdom and *dhikrullāh* takes you out of Hellfire and takes you to Paradise!

وقال (عليه السّلام) : « من قال : لا حول ولا قوة إلاّ بالله مائة مرة في كل يوم لم يصبه فقر أبداً

The Prophet ﷺ said, "The one who recites, 'Lā ḥawla wa lā quwatta illa billāhi 'l-ʿAlīyyu 'l-ʿAẓīm' a hundred times daily will never see poverty."[174]

It means he will be rich. So if you are poor, say, *"Lā ḥawla wa lā quwatta illa billāh."* What kind of poverty? Two kinds: *dunyā* and *Ākhirah.* "You will not see poverty in *dunyā*" means Allāh will grant you to eat and drink enough. That is what you will get and you will not sleep hungry. And in *Ākhirah,* you will have no poverty and you will enter Paradise with no account. "Welcome, My servants!" the angels will be bringing you directly to Paradise. *Allāhumma ṣalli ʿalā Sayyīdinā Muḥammadin wa ʿalā āli Muḥammadin wa sallim! Allāhumma ṣalli ʿalā Sayyīdinā Muḥammad wa ʿalā āli Sayyīdinā Muḥammad.*

Dhikrullāh will also increase memory. Sometimes we complain of losing our memory. If you recite, *"Lā ḥawla wa lā quwatta illa billāhi 'l-ʿAlīyyu 'l-ʿAẓīm,"* it will increase your memory. Recite it and Allāh will send many chips of memory and software in your brain programmed by angels. You don't need to program it as angels will give that to you by *dhikrullāh. Dhikrullāh* programs any program you need. What program do you need? You will be programmed for Paradise, so *dhikrullāh* will take you to be focused directly and will increase our memory.

Look, O viewers! How many are we on Earth? They say 6.5 billion. Everyone has a different brain and intelligence, and everyone has different manners and characters. Why can you not find two the same? Because of different programs and software. Allāh gave us a brain like the hardware of a computer. He put a small chip the size of a lentil in the brain where all memory and intelligence is there. Today you need thousands and thousands of engineers to make a program and make computers to speak to one

---

[174] Ibn Abi 'd-Dunyā.

another. How many languages are there between computers? Hundreds, and they want to program them to communicate with each other. And how many human languages? There are millions. Even in China alone there 10,000 languages. All these languages can be understood by the brain.

اطلبوا العلم ولو في الصين

Seek knowledge even unto China.[175]

What kind of knowledge? "Seek the miracles in China. Look at what the young men there are doing. Learn from them to understand the Greatness of Allāh ﷻ. They are not Believers, but learn from them their languages and technology, as they are going to be ahead of everyone," as the Prophet ﷺ is predicting they are going to be ahead of everyone. And how much software we have for human beings? There are 6.5 billion different software. Who can do 6.5 different programs of software?

O Muslims! *Dhikrullāh* is the container of software for Paradise and in different ways the Prophet ﷺ gave to do *dhikrullāh,* and Allāh said, *w 'adhkurūllāh dhikran kathīra,* "Make excessive remembrance of Allāh." That means there are countless ways of remembering Allāh, and through that He will take you from darkness to Light! He will order His angels to make *ṣalāt* on you, meaning they will praise you, defend you and raise you higher and higher, and take you from ignorance to knowledge. *Allāhu Akbar*! *Allāhu Akbar*!

وَلَقَدْ يَسَّرْنَا الْقُرْآنَ لِلذِّكْرِ فَهَلْ مِن مُّدَّكِرٍ

And We have certainly made the Qur'an easy for remembrance,
so is there any who will remember?[176]

"And we have made the Holy Qur'an a way for *dhikrullāh*; we have revealed the Holy Qur'an for *dhikrullāh.*" It is called *'dhikrullāh,'* which means any word or even letter in it is *dhikrullāh.* Even "*Alif. Lām. Mīm,*" are *dhikrullāh.* Each is a code and if you know how to open this code all *Sūrat al-Baqarah* will be opened to you. The whole constitution of Islam is in *Sūrat al-*

---

[175] Bayhaqī.
[176] Sūrat al-Qamar, 54:40.

Baqarah. If you know the code, *"Alif. Lām. Mīm,"* it will open for you oceans of knowledge.

إِنَّا نَحْنُ نَزَّلْنَا الذِّكْرَ وَإِنَّا لَهُ لَحَافِظُونَ

Behold! It is We Ourselves Who have bestowed from on high, step by step, this reminder and behold, it is We Who shall truly guard it (from all corruption).[177]

"We have sent down the *dhikrullāh* and we are preserving and protecting it." Allāh ﷻ is protecting it from any kind of changes, it is a perfect moon. That is Holy Qur'an! I will mention one or two *aḥādīth.*

ما اجتمع قوم في بيت من بيوت الله يتلون كتاب الله، ويتدارسونه بينهم، إلا نزلت عليهم السكينة، وغشيتهم الرحمة، وحفتهم الملائكة، وذكرهم الله فيمن عنده"

Abū Hurayrah ؓ said that the Prophet ﷺ said:

Any group of people that assemble in one of the Houses of Allāh to study the Qur'an, tranquility will descend upon them, mercy will engulf them, angels will surround them and Allāh will make mention of them to those (angels) in His proximity.[178]

If a group of people meet in a house or in a *masjid* and put the Book of Allāh and begin to study it, "My tranquility will descend on these people and My Mercy will overtake them and the angels will come and surround them up to Heavens, and Allāh will mention them in His gathering." That is if we are reading Holy Qur'an, because Holy Qur'an is *dhikrullāh.*

أَلاَ أُعَلِّمُكَ أَعْظَمَ سُورَةٍ فِي الْقُرْآنِ قَبْلَ أَنْ تَخْرُجَ مِنَ الْمَسْجِدِ ". فَأَخَذَ بِيَدِي فَلَمَّا أَرَدْنَا أَنْ نَخْرُجَ قُلْتُ يَا رَسُولَ اللَّهِ إِنَّكَ قُلْتَ لأُعَلِّمَنَّكَ أَعْظَمَ سُورَةٍ مِنَ الْقُرْآنِ. قَالَ "{الْحَمْدُ لِلَّهِ رَبِّ الْعَالَمِينَ} هِيَ السَّبْعُ الْمَثَانِي وَالْقُرْآنُ الْعَظِيمُ الَّذِي أُوتِيتُهُ

The Messenger of Allāh ﷺ said, "Shall I teach you the greatest sūrah in the Qur'an before you leave the mosque?" Then he ﷺ took me by the hand and when we were about to step out, I reminded him of his promise to teach me the greatest sūrah in the Qur'an. He ﷺ said, "It is, 'Praise be to Allāh, the Lord of the Worlds,' (i.e.,

---

[177] Sūrat al-Ḥijr, 15:9.
[178] Sahih Muslim.

Sūrat al-Fātiḥah), which consists of seven repeatedly recited verses and the Magnificent Qur'an which was given to me."[179]

"The Prophet ﷺ asked me, 'Do you want me to teach you a *sūrah* of Holy Qur'an that is the greatest *sūrah*?' and he took my hand and began to take me out of the *masjid*, and I asked him, 'Will you not teach me the *sūrah* you mentioned?'" and the Prophet ﷺ taught him *Sūrat al-Fātiḥah.*

The entire Holy Qur'ān has been put into *Sūrat al-Fātiḥah.* It is said that *Yāsīn*, Prophet ﷺ, is *Qalb al-Qur'ān*, the heart of Holy Qur'an, and *Sūrat al-Fātiḥah* is the heart of *Yāsīn*.

May Allāh bless us in this session on this Monday morning, and our thanks to Ummah TV for broadcasting this around the world.

May Allāh forgive us and may Allāh bless us.

Wa min Allāhi 't-tawfiq, bi ḥurmati 'l-ḥabīb, bi ḥurmati 'l-Fātiḥah.
And with Allāh is success. For the sake of the Beloved, for his sake we recite the opening chapter of Holy Qur'ān.

[179] Ḥadīth of Abū Sa'īd reported by Bukhārī.

Some of the Magnificent Benefits of Dhikr

A'ūdhu billāhi min ash-Shayṭāni 'r-rajīm. Bismillāhi' r-Raḥmāni 'r-Raḥīm.
Nawaytu 'l-arbā'īn, nawaytu 'l-'itikāf, nawaytu 'l-khalwah, nawaytu 'l-'uzlah,
nawaytu 'r-riyāḍa, nawaytu 's-sulūk, lillāhi Ta'alā fī hādhā 'l-masjid.
Atī'ūllāha wa atī'ū 'r-Rasūla wa ūli 'l-amri minkum. (4:59)

As-salāmu 'alaykum wa raḥmatullāhi wa barakātuh. Alḥamdulillāh that Allāh ﷻ is giving us and everyone a good life. *Mashā-Allāh,* we are not sleeping hungry, everyone has enough for himself and his family. When you go to the supermarket you have a list of what you want to buy, there are many items on the list. Also, if we want to buy *Ākhirah,* we have to mention everything we need for *Ākhirah* by name through *dhikrullāh,* as without *dhikrullāh* there is no benefit!

Allāh has His Ninety-nine Names.

وَلِلّهِ الأَسْمَاء الْحُسْنَى فَادْعُوهُ بِهَا وَذَرُواْ الَّذِينَ يُلْحِدُونَ فِي أَسْمَآئِهِ سَيُجْزَوْنَ مَا كَانُواْ يَعْمَلُونَ

The Most Beautiful Names belong to Allāh, so invoke Him by them.
And leave (the company of) those who practice deviation concerning
His Names. They will be recompensed for what they have been doing.[180]

Allāh ﷻ has His Beautiful Ninety-nine Names and Attributes (and says), "Ask Me through these Names, *fad'ūhu bihā,* call on Me in *du'ā* through these Names. If you mention these Names, I trust you at that time and say, '*Ṣadaqa 'abdī*!" If Allāh trusts His servant, saying, "My servant has said the truth," what do you think Allāh is going to give that '*abd*? If He says, "*Ṣadaqa 'abdī*!" He is happy with him and He will give him, *mā lā 'aynun rā'at wa lā udhunun sami'at wa lā khaṭar 'alā qalbi bashar,* "What no eye has seen, no ear has heard and what never came to the mind!"

We spend more time on *dunyā* than on *Ākhirah.* How many prayers are there? Let us say ten *raka'ats.* So we spend 10-15 minutes for our prayers and the total for five prayers is less than one hour. Is anyone doing more? No, in

[180] Sūrat al-'Arāf, 7:180.

fact, we are doing less. So Allāh is asking something very small in return for something very big!

From Our Dhikrullāh, Allāh Will Say "My Servant Said the Truth!"

Dhikrullāh is something to show Allāh, "My servant said the truth," and for whomever Allāh said, "My servant said the truth," will never be with the *kādhibīn*, those who lied to Allāh!

Where does Allāh send those about whom He said are trustworthy? He will put them with those who are trustworthy, like Sayyīdinā Abū Bakr aṣ-Ṣiddīq ﷺ, whom Allāh called *aṣ-Ṣiddīq*, "The Trustworthy One." So *ṣādiq* with *ṣādiq*, trusted one with trusted one, and liar with liar, as Allāh keeps a balance. To be with the prophets, trustworthy ones, martyrs and the righteous:

مَعَ الَّذِينَ أَنْعَمَ اللهُ عَلَيْهِم مِّنَ النَّبِيِّينَ وَالصِّدِّيقِينَ وَالشُّهَدَاءِ وَالصَّالِحِينَ وَحَسُنَ أُولَـئِكَ رَفِيقًا

In the company of the prophets (who teach), the sincere (lovers of Truth), the witnesses (who testify), and the righteous (who do good). Ah, what a beautiful fellowship![181]

وعن أبي سعيد الخدري وأبي هريرة، رضي الله عنهما، أنهما شهدا علي رسول الله ، صلى الله عليه وسلم ، أنه قال: "من قال: لا إله إلا الله والله اكبر ، صدقه ربه، فقال: لا إله إلا أنا وأنا أكبر. وإذا قال: لا إله إلا الله وحده لا شريك له، قال: يقول: لا إله إلا أنا وحدي لا شريك لي. وإذا قال: لا إله إلا الله له الملك وله الحمد، قال: لا إله إلا أنا لي الملك ولي الحمد. وإذا قال: لا إله إلا الله ولا حول ولا قوة إلا بالله، قال: لا إله إلا أنا ولا حول ولا قوة إلا بي"

The Messenger of Allāh ﷺ said, "If a person says, 'Lā ilāha illa-Llāhu w 'Allāhu Akbar (there is no true god except Allāh and Allāh is Greatest)', his Lord responds to him and affirms, '[Yes!] There is no true god except I and I am the Greatest.' When he says, 'Lā ilāha illa-Llāhu waḥdahu lā sharīka lahu (there is no true god except Allāh, the One, He has no partner),' Allāh ﷻ affirms, '[Yes!] There is no true god except I. I have no partner.' When he says, 'Lā ilāha illa-Llāh lahu 'l-mulku wa lahu 'l-ḥamd (the sovereignty belongs to Him and all the praise is due to Him),' He ﷻ affirms, '[Yes!] There is no true god except I, Mine is the praise and to Me

181 Sūrat an-Nisā, 4:69.

belongs the sovereignty.' When he says, 'Lā ilāha illa-Llāhu wa lā ḥawla wa lā quwwata illā billāh (there is no true god except Allāh and there is no might and power but with Allāh,' He ﷻ affirms, '[Yes!] There is no true god except Me and there is no might and power but with Me.'"[182]

When you mention *Kalimat at-Tawḥīd,* Allāh will say, "You said the truth, *ṣadaqa ʿabdī!*" and will put the servant with the *ṣādiqīn,* like Sayyīdinā Abū Bakr aṣ-Ṣiddīq ؓ. Allāh will say by Himself to Himself, *"Lā ilāha illā Anā wa Anā Akbar,* there is no god but Me and I am Greater." And if the servant says, *"Lā ilāha illa-Llāhu waḥdah,* there is no god but Allāh by Himself," then Allāh says, "Yes, *ṣadaqa ʿabdī.* There is no god but Me, One, by Myself." Then, *"Lā ilāha illa-Llāhu waḥdahu lā sharīka lahu,"* and Allāh says, *"Ṣadaqa ʿabdī. Lā ilāha illā Anā lā sharīka lā.* My servant spoke truth and there is no god but Me and I have no partner." When the servant says, *"Lā ilāha illa-Llāh lahu 'l-mulku wa lahu 'l-ḥamd,"* Allāh says, "My servant spoke the truth and there is no god but Me and to Me is the Kingdom and the Praise!" When he says, *"Lā ilāha illa-Llāh wa lā ḥawla wa lā quwwata illā billāh,"* then Allāh says, "My servant spoke truth and there is no god but Me and there is no power and no might except in Me."

Heavenly Palaces are Built on Our Dhikrullāh

Those servants who say these words are stamped with *ṣidq,* truthfulness, as Sayyīdinā Abū Bakr aṣ-Ṣiddīq ؓ was called *"aṣ-Ṣiddīq."* He said, *"Ṣadaqata,* you told the truth," without question to whatever the Prophet ﷺ said. On the other hand, Sayyīdinā ʿUmar ؓ sometimes had a question. When the Prophet ﷺ went for *Isrā' wa 'l-Miʿrāj,* Sayyīdinā ʿUmar ؓ went to Sayyīdinā Abū Bakr aṣ-Ṣiddīq ؓ and said, "Look what the Prophet ﷺ is saying," and Sayyīdinā Abū Bakr aṣ-Ṣiddīq ؓ said, "He spoke the Truth, *ṣadaqa Rasūlullāh.*" He had no questions or doubts.

What will Allāh give such people? Heavenly paradises and palaces, if we can call them that. They are built from pure pearls, as huge as Allāh likes. What we see in *dunyā* is a miniature pearl, but what Allāh gives to those who do *dhikrullāh,* is huge.

---

[182] Tirmidhī.

So these palaces are built by *dhikr*, the houses of Paradise are built by *dhikrullāh*. When you make *dhikrullāh*, they put one brick for you in Paradise; if you do *dhikrullāh* two times, two bricks; three times, three bricks; ten times, ten bricks, and so on. If you stop, they stop. This is how they build your Paradise. Allāh grants for you angels who build for you, it depends on how much *dhikrullāh* you do. One brick might be the size of this *dunyā* or more. It has no comparison to *dunyā*. Allāh gives to the *ṣādiqīn* something they never expected. When the one doing *dhikr* stops his *dhikr*, the angels stop building his palace in Paradise.

إن بيوت الجنة تبنى بالذكر ، إذا أمسك الذاكر عن الذكر أمسكت الملائكة عن البناء

Truly our houses are built with dhikr in Jannah, then when someone stops dhikr, the angels stop building the house.[183]

Allāh ordered the angels, "When My servant stops *dhikrullāh* then stop building his palace." So some people will have small palaces in Paradise. The teacher wants his students to have the best palace in Paradise so he gives the Initiate to recite *"Allāh, Allāh"* 1,500 times. He assigns the student at the level of *Mustaʿid*, "Prepared", to recite *"Allāh, Allāh"* 5,000 times out loud and silent. Sadly, we don't trust our shaykh, but our ego, as we question him. In turn, you build a doubt in yourself and that doubt never goes away, it always comes to take you from Allāh's Hands to the hands of Shayṭān. This is supported in a *ḥadīth* of the Prophet ﷺ that Abū Hurayrah ﵁ reported the Prophet ﷺ said:

من قال سبحان الله وبحمده سبحان الله العظيم سبع مرات بني له برج في الجنة

Who says, "SubḥānAllāh wa bi-ḥamdihi subḥānAllāh al-ʿAẓīm," seven times, Allāh will build a tower for him in Paradise.[184]

There was no tower in the time of the Prophet ﷺ as the maximum height for a home or building was two or three storeys. The Prophet ﷺ disliked any structure or building to be above two stories, he recommended one-storey houses. Today everyone has condominiums and Shayṭān likes that. Three stories, but still in limits. The Prophet ﷺ predicted that in

---

[183] Ibn Qayyim al-Jawzīyya, *Al-Wābil as-Ṣayyib*.
[184] Ibn Abī 'd-Dunyā.

Paradise Allāh will give us a tower. What do we say in *sujūd*? *"Subḥāna rabbī al-'alā wa bi-ḥamdih,"* so don't forget *"wa bi-ḥamdih."* If you say it one time you will get one tower, two times you will get two towers. Can you describe the tower? No, it is according to Allāh's Greatness.

Heavenly Trees Sprout from Our Dhikrullāh

What are the trees of Paradise? They are the trees of *dhikr*: You make *dhikrullāh* once and one tree of *dhikr* will come out making *dhikrullāh* for you, as it is mentioned by the Prophet ﷺ in a story about Sayyīdinā Ibrāhīm ؑ:

لَقِيتُ إِبْرَاهِيمَ لَيْلَةَ أُسْرِيَ بِي فَقَالَ يَا مُحَمَّدُ أَقْرِئْ أُمَّتَكَ مِنِّي السَّلَامَ وَأَخْبِرْهُمْ أَنَّ الْجَنَّةَ طَيِّبَةُ التُّرْبَةِ عَذْبَةُ الْمَاءِ وَأَنَّهَا قِيعَانٌ وَأَنَّ غِرَاسَهَا سُبْحَانَ اللَّهِ وَالْحَمْدُ لِلَّهِ وَلاَ إِلَهَ إِلاَّ اللَّهُ وَاللَّهُ أَكْبَرُ

> *I met Ibrāhīm ؑ on the night of my ascent, so he said, "O Muḥammad! Recite salām from me to your nation, and inform them that Paradise has pure soil and delicious water, and that it is a flat treeless plain, and that its seeds are: SubḥānAllāh (Glory is to Allāh), Alḥamdulillāh (all praise is due to Allāh), Lā ilāha illa-Llāh (none has the right to be worshipped but Allāh), and Allāhu Akbar (Allāh is the greatest)."*[185]

So when you recite this, you have planted a tree. If you say it two times, you get two trees. Everyone now said it two times, so they will have two trees. How many are we here? Two hundred and so it is on the number of people in *jama'ah*. You do it on your own you take one tree and if you are doing it together, you get according to the number of the *jama'ah*. When you pray in *jama'ah* the rewards are twenty-seven times more. So are we correct or not? Allāh is The Generous; remember Him and He remembers you. With *dhikrullāh* you build a palace and fill it with trees.

One time I went to Brunei with my shaykh, Mawlana Shaykh Nazim, may Allāh grant him long life. We visited the Sulṭān of Brunei accompanied by the Minister of Education, who is at the level of prime minister. They took us to the palace and through the main door, where you would find something resembling a river passing through the palace, whose entrance is like a bridge. You pass inside and there is water. In the water are goldfish and on both sides are trees, but not normal trees. They are made from

---

[185] Tirmidhī.

jewels: the trunk is a gem put together and then the branches, the leaves are emerald, the flowers are different colors of gems from sapphires to emeralds to rubies and in the middle is a diamond. These are the flowers of the trees, and many of these trees, everything is in gold and diamonds: couches, trays and chairs. This is a man to whom Allāh gave in *dunyā*. What do you think of *Ākhirah*, what will Allāh give? That is not too much for Allāh when you say, "*Subḥāna rabbī al-'Aẓīm wa bi-ḥamdih.*" That is a tree that a man gives. What about the tree that Allāh gives? Allāh gives without asking, but be sincere with Him. If you make a sin, repent and Allāh will forgive.

Islam is spread through the narration of stories. How did the Sulṭān of Brunei become rich? His father used to go to India to collect money from the British for the employees in the government. Suddenly, they stopped giving. He used to go to India, because he cared for his people. He slept and saw a dream in which a shaykh was telling him, "As soon as you arrive back home by boat, hit your stick on the soil." So it was finished, the British did not give him money and he went back to his country. There, as he arrived, he took his stick and hit it on the ground and sat. The processions of welcomers came for one hour and he was beginning to smell oil. He took the stick and it was black. His stick had struck oil and it began coming from the ground! For seven miles out of this island in front of Brunei is oil and if you go to both sides in Indonesia there is nothing.

So when Allāh is happy with His servant, He gives. Allāh gave the pious king, and we say, "O Allāh! Give us in *dunyā* and *Ākhirah*." Allāh is Generous to give you whatever you like.

The Prophet ﷺ said:

أكثروا من غراس الجنة قالوا يا رسول الله وما غرسها ؟ قال ما شاء الله ولا قوة إلا بالله

Try as much as possible to plant trees of Paradise. Ṣaḥābah asked, "What are the trees of Paradise?" The Prophet ﷺ said, "Mashā-Allāh lā ḥawla wa lā quwatta illāh billāh." The Prophet ﷺ is giving us many choices, you may use any one and get these trees in Paradise.

The Fence between You and Hellfire and the Dhikr of Stones

It is said that *dhikrullāh* is a fence between you and Hellfire. When you do *dhikrullāh* you are building a fence against Hellfire approaching you. If the 'abd did something wrong and was judged to go to Hellfire, *dhikrullāh* will come and block the door to Hellfire, putting a fence in front of Hellfire and pulling you out. You will be saved by *dhikrullāh*!

'Abd al-'Azīz Ibn al-Rawād related that a man built a *masjid* of wood in a desert and placed seven stones facing the *qiblah. Kāna idhā qaḍā ṣalātahu qāl,* whenever he finished his prayers he called: *Yā aḥjār ush-hidukum annahu lā ilāha illa-Llāh.* The Bedouins live in the desert; they don't drink, as they are accustomed to having their own ways. So he placed these seven stones and when he finished his prayer, he said, *yā aḥjār ush-hidukum annahu lā ilāha illa-Llāh,* "I take you stones as witness that there is no god but Allāh," as everything makes *tasbīḥ*, stones also make *dhikrullāh*:

وَإِن مِّن شَيْءٍ إِلاَّ يُسَبِّحُ بِحَمْدِهِ

And there is not a thing but celebrates His praise![186]

There is not one thing that does not do *dhikrullāh*, so it is "a thing." The *miswāk* does *tasbīḥ*, as everything does *tasbīḥ*. If you cut it into pieces, each piece does *dhikrullāh*. He said to the stones, "I make you my witness that I said *'Lā ilāha illa-Llāh.'*" After a while, that man got sick, the angels took his soul and ascended with it. He said, "I saw in my dream as if I am passing through Hellfire and I saw one of these stones coming and saying, 'O, I know this person! Where are you taking him?'" With all his prayers, he was still going towards Hellfire. "Then the second stone came and said, 'I know that one!' and the gates of Hellfire that I was facing were closed. Then they took me to another door and another stone came, all of them were coming one after another covering the doors to Hellfire." He was saved because he had made them his witness, that Allāh ﷻ and has no partner. So when you make to witness the angels and the creations of Allāh, then you close Hellfire in front of you. There are so many *du'ās* that they cannot be written down, *subḥānAllāh*!

Angels Ask Allāh for Our Forgiveness and Continue our Dhikr

The angels are given specialty to ask forgiveness for the one making *dhikr*. As much as he does *dhikr*, as much they ask forgiveness. I found in the Book revealed to the Prophet ﷺ that if the servant says, *"Alḥamdulillāh,"* the angels

[186] Sūrat al-'Isrā, 17:44.

continue the *āyah* saying, *"Rabbī 'l-ʿalāmīn,"* and the angels will continue. And if he says, *"Alḥamdulillāhi Rabbī 'l-ʿalāmīn,"* then the angels say, "O Allāh! Forgive that person." If he says, *"SubḥānAllāh,"* the angels say, *"Wa bi-ḥamdihi,"* and if he says, *"SubḥānAllāh wa bi-ḥamdihi,"* angels say, *"Allāhumma ighfir li ʿabdika."*

So what do we have to say in *sajda*? *"Subḥāna rabbī al-ʿalā wa bi-ḥamdih,"* and the angels will ask forgiveness of him. We will end by this, that the mountains and deserts, *qifār*, are all given a name by Allāh ﷻ. This is related by Ibn Masʿūd ؓ and narrated by Tabarani:

وعن ابن مسعود قال: إن الجبل ينادي الجبل باسمه: أي فلان هل مر بك [اليوم] أحد ذكر الله؟ فإذا قال: نعم استبشر.

The mountain will call the other mountain by name (and ask), "Did anyone pass by you making *dhikrullāh* today?" The mountains speak to each other in their language and if the mountain says, "Yes," the other will mountain gets happy. Ibn Qayyim said deserts or villages are known by names and Allāh gave everything a name:

وَعَلَّمَ آدَمَ الأَسْمَاء كُلَّهَا

And He taught Ādam the names of all things.[187]

So they ask, "Did anyone doing *dhikrullāh* pass by you?" If they say, "No," the mountains are not happy, if they say, "Yes," then they are happy and they make *tasbīḥ* and *istighfār*, and Allāh records it in His book for that servant. So the *dhākir* becomes like a spotlight attracting anyone who looks at him. Even if you are the ugliest one in *dunyā,* with *dhikrullāh* (Allāh) makes you the most beautiful one in Paradise. Don't say, "Why did Allāh create me like this or like that?" If you make *dhikrullāh,* then you will be most beautiful one in Paradise. May Allāh guide us to His *dhikrullāh*. There are so many benefits over 100 and we went through 20-30. It needs days and nights to mention all these!

[187] Sūrat al-Baqarah, 2:31.

How much *Ṣaḥābah* ﷺ made *dhikrullāh*! They sat behind the Prophet's house and made *dhikrullāh* so often that they became known as *Āhl as-Suffa*, People of the Bench.

وَاصْبِرْ نَفْسَكَ مَعَ الَّذِينَ يَدْعُونَ رَبَّهُم بِالْغَدَاةِ وَالْعَشِيِّ يُرِيدُونَ وَجْهَهُ وَلَا تَعْدُ عَيْنَاكَ عَنْهُمْ تُرِيدُ زِينَةَ الْحَيَاةِ الدُّنْيَا وَلَا تُطِعْ مَنْ أَغْفَلْنَا قَلْبَهُ عَن ذِكْرِنَا وَاتَّبَعَ هَوَاهُ وَكَانَ أَمْرُهُ فُرُطًا

And keep yourself patient (by being) with those who call upon their Lord in the morning and the evening, seeking His countenance. And let not your eyes pass beyond them, desiring adornments of the worldly life, and do not obey one whose heart We have made heedless of Our remembrance and who follows his desire and whose affair is ever (in) neglect.[188]

Wa lā ta'daw 'aynāk 'anhum turīdu zīnat al-ḥayāt ad-dunyā, "Don't turn your eyes from them, *yā Rasūlullāh*! They are sitting making *dhikrullāh*." When the Prophet ﷺ went out from his house, in the back were the *Āhl as-Suffa* who were workers during the day and rememberers during the night. Allāh told the Prophet ﷺ strongly, "Give them your eye, gaze upon them that they be happy." May Allāh ﷻ and Prophet ﷺ give us a gaze and to *Āhlu 's-Sunnah wa 'l-Jama'ah* for their benefit wherever they are, for our benefit and repentance to take our sins away.

Wa min Allāhi 't-tawfiq, bi ḥurmati 'l-Fātiḥah.

This shows us how much we are so small, miniature. Did you see how the Persians used to draw miniature drawings? *Ṣaḥābah* ﷺ were towers, *abrāj*, stars! If they make us stars, we accept also. Allāh is Great. *Yā Rabb!* You give from Your Generosity, we ask for the sake of the Prophet ﷺ to dress us from Your Generosity:

وَمَا ذَٰلِكَ عَلَى اللَّهِ بِعَزِيزٍ

That is not at all difficult for Allāh, Who has no equal.[189]

That is not difficult for Allāh. Allāh looks at hearts and intentions. People have strong intentions. Forget your work and *dunyā*, but intention of *Āhlu 's-Sunnah wa 'l-Jama'ah* is love of the Prophet ﷺ. That is enough. That

---

[188] Sūrat al-Kahf, 18:28.
[189] Sūrat Ibrāhīm, 14:20.

doesn't mean you don't pray, but it is enough to go to Paradise, like someone who has a tray of *ḥalwā* and on the other side a tray of water, and *ḥalwā* is *Āhlu 'l-Bayt*. Do you take them or not? Or a tray of *ḥalwā* and a tray of poison.

Āhlu 'l-Bayt are our way to Paradise, they are our light, our moon, our sun; they are our everything that is all in the hands of the Prophet ﷺ. Good tidings who are from the line of the Prophet ﷺ! That means, Allāh honored them without doing anything, but because they are related to the Prophet ﷺ, finished. And *Āhlu 's-Sunnah wa 'l-Jama'ah* are all related to love of the Prophet ﷺ. That is for our *Ākhirah,* which will save us. Don't listen to those squares. I will give you an example. Look how happy the children are with shirts on which is written Superman or Batman or poison man or redneck. They are happy with it or not? They are happy with what is garbage; they are happy with that in Muslim countries and buying it for them around the world, and parents are happy to buy them with pictures. What do you think about seeing the Prophet ﷺ? What about the *Ṣaḥābah* ؓ who saw the Prophet ﷺ? Do you like to see the Prophet ﷺ? Yes, everyone likes to see the Prophet ﷺ. *Inshā-Allāh* you will see him in *dunyā* and *Ākhirah.*

So there is no comparison between seeing the Prophet ﷺ and seeing Superman, that is garbage, that is games. And the Prophet ﷺ, we are resting and sleeping and the Prophet ﷺ is observing our *'amal* in his holy place and asking forgiveness of Allāh in his Holy Grave. What you want more than that? Give your life to the Prophet ﷺ, give your love to His Family. He asked us for His Family: I am not asking you anything, but to take care of My Family. They don't need our care. Allāh said in the Holy Qur'an, "Say to them, 'I don't ask from you any reward except that you take care of My Family.'"

قُل لَّا أَسْأَلُكُمْ عَلَيْهِ أَجْرًا إِلَّا الْمَوَدَّةَ فِي الْقُرْبَى

Say, "No reward do I ask of you for this except the love of those near of kin."[190]

Yā Rasūlullāh! If you are taking care of us, then your family is taking care of all of us. But only to take care to remember His Family in order he takes care of us, and it is a double situation that the Prophet ﷺ asked us to

---

[190] Sūrat ash-Shūrā, 42:23.

take care of the Family of the Prophet ﷺ. When we begin to take care of His family, it is a cause to pull us towards Paradise. We cannot take care of ourselves, but when we make *ṣalawāt* on *Āhl al-Bayt,* "Say! 'I don't ask anything of you but love of my Family,'" *Allāhumma ṣalli ʿalā Muḥammad wa ʿalā āli Muḥammad.*

May Allāh teach us wisdom to understand what is in secrets of Holy Qur'an and secrets of *ḥadīth.* May the Prophet ﷺ dip us in the Ocean of Knowledge and Wisdom as he dipped *awlīyāullāh.* We thank those broadcasting this around the world, Ummah TV and their listeners.

May Allāh forgive us and may Allāh bless us.

Wa min Allāhi 't-tawfiq, bi ḥurmati 'l-ḥabīb, bi ḥurmati 'l-Fātiḥah.
And with Allāh is success. For the sake of the Beloved, for his sake we recite the opening chapter of Holy Qur'ān.

Dhikrullāh Brightens Your Face

Aʿūdhu billāhi min ash-Shayṭāni 'r-rajīm. Bismillāhi' r-Raḥmāni 'r-Raḥīm. Nawaytu 'l-arbāʿīn, nawaytu 'l-ʿitikāf, nawaytu 'l-khalwah, nawaytu 'l-ʿuzlah, nawaytu 'r-riyāḍa, nawaytu 's-sulūk, lillāhi Taʿalā fī hādhā 'l-masjid. Atīʿūllāha wa atīʿū 'r-Rasūla wa ūli 'l-amri minkum. (4:59)

As-salāmu ʿalaykum wa raḥmatullāhi taʿalā wa barakātuh. When we say *salām*, Allāh sends angels to answer us with His *Salām*. It is better that all of us repeat. The *Ṣaḥābah* ❀ used to compete with each other to say, *"As-'salām ʿalaykum wa raḥmatullāhi wa barakātuh,* and Prophet ﷺ used to answer with: *"Wa ʿalaykum as-salām wa raḥmatullāhi wa barakātuh,"* that will bring Allāh's Favors on us.

Dhikrullāh will make as it is said, give you "brightness in the face". You might not see the brightness but those who look at you see the brightness, because when your face become more and more bright people can notice, but you are not noticing. Can you see your own face? That is why the Prophet ﷺ said:

المؤمن مرآة أخيه

The mu'min is the mirror of his brother.[191]

The *mu'min* is the mirror of the Believer, his brother, the other one who cannot see; he is a mirror for him and you are seeing the reflection of him on you because he has bright face from *dhikrullāh.* So *dhikrullāh* is important so that it gives us brightness in *dunyā* and in *Ākhirah* it will give you *nūr*. The Prophet ﷺ said *dunyā* is ending, and everyone wants to run to Paradise, don't think it's going to be too long, Everyone is planning plans, but *awlīyāullāh* don't plan plans. If *awlīyāullāh* like you they make you a mirror, they make you someone not in need for anyone, Allāh sends.

من قال كل يوم مائة مرة لا إله إلا الله وحده لا شريك له له الملك وله الحمد يحيي ويميت وهو على كل شيء قدير أتى الله تعالى يوم القيامة ووجهه أشد بياضا من القمر ليلة البدر

[191] Bukhārī, Adab al-Mufrad.

So the Prophet ﷺ said, "Whoever says every day, *man qāla kulla yawmin miata marrah: lā ilāha illa-Llāh waḥdahu lā sharīka lahu lahu 'l-mulku wa lahu 'l-ḥamdu yuḥīyy wa yumīt wa Hūwa ʿalā kulla shay'in qadīr*[192], he will enter Paradise and his face will be brighter than the full moon, (the amongst all the people of Paradise).

It means anyone saying *"Lā ilāha illa-Llāh waḥdahu lā sharīka lahu lahu 'l-mulku wa lahu 'l-ḥamdu yuḥīyy wa yumīt wa Hūwa ʿalā kulla shay'in qadīr,"* will be taken you to Paradise. That is why the *Ṣaḥābah* ؓ used to collect these different *adhkār* that Prophet ﷺ used to mention, and put them in small books, as Imam Nawawi explained in his own book, *al-Adhkār*. All these *aḥādīth* are written there, what you have to recite day and night. We can get all the *ḥadīth* we had from the beginning if anyone wants.

We will jump to another subject, since it is the last day of *Ramaḍān*—might be today or tomorrow, but the majority say that it is today—since it is the last day I will mention some *ḥadīth* about *siyām*, fasting, to show its importance and then we will go to a long *ḥadīth*, I don't know if there is sufficient time to explain, but that is one of the most important *ḥadīth* that contains everything.

Important Holy Days of Fasting

The Prophet ﷺ was asked about *ṣawmi ʿArafah*, fasting of ʿArafāt, and these *aḥādīth* will show the important days in the year to fast.

أَنَّ رَسُولَ اَللَّهِ - صلى الله عليه وسلم -سُئِلَ عَنْ صَوْمِ يَوْمِ عَرَفَةَ. قَالَ: " يُكَفِّرُ اَلسَّنَةَ اَلْمَاضِيَةَ وَالْبَاقِيَةَ ", وَسُئِلَ عَنْ صِيَامِ يَوْمِ عَاشُورَاءَ. قَالَ: " يُكَفِّرُ اَلسَّنَةَ اَلْمَاضِيَةَ " وَسُئِلَ عَنْ صَوْمِ يَوْمِ اَلِاثْنَيْنِ, قَالَ: " ذَاكَ يَوْمٌ وُلِدْتُ فِيهِ, وَبُعِثْتُ فِيهِ, أَوْ أُنْزِلَ عَلَيَّ فِيهِ "

The Messenger of Allāh ﷺ was asked about fasting on the day of ʿArafah (the 9th of the month of Dhu 'l-Ḥijjah). He replied, "Fasting on the day of ʿArafah is expiation for the preceding year and the following year." He was also asked about fasting on the day of ʿĀshūrā (the 10th of the month of Muḥarram). He replied, "Fasting on the day of ʿAshūrā is expiation for the preceding year." The Messenger of Allāh ﷺ was also asked about fasting on Monday, and he replied, "This is the day on which I

[192] Followers of *Ṭarīqat an-Naqshbandīyya-Nāẓimīyya* recite this after every prayer.

was born and the day on which I was sent (with the Message of Islam) and the day on which I received Revelation.[193]

Yukaffiru as-sannat al-māḍīyya wa 'l-bāqīyya, whoever fasts ʿArafāt, Allāh will erase his sins of the current year and the prior year. That is through fasting one day when pilgrims go to ʿArafāt, which will erase the sins of the year and those of the last year, so who doesn't want that? So you must jump to fulfill that *ḥadīth* from childhood, because whatever you do of sins it gets erased and what is left of the current year will be erased, so it will be as if you were newly born since you fast that day of ʿArafāt. And he ﷺ was asked about fasting on Mondays. Look, the best answer for square, not rectangular; from four sides it is square. He was asked about the day he was born. Why did they ask about the day the Prophet ﷺ was born if they were not celebrating or interested in that day? He didn't tell them to ask about it, about Monday, but the *Ṣaḥābah* came and asked, "*Yā Rasūlullāh,* what about fasting on Monday?" And he said, "That is the day I was born and that was the day that Allāh sent the message of the Holy Qur'ān, the day of the first revelation."

اقْرَأْ بِاسْمِ رَبِّكَ الَّذِي خَلَقَ خَلَقَ الْإِنسَانَ مِنْ عَلَقٍ اقْرَأْ وَرَبُّكَ الْأَكْرَمُ الَّذِي عَلَّمَ بِالْقَلَمِ عَلَّمَ الْإِنسَانَ مَا لَمْ يَعْلَمْ

Read! In the Name of your Lord Who created, Who created Man from a clot. Read! And your Lord is Most Bountiful, He Who taught (the use of) the pen taught Man that which he knew not.[194]

We understand the first part, *Iqrā bismi rabbik alladhī khalaq,* "Read in the Name of your Lord," there is an interpretational aspect, but we won't go into that now. Then He said, *"Iqrā wa rabbuka 'l-akram alladhī ʿallāma bi 'l-qalam,* "Read and your Lord is more Generous," but more generous on what? It means there is something He is giving to Prophet ﷺ, repeating to him, "Read another time, I will be more generous with you." Why?

First, Allāh said, "Read in the Name of the One Who Created," and He could have said to him, "Read in the Name of Allāh," but why he said,

---

193 Sahih Muslim, narrated by Abū Qatadah al-Anṣāri.

194 Sūrat al-ʿAlaq: 96:1-5.

"*Alladhī khalaq,* the One Who Created." Because He wants to pour the knowledge of Creation, of what He has created, into the heart of Prophet ﷺ.

Then He said, *Iqrā wa rabbuka 'l-akram,* "Read, I will be more Generous, I will give you more knowledge." That is when Allāh gave him Knowledge of Before and After with no limits, then the Prophet ﷺ can open every door. He is the Favored One on every Creation: on angels, in Paradises, on other creations that we don't know, on Earth, on every place that Allāh created. That is why the Prophet ﷺ said, "*Buʿithtu fīhi,* On that day I was sent, and that day *wa unzila ʿalayya fīhi,* Allāh sent the first *āyah,* revealed it on that day, *ʿallama bi 'l-qalam,* "taught Man by means of the Pen." Stone Age people were not writing, but that doesn't mean Allāh didn't teach them by the Pen.

وَعَلَّمَ آدَمَ الأَسْمَاءَ كُلَّهَا

And He taught Ādam all the names.[195]

"He taught Ādam all the names," it means all the knowledges of *dunyā* and the first thing Allāh created from the *Nūr*/Light of the Prophet ﷺ was the *Qalam,* the Pen. It is said in one *ḥadīth* of Prophet ﷺ that what Allāh created first was the *ʿArsh* from the *Nūr,* the Light of the Prophet ﷺ, then the *Kursīyy* and then the *Qalam.* That means there are Creations of Allāh that are writing. Who are these? First are two angels on the right and left shoulder who write your deeds, writing with a *qalam.* What pen? Do they write with an ink pen or like today they have dry ink or ballpoint; do they write with such a pen or a Heavenly Pen? It is a Heavenly Pen.

So the Prophet ﷺ said, "On that day, Monday, I was born and on that day I had revelation on me, so fast that day." (*Muslim*)

That is the importance of *ṣīyām* on that day. In another *ḥadīth* from Abū Ayyūb al-Anṣārī ؓ, the Prophet ﷺ said:

مَنْ صَامَ رَمَضَانَ ثُمَّ أَتْبَعَهُ سِتًّا مِنْ شَوَّالٍ فَذَلِكَ صِيَامُ الدَّهْرِ

Whoever fasts Ramaḍān, then follows it with six from Shawwāl, then that is (equal in reward) to fasting every day.[196]

---

[195] Sūrat al-Baqarah, 2:31.

Whoever fasts *Ramaḍān* and then follows it by fasting the six days of *Shawwāl* will be as if he fasted the whole year. Correct? (Yes.) How? How many days are in *Ramaḍān*, in general? Thirty days, multiply it by ten as every *ḥasanāt* is ten, which is Allāh's normal rewards, so it is 300. And then the six days of *Shawwāl*, and every *ḥasanāt* by ten, which is like sixty days, plus 300 equals 360 days, which is a whole year in the lunar calendar that he will get benefit of that fasting that no one knows what reward Allāh will give, because He said:

الصوم لي وانا أجزي به

Fasting is for Me and I will reward it.[197]

"*Ramaḍān* is for Me and I will reward it," so no one knows that, they will receive a reward that is unexpected that the angels cannot write it, immediately the fasting will come to My Presence and I will reward that '*abd* who fasted that day, but be careful of backbiting.

Then Abū Dharr ؓ said the Prophet ﷺ ordered us to fast three days every month, *Ayām al-Bīḍ*, the White Days[198] and he said the 13th, 14th, and 15th.

عَنْ مِلْحَانَ الْقَيْسِيِّ ، قَالَ كَانَ رَسُولُ اللَّهِ عَلَيْهِ السَّلَامُ يَأْمُرُنَا أَنْ نَصُومَ الْبِيضَ : ثَلَاثَ عَشْرَةَ ، وَأَرْبَعَ عَشْرَةَ ، وَخَمْسَ عَشْرَةَ. وَقَالَ : هُوَ كَهَيْئَةِ الدَّهْرِ

The Messenger of Allāh commanded us to fast the three White Days (Ayām al-Bīḍ), the thirteenth, fourteenth and fifteenth.[199]

So you fast these days, he ordered us to fast them, and for *barakah* of these days the *Ṣaḥābah* ؓ used to fast these days.

Abū Saʿīd al-Khuḍrī ؓ said that the Prophet ﷺ forbade fasting two days, the day of *ʿĒid al-Fiṭr* and the first day of *al-Aḍḥā*, where they sacrifice and give to the poor.

---

[196] Tirmidhī.
[197] Ḥadīth Qudsī related by Muslim.
[198] Referring to the moon's brightness.
[199] Related by Abū Dāwūd, an-Nasāī and Tirmidhī.

عَنْ أَبِي سَعِيدٍ الْخُدْرِيِّ رَضِيَ اللَّهُ عَنْهُ رَسُولَ اللَّهِ صَلَّى اللَّهُ عَلَيْهِ وَسَلَّمَ : " نَهَى عَنْ صِيَامِ يَوْمَيْنِ : يَوْمِ الْفِطْرِ ، وَيَوْمِ النَّحْرِ "

The Messenger of Allāh ﷺ has prohibited fasting on two days: the day of Fiṭr (breaking the fast of Ramaḍān) and on the day of sacrifice (ʿĒid ul-Aḍḥā). (Bukhārī and Muslim)

Also the three days of *Mina*, first is *ʿĒid* which is the 10th, and then 11th, 12th, and 13th, these four days you cannot fast and *ʿĒid al-Fiṭr* you cannot fast, so five days in the year there is no fasting, but other than these, fast do as much as you want. May Allāh ﷻ bless us in this *Ramaḍān*, and we quote what Abū Hurayrah ؓ said about this month.

من صام رمضان إيمانا واحتسابا غفر له ما تقدم من ذنبه

Whoever fasts during Ramaḍān with faith and seeking his reward (from Allāh), all his past sins will be forgiven.[200]

Whoever fasts *Ramaḍān* and *qāma*, did night prayers, *īmānan*, faithfully, *w 'aḥtisāban* by remembering that you are going to be asked one day, *ghufira lahu mā taqaddama min dhanbih* you will be saved from all sins not just for the last year, *mā taqaddama* whatever sins he made in his life, from that day all the way back will be forgiven.

That is *Ramaḍān*. May Allāh bless us with *Ramaḍān*, and correct our lives in this life and the Next!

Redeeming Acts in the Ḥadīth, "I Saw a Man from my Ummah"

This *ḥadīth* is recorded by Abū Saʿīd al-Khudrī ؓ and ʿAbdur-Raḥmān ibn Samra al-Jundab ؓ related it in a long *ḥadīth*, but we will take some parts of it:

عن عبد الرحمن بن سمرة بن جندب قال : خرج علينا رسول الله صلى الله عليه و سلم يوما وكنا في صفه بالمدينة فقام علينا فقال : إني رأيت البارحة عجبا : رأيت رجلا من أمتي أتاه ملك الموت ليقبض روحه فجاءه بره والديه فرد ملك الموت عنه...

---

[200] Bukhārī and Muslim.

One day the Prophet ﷺ came to meet us. We were in the Ṣuffah, in Madīnatu 'l-Munawwara, and he ﷺ stood up and said, "I saw something amazing yesterday. I saw a man from my community with the Angel of Death coming to him to take his soul, then came good dealings with his parents (to intercede for him) and the Angel of Death left him....[201]

Innī ra'aytu al-bāriḥa 'ajaban, "Yesterday I saw something amazing, *'ajaban.* I saw one person of my *Ummah* and the Angel of Death coming to take his soul," *fa jā'ahu birrihi bi 'l-wālidayyi fa raddu malaku'l-mawt 'anhu,* his sincerity and respect to his parents and keeping that relationship, *birri bi 'l-wālidayn* which is important, to give them what they have given you all your life. They did everything for you in your life, they looked after you and you have to look after them when they are old. Don't throw them in senior citizens houses like they are doing in some countries. No, never in our culture do we put our mother or father in a senior's house. Do you put them in senior homes in your country? No, they take care of them in their homes, it is the responsibility of the children. So that goodness to his parents, *birr al-wālidayn,* the goodness for his parents immediately came and made a fence from the Angel of Death where he was unable to take his soul, so he left. (*Ḥadīth* continues.)

ورأيت رجلا من أمتي قد بسط عليه عذاب القبر فجاءه وضوؤه فاستنقذه من ذلك

Then I saw a man whose punishment in the grave was being laid out for him, then came his ablutions and he was rescued by them.

And the Prophet ﷺ said, "I saw another man who was judged to go to Hellfire," because he said, "I was amazed." Immediately at that moment his ablution came, (as he was keeping his ablution 24 hours: when he sleeps keeping ablution and when he awakes he makes new *wuḍū* and does that every time during the day) and that *wuḍū* came and blocked the punishment of the grave from Hellfire.

ورأيت رجلا من أمتي قد احتوشته الشياطين فجاءه ذكر الله عز
و جل فطرد الشيطان عنه

---

[201] Ibn Qayyim, al-Wābil aṣ-Ṣayyib.

Then I saw a man from my community who was surrounded by devils, then came the remembrance of Allāh and the devils were driven away from him.

Do you see? First is *birr al-walīdayn,* taking care of the parents; second is the ablution, how many miracles the ablution is doing; and third is *wa ra'aytu rajulan qad ihtawajah-tu 'sh-shayāṭīn,* "I saw a man from my *Ummah* and the *shayātīn* are taking him in." *Fa jā'hu dhikrullāhi ʿazza wa jalla faṭurada 'sh-shayāṭīn ʿanhu,* "Then his *dhikrullāh* came immediately and chased the devils away." See how merciful Allāh ﷻ is with His servants! Everything (bad) you do Allāh gave you a remedy, a way out during your life: *birr al-wālidayn,* ablution and *dhikrullāh.*

ورأيت رجلا من أمتي قد احتوشته ملائكة العذاب فجاءته صلاته فاستنقذته من أيديهم

And I saw a man of my community who was surrounded by the Angels of Punishment, then there came his prayers and he was rescued from their hands.

"And I saw a man who the Angels of Punishment were grabbing for punishment," and his prayers came and blocked them and took him from their hands." So first is *birr al-wālidayn,* being good to parents, second ablution, third is *dhikrullāh* and fourth is *ṣalāt,* prayers. So what you want better than that?

ورأيت رجلا من أمتي يلهب - وفي رواية يلهث -عطشا كلما دنا
من حوض منع وطرد فجاءه صيام شهر رمضان فأسقاه وأرواه

And I saw a man from my community who was panting from thirst. When he got close to them, he was prevented from every jug of water and they were taken away from him. Then came his fasting of the month of Ramaḍān and, therefore, he drank and was satisfied.

Then the Prophet ﷺ said, "And I saw a man from my *Ummah* very thirsty; whenever he comes to drink from the *Ḥawd,* a river from Paradise, he has been kicked out and not allowed to enter. Then comes the fast of *Ramaḍān,* because in *Ramaḍān* he kept himself thirsty. Now when he goes to quench his thirst from Paradise they prevent him, and *Ramaḍān* is making *shafaʿah* for him, interceding for him. So the fast of *Ramaḍān* came and gave him the drink to drink, allowed him to drink from *Ḥawd al-Kawthar.*

ورأيت رجلا من أمتي ورأيت النبيين جلوسا حلقا حلقا كلما دنا إلى حلقة طرد فجاءه غسله من الجنابة فأخذ بيده فأقعده إلى جنبي

I saw a man from my community and I saw prophets sitting in groups. Every time the man went to the circles he was driven away. Then came his bathing as purification from major defilement, and took him by his hand and sat him besides me.

And the Prophet ﷺ said, "I saw a man from my *Ummah* and I saw prophets of my *Ummah* sitting in circles; whenever that man tried to enter the circle of prophets he was chased out. He was good, but because he was doing something not good, they were preventing him from entering the circle because he needs to be clean." So if you want to enter their circle you have to be clean. So what came to save him? "His *ghusl* after *janāba* came and put him next to me," as he never went out to work in a state of *janāba* without taking a necessary shower. "That *ghusl* took him by his hand and sat him by me," by Prophet ﷺ. That means to take a shower (after), not before *janāba*, as many people do, especially in western countries: they take a shower and then they go do it. Then you have to take shower, but they don't because they took it before. No, you have to take it after. That is purity, so that *ghusl* came and put him close to the Prophet ﷺ.

ورأيت رجلا من أمتي بين يديه ظلمة ومن خلفه ظلمة وعن يمينه ظلمة وعن يساره ظلمة ومن فوقه ظلمة ومن تحته ظلمة وهو متحير فيها فجاءه حجه وعمرته فاستخرجاه من الظلمة وأدخلاه في النور

And I saw a man from my community, in front of him was darkness, behind him was darkness, on his right was darkness, and on his left was darkness, and above him was darkness, and below him was darkness, and he was lost in the darkness. Then there came his pilgrimage and lesser pilgrimage and they took him out of the darkness and entered him into light.

And the Prophet ﷺ said, "I saw a man from my *Ummah,* in front of him darkness, behind him darkness, and on his left darkness, on his right darkness, above and under darkness, he was confused and didn't know what to do," like these new generation of Muslim scholars, they put everyone in a box: you go straight it is *shirk,* you go left it is *harām,* if you go right, *bida*ʿ, you go back it is *kufr*. So that one does not know what to do...*ẓulma* from everywhere! his *Hajj* and *ʿUmrah* came and took him out of the darkness and put him in light, dressed him with *nūr*.

ورأيت رجلامن أمتي يتقي بيده وهج النار وشرره فجاءته صدقته فصارت سترة بينه وبين النار وظللت على رأسه

And I saw a man from my community who was being burned by a fire. Then there came his charity and it formed a cover between him and the fire, and it provided a shade over his head.

"And I saw a man from my *Ummah* trying to push the flame of the Fire and the heat of the Fire away from him, but he was unable. Then quickly came his *ṣadaqah,* charity, and it was a fence between him and the Fire and covered his head and made a shade above his head from the intensity of the heat of the Fire."

ورأيت رجلا من أمتي يكلم المؤمنين ولا يكلمونه فجاءته صلته لرحمه فقالت : يا معشر المسلمين إنه كان وصولا لرحمه فكلموه فكلمه المؤمنون وصافحوه وصافحهم

And I saw a man from my community who was talking to the Believers, but they would not talk to him. Then there came his keeping of family relations and it said, "O gathering of Muslims! He kept together family ties, so speak with him." Therefore, the Believers talked to him and they shook his hand.

"And I saw a man from my *Ummah* that the *mu'min* would not speak with and he could not speak with them, but his *ṣilat ar-raḥim* saved him," because he kept relations with his relatives, called *'ṣilat ar-raḥim'* in Arabic, relations, connections of the womb. "So that came and brought him to sit with the *mu'mins* and to speak with the other Muslims." That *ṣilat ar-raḥim* was speaking, saying, "O Muslims! That man was keeping relations with all his families, as Allāh ﷻ ordered in the Holy Qur'ān, so please speak with him." And they spoke with him, "He shook hands with them and said *'salām'* and he was one of them."

Don't break relationships, but try to connect, as the Prophet ﷺ said:

تصل مَنْ قطعك

Connect with the one who cuts you off.[202]

ورأيت رجلا من أمتي قد احتوشته الزبانية فجاءه أمره بالمعروف
ونهيه عن المنكر فاستنقذه من أيديهم وأدخله في ملائكة الرحمة

And I saw a man of my community who was encircled by the angels who throw the disbelievers into Hell. Then there came his ordering the good and forbidding the evil, so he was rescued from their hands. And he was entered among the Angels of Mercy.

"And I saw a man from my *Ummah* that the *zabānīyya,* Angels of Punishment of *Jahannam*[203], *ʿalayhā tisʿata ʿashar, fa jā'a amruhu bi 'l-mʿarūfin wa nahīyyhu ʿani 'l-munkar,* then immediately came in front of them, because in his life he was calling for good and preventing what is bad, they came and saved him from their hands."

ورأيت رجلا من أمتي جاثيا على ركبتيه وبينه وبين الله عز وجل حجاب فجاءه حسن خلقه
فأخذ بيده فأدخله على الله عز و جل

And I saw a man from my community who was kneeling and between him and Allāh there was a curtain. Then there came his good character and he was taken by his hand and permitted to be with Allāh.

"And I saw a man from my *Ummah* sitting on his knees and between him and Allāh ﷻ is a veil, and immediately *ḥusnu khuluqihi,* his good manners came and brought him to the Presence of Allāh Almighty," that is:

انما بعثت لاتمم مكارم الاخلاق

I have been sent to perfect the best of conduct (your behavior and character).[204]

"Surely, I was sent to complete and perfect good manners." So his good manners, might be that that he was not doing something of his five obligations, might be he is delaying them or there is some problem, so Allāh

---

202 Bayhaqī.
203 The nineteen Angels for Punishment who are very powerful; in their small finger they turn *Jahannam* upside down and they caught him.
204 Bazzār.

ﷺ made his *ḥusnu 'l-khuluq*, his good character, to speak nicely with people, slowly, not rude, and it came and saved him from Hell.

ورأيت رجلا من أمتي قد ذهبت صحيفته من قبل شماله فجاءه خوفه من الله عز و جل فأخذ صحيفته فوضعها في يمينه

And I saw a man from my community whose recorded deeds were taken from his left hand. Then there came his fear of Allāh and he took his record of deeds and them placed on his right hand.

And I saw a man from my *Ummah* who had the right notebook kept down on his shoulder and on his left shoulder was coming first because of too many bad deeds in it," more than the good *'amal*, and all his life he was afraid of Allāh but he was making mistakes, but he had *khawf*, fear, "and immediately his fear of Allāh came and took him and saved him and put his notebook which was on his left, and moved to his right side," means everything was erased.

ورأيت رجلا من أمتي خف ميزانه فجاءه أفراطه

And I saw a man from my community whose deeds in the Scale were very light, and who had children who died. Then there came his young children who had died and his deeds weight in the Scale was increased.

I saw a man of my *Ummah* whose right-hand scale was light weight and he did not have too much good *'amal* and he is supposed to go to Hellfire. "Immediately all his children who died in his life came," because if you have a child that died at an early age before maturity, girl or boy, they will take you to Paradise with no account, they take your hand and go, Allāh gave them that authority because they are innocent, "and they took him, *fa thaqqalu mīzanah* they made his balance very heavy and took him to Paradise."

ورأيت رجلا من أمتي قائما على شفير جهنم فجاءه رجاؤه في الله عز و جل فاستنقذه من ذلك ومضى

And I saw a man from my Ummah and he was standing on the edge of Hellfire and might fall down, and then Allāh's Mercy came on him and took him and he went to Paradise."

ورأيت رجلا من أمتي قد أهوى في النار فجاءته دمعته التي بكى من خشية الله فاستنقذته من ذلك

I saw a man from my community who was thrown in the fire. Then there came his tears that he cried out of fear of Allāh and he was rescued from that.

And I saw a man of my *Ummah* who was thrown in Hellfire and *subḥānallāh,* he was thrown in Hellfire, what came to him? "One tear came to him, *khawfun min Allāh,* that was coming out from fear of Allāh, shedding from his eyes that tear was pulling him out and taking him out of Hellfire." How many people cry when they remember Allāh ﷻ and how tears come when they remember the Prophet ﷺ, and how many tears come when they remember *Ṣaḥābah* ؓ gave their lives for Allāh and His Prophet ﷺ and how they have been killed, and how many tears come from thinking of the *Āhl al-Bayt* and how they were killed, and pieces and pieces.

ورأيت رجلا من أمتي قائما على الصراط يرعد كما ترعد السعفة في ريح عاصف فجاءه حسن ظنه بالله عز و جل فسكن رعدته ومضى

And I saw a man from my community standing along a path that was shuddering in the same way that a limb of a palm tree shudders on a stormy night. Then there came to him, the good thoughts he had had about Allāh and the shuddering stopped.

And I saw a man of my *Ummah* standing on the *Ṣirāṭ* he was shaking and making a sound," when you see lightning you hear *raʿd,* thunder and like the date tree in thunderstorm, *raʿd,* "and he was shaking like that on the Bridge," and what comes to him? Look at Allāh's Kindness towards His servants. "and that person always used to have good thoughts, never bad thoughts." The Prophet ﷺ said, "Have good doubts, not bad doubts, *inna baʿd aẓ-ẓanni ithm,"* Allāh said in the Holy Qur'ān that from bad thoughts there might be punishment as you might think different of what the reality is. So that good thought came to him, *fasakana rʿadat-hu* and calmed him down and made him to enter Paradise.

ورأيت رجلا من أمتي يزحف على الصراط ويحبوأحيانا فجاءته صلاته علي فأقامته على قدميه وأنقذته

And I saw a man from my community crawling on the Bridge (over Hellfire). Sometimes he was crawling on it and sometimes he was hanging from it.

Then there came his invoking blessings upon the Prophet ﷺ and he was made to stand on his feet and he passed over it.

"And I saw a man crawling on the *Sirāt* and sometimes *yahbū*, he comes down on his knees crawling and *wa yataʿalāq ahyānan*, sometimes he holds onto something on *Ṣirāṭ al-Mustaqīm*, and immediately then his *ṣalawāt* he sent on me came and took him and saved him." How much we have to make *ṣalawāt an-Nabī*?

Salawāt al-Fātiḥ

اللهم صل على سيدنا محمد الفاتح لما أغلق و الخاتم لما سبق ناصر الحق بالحق
و الهادي إلى صراطك المستقيم و على آله حق قدره و مقداره العظيم

Allāhumma ṣalli ʿalā Sayyīdinā Muḥammadi 'l-fātiḥi limā ughliqa wa 'l-khātimi limā sabaqa nāṣiri 'l-ḥaqqi bi 'l-ḥaqqi wa 'l-hādī ilā ṣirāṭika 'l-mustaqīma ṣall 'Llāhu ʿalayhi wa ʿalā ālihi wa aṣ-ḥābihi ḥaqqa qadrihi wa miqdārihi 'l-ʿAẓīm.

O Allāh! Bless our Master Muḥammad ﷺ, who opened what was closed and who is the Seal of what went before, he who makes the Truth victorious by the Truth, the guide to Your Straight Path, and bless his Household as is the due of his immense position and grandeur.[205]

How much that *ṣalawāt* will open for us everything that is locked, it will save us!

ورأيت رجلا من أمتي انتهى إلى أبواب الجنة فغلقت الأبواب دونه فجاءته شهادة أن لا إله
إلا الله ففتحت له الأبواب وأدخلته الجنة

And I saw a man from my community who came to the doors of Paradise and they were closed in front of him. Then there came his testifying that there is no god except Allāh and the doors were opened for him and he entered into Paradise.

And I saw one of my *Ummah* reached the doors of Paradises but they were closed in front of his face," not allowing him to enter. What will allow you to enter Paradise? *Shahadah. Ash-hadu an lā ilāha illa-Llāh wa ash-hadu*

---

[205] From Sufilive.com/salawat.

anna Muḥammadu 'r-Rasūlullāh immediately came and opened for him the doors and made him to enter Paradise.

من قال لا اله الا الله دخل الجنة

Whoever said 'lā ilāha illa-Llāh' entered Paradise.

It is mentioned by many scholars, and its chain is *ḥasanun jiddan*, related by Saʿīd ibn Mūsāyyib ﵁, and it is a strong *ḥadīth* and very important *ḥadīth* that people should know and memorize. It is a long *ḥadīth*, but a beneficial one.

May Allāh ﷻ forgive us and that was the last day of *Ramaḍān*, thirty days and we reached that *ḥadīth*. There are many other nice *aḥādīth* and all *aḥādīth* are nice, all of them show how much mercy Allāh ﷻ gave to *Ummat an-Nabī* ﷺ!

May Allāh forgive us and may Allāh bless us.

Wa min Allāhi 't-tawfīq, bi ḥurmati 'l-ḥabīb, bi ḥurmati 'l-Fātiḥah.
And with Allāh is success. For the sake of the Beloved, for his sake we recite the opening chapter of Holy Qur'ān.

Advice is the Structure of Islam

Aʿūdhu billāhi min ash-Shayṭāni 'r-rajīm. Bismillāhi' r-Raḥmāni 'r-Raḥīm. Nawaytu 'l-arbāʿīn, nawaytu 'l-ʿitikāf, nawaytu 'l-khalwah, nawaytu 'l-ʿuzlah, nawaytu 'r-riyāḍa, nawaytu 's-sulūk, lillāhi Taʿalā fī hādhā 'l-masjid. Atīʿūllāha wa atīʿū 'r-Rasūla wa ūli 'l-amri minkum. (4:59)

Kālimātani khafifatān ʿalā al-lisān thaqīlatān fī 'l-mīzān subḥānAllāh wa biḥamdihi subḥānAllāhi 'l-ʿAẓīm astaghfirullāh. Allāh ﷻ said in the Holy Qur'ān that every time you see each other, remind each other of Islam, remind each other of the Prophet ﷺ, remind each other of *tawḥīdullāh ʿazza wa jal*. And Allāh loves the most that we remind us of:

> *Bismillāhi' r-Raḥmāni 'r-Raḥīm. Qūl Hūwa Allāhu Āḥad, Allāhu 'ṣ-Ṣamad lam yalid wa lam yūlad, wa lam yakun lahu kufūwan Āḥad.*
>
> *Bismillāhi' r-Raḥmāni 'r-Raḥīm. Qūl Hūwa Allāhu Āḥad, Allāhu 'ṣ-Ṣamad lam yalid wa lam yūlad, wa lam yakun lahu kufūwan Āḥad.*
>
> *Bismillāhi' r-Raḥmāni 'r-Raḥīm. Qūl Hūwa Allāhu Āḥad, Allāhu 'ṣ-Ṣamad lam yalid wa lam yūlad, wa lam yakun lahu kufūwan Āḥad.*

Three times, *subḥānAllāh,* how much Allāh is Merciful. They say, "We don't know how to read Qur'ān." For three times' recitation of *Qūl Huwa Allāhu Āḥad,* you will be rewarded as if you read the whole Qur'ān, as if you mentioned 6,666 verses and you have read them all and all 114 *sūrahs,* as if you have accomplished reading them all! So in such an association, although it is *ʿĒid* tomorrow, but in *ʿĒid* it is all the days of *farḥ,* joy and happiness, and *ṣilat ar-raḥim,* to go make *zīyāra* to each other and to make *zīyārah* to someone you love, like to Mawlana Shaykh Nazim, may Allāh give him long life.

To make *zīyāra* there is *ṣilat ar-raḥim,* you are connecting with your teacher, with his representative, with his deputies, with his *khulafā*; you are accomplishing something that is accepted and very well-demanded in Islam, *ṣilat ar-raḥim.* So in such associations, although it is *ʿĒid* tomorrow, but for ten or fifteen minutes it is better to end our fasting of *Ramaḍān* with a small *naṣīḥa,* as Prophet ﷺ said:

الدين نصيحة

Religion is advice.[206]

Our religion is based on advice, so the infrastructure is advice. Without advice how can people know each other, how can people understand knowledge, how can people understand Sharīʿah? It is by *naṣīḥa,* advice. So advice is the guide, if we really go deep into the secret of the meaning of *naṣīḥa;* it is the guidance, it is an advice that guides you through your heart. If you don't have a teacher to guide you, then through your heart Allāh will guide you.

So *naṣīḥa* really is the *nūr* that Islam came with and made advice part of Islam to accomplish what you need. Prophet ﷺ came at the beginning of the *naṣīḥa,* giving advice to people to drop worshipping of idols and to worship Allāh ﷻ. That was the *naṣīḥa* and many people went into it. After that, it began to build up. So the basis, the infrastructure of *naṣīḥa* is *Tawḥīd.* Without *Tawḥīd,* all your *naṣīḥa* is thrown in your faces. *Tawḥīd* is the main infrastructure for *naṣīḥa* and on top of it, after *Tawḥīd,* we have the Five Pillars of Islam, of which the first one is *Tawḥīd: Ash-hadu an lā ilāha illa-Llāh wa ash-hadu anna Muḥammadu 'r-Rasūlullāh.*

That is the infrastructure that you make sure to always check, has something been rusted? Has it been covered in some rust from our rusted heart or is that *Shahadah* we are bringing, that *Tawḥīd,* still clean and pure? We recite it every day, morning and evening, when we wake up and when we sleep with *"Ash-hadu an lā ilāha illa-Llāh wa ash-hadu anna Muḥammadu 'r-Rasūlullāh,"* so do we have a very strong infrastructure? Then if any earthquake comes, that cannot change it, take it, or demolish it. 'Earthquake' means any *shayṭānic,* false gossips or information that comes to your mind is thrown on the face of Shayṭān when you are saying *Shahadah, "Ash-hadu an lā ilāha illa-Llāh wa ash-hadu anna Muḥammadu 'r-Rasūlullāh."*

So *ad-dīnu naṣīḥa,* for Allāh, for His Prophet ﷺ and for the *Ummah.* Allāh loves people who advise each other and so, *alḥamdulillāh,* this *Ramaḍān* all the people attending the *naṣīḥa,* our associations here, they didn't go empty. One of the most important benefits is that we were all on one heart

[206] Abū Dāwūd.

and our heart was on one direction; we didn't go right or left, but in one direction, straight-forward, connecting our hearts with our teacher, Mawlana Shaykh Muḥammad Nazim ʿAdil al-Ḥaqqānī, may Allāh give him long life, from him to Prophet ﷺ! Or we can say from him passing through the chain of *awlīyāullāh*, passing through Grandshaykh Sayyidi Shaykh ʿAbdAllāh al-Fā'iz ad-Dāghestānī ق, *Sulṭān al-Awlīyā*, and from one to another to another in a chain of *awlīyāullāh*.

Mentioning Names of Awlīyāullāh Brings Barakah

We are lucky that we are part of the students of someone who refused to take the *khilafah* of the Naqshbandi Order without getting it from Prophet ﷺ and *awlīyāullāh*, and his request is that anyone that sits in his association has to be in the same level with him in *dunyā* and in *Ākhirah*! That was Grandshaykh ʿAbdAllāh ق! When the message from Shaykh Sharafuddīn ق was passed to him, the *khilafah* of the Naqshbandi Order, he asked that anyone who sits in his association will be raised to his level and to be with him *dunyā* and *Ākhirah*. And *alḥamdulillāh*, all Shaykh Nazim's students or followers are also, in the same time, followers of Grandshaykh ʿAbdAllāh al-Fā'iz ad-Dāghestānī ق.

Sayyīdinā ʿAbdu 'r-Raūf al-Yamānī, may Allāh bless his presence, for a long time we didn't mention his name and now he is indicating to mention his name. Any *walī*, when you mention their name, they are present or he looks from far and his presence comes with a high level of enlightenment that he will dress us with by permission of *awlīyāullāh*, by permission of Mawlana Shaykh Nazim ق, as they don't overlap and each has his own students. By permission he took every one of us in his presence, and he will for sure present them to Prophet ﷺ on behalf of Grandshaykh ق and Mawlana Shaykh Nazim ق as he wants to do that favor to their followers. He wants to make that favor, because he is appreciating the level where Grandshaykh ق is putting us, he is appreciating and feeling that he is obliged to give us a gift and that gift from *awlīyāullāh* between each other is highly recommended, because they always give gifts to each other. And this *Ramaḍān*, his gift was to present us and carry all our burdens and present us to Mawlana Shaykh Nazim ق, to Grandshaykh ق, and all the way up to the Prophet ﷺ! May Allāh keep us with them, because we benefit a lot from them. People who are here or people who are somewhere else have been blessed this *Ramaḍān* with this gift!

Spiritual gifts are more accepted and valuable than *dunyā* gifts, while in *dunyā* it is nice to give each other gifts, but *Ākhirah* gifts are more important. *Ākhirah* gifts are not to attack someone else or to criticize someone else. Allāh ﷻ tests His servants. Look at Sayyīdinā Shāh Bahāuddīn Naqshband ق. He was a rich person and a big scholar. *Awlīyāullāh* do a test. They don't say, "This is *Sulṭān al-Awlīyā*," and "This is not *Sulṭān al-Awlīyā*." Everyone is under a big test, especially *awlīyāullāh*. Don't think they are sitting happy and enjoying, no, no! The burden on their heads and shoulders cannot be described. There are a lot of burdens from the badness they see from their followers, because all of us have rusted hearts, if not entirely then part of the heart or a little bit of the heart, but there is rust. So one day Sayyīdinā Shah Baha'uddīn Naqshband ق was in a trance and as he was thinking:

تفكر ساعة خير من عبادة سبعين سنة

To remember (contemplate or meditate) Allāh ﷻ for one hour is better than seventy years of worship.

I don't know from where some people say, "There is no *tafakkur* in Islam or there is no *murāqabah*, there is no *rābiṭah*, you don't do that, only Hindus do that!" *Allāhu Akbar! Ajīb*, it's strange. Prophet ﷺ said, *Tafakarru sa'atan khayrun min 'ibādati sannah*, and in some narrations, *khayrun min 'ibādati saba'īn sannah*, "To think for one hour you will be rewarded as if you worshipped one year, or seventy years." So how there is no *tafakkur* (contemplation, meditation) in Islam?

So he was in *tafakkur* on all the problems that came on him from his brothers, sisters, wives, families, children, students, too many attacks from right and left. As we said this morning, don't think the *walī* is out of burdens, he is full of burdens! Don't run to be a shepherd, as we said in morning, don't ask to be shepherd, be a sheep, it is better for you. Presidents don't sleep, Grandshaykh ق always used to pray for presidents.

They asked "*Yā Sayyīdī*, some of them are bad!"

He said, "At least we are sleeping okay in our homes, sleeping in our beds. They are not sleeping, they are thinking day and night; whether they are good or bad they are thinking day and night how to rule their country."

So we are sleeping, so why we have to be shepherds? And *awlīyāullāh* don't like to be a shepherds, but they have been put in their positions. It is not with their efforts or their choice; if they would be asked their choice, they don't want it. Grandshaykh ق, after Shaykh Sharafuddīn ad-Dāghestānī ق died, he tore up the will and said, "I don't want to be known by anything except '*Hajji*'."

Open the Box of Your Limited Mind!

Can you imagine the Prophet ﷺ was 23 years with the *Ṣaḥābah* ﵃, day and night, day and night, day and night he was with the *Ṣaḥābah*, and not one single moment without an advice or a *ḥadīth* or an issue or a problem, or a sickness or a revelation. He was always 24 hours with speeches, delivering the Message of Allāh ﷻ. And they come and say, "There are only 3,000 *aḥādīth*." *ʿUlamā* of *Āhl as-Sunnah wa 'l-Jamaʿah* say, "Are you crazy? He was speaking to them day and night, advising them!" Sayyīdinā Abū Bakr aṣ-Ṣiddīq ؓ related only 23-23 *aḥādīth*? Where are these *aḥādīth*?

Open this box! Let us smell the breeze of the cool air that we don't find it now here, the fans are not working well. Open the box that everyone can breathe nicely! Shah Bahaʿuddīn Naqshband ق was in that *tafakkur*, he was "opening the box." When you open the box you are in the light 25 *aḥādīth* and he was Prophet's friend in the cave, he was with him day and night, but only everywhere, under the sun, under the *nūr*. He was in that trance and felt himself standing up, opening the door of the house and moving in the alley and moving out of house, following that smell that was coming to him, a spiritual smell coming to him that was full of beautiful incense, perfumes, following, guiding him where to go. He was pulled by that smell. Like today some children say, "Oh! I smell nice food," coming from outside to kitchen. "What is that smell? Come and eat." We are children and it is good if we smell something like Shāh Bahāuddīn Naqshband ق, so make *tafakkur* and you will smell.

So he was smelling and following, following until he reached from one side of the alley to the other side, until he reached the door of Sayyīdinā Amīr al-Kulāl ق, who was his shaykh but not yet. He reached him and was standing by the door. You cannot enter the door without asking permission, *isti'dhān*, you have to ask permission to enter.

So the shaykh looked at him and immediately said to his people, "Who is this? Who is this?"

They said, "*Yā Sayyidī*, this is the famous Muḥammad Bahāuddīn Naqshband ق, the famous one that his reputation is East and West in the world. All Central Asia comes and learns from his *ḥadīth* and Sharī'ah and *tafsīr*."

He said to them, "Take him and throw him out, we don't need such things here."

That was a big slap in his face. Can you take that? If the shaykh takes your hand and gives you a slap, spiritual, not physical, "I don't want you here. Go!" Slap from left, slap from right and from bottom, and from the top, everywhere you are being slapped. And then at the end they shout at you and curse you, in polite cursing, and your heart will be broken. Shah Baha'uddīn Naqshband's ق heart was broken. A *walī* through *tafakkur*, instead of his heart getting more and more light, his heart was broken. Don't say the *walī's* heart is not broken. Yes, they are but they keep quiet. The treatment they receive, especially from those who are around them, is not nice. Some, not all of them. May Allāh ﷻ relieve Mawlana from any bad hands and relieve us from any bad hands.

So he went with a broken heart and Shayṭān began to play. A *walī*, does Shayṭān come? Yes, of course. Shayṭān did not leave Sayyīdinā Ādam ؏ free, and Iblīs came to the Prophet ﷺ, but he cannot go without permission of Allāh. "You want to go to My Prophet ﷺ? Then go." And he got a big slap from the Prophet ﷺ. He came to the Prophet ﷺ with a long list of questions in his heart. So Sayyīdinā Jibrīl ؏ came to the Prophet ﷺ and said, "Allāh sends His greetings on you and says He gave permission for Iblees to speak to you. He has a lot of questions for you and these are the answers." Iblīs, *la'anahullāh*, came to the presence of the Prophet ﷺ, (and Prophet said), "Iblees, you are cursed! These are your questions and these are the answers," and the Prophet ﷺ said, '*fooooh* on him!' and then he was thrown 700 years a horse-rider's distance into a ditch and he was vomiting continuously. And as Grandshaykh ق said, that is his part of the story, the first part is *ḥadīth*. So Grandshaykh said he was thrown far away and he was vomiting from up and from down, and after a while when he woke up, he was seeing a shoot coming up from his vomit and he was so happy. And he said, "Now I have power to destroy everyone, Muslim and non-Muslim," with that shoot which has many leaves on it from his vomit.

What was that? Tobacco, and from that they got cigarettes! Those who smoke, all of them have bad characters; they are the worst in character, they cannot control themselves, they are angry and they want to smoke. So he was busy spreading that plant with all his devils in different areas in order to spoil people after the Prophet ﷺ would leave *dunyā*.

In any case, Sayyīdinā Shāh Bahāuddīn Naqshband ق was broken-hearted and Shayṭān was coming to play with him and his ego was saying to him, "Who are these Sufis? You don't need him," like they come now and say, "What is 'Sufi'?" They are the grandchildren of those who denied *Taṣawwuf*. "What is this? Your heart is being broken, you are the big *ʿalīm*, you go make your own," like today many representatives make their own groups now. "Do what you want, leave him."

And he said, "I was in that struggle," and finally he said to himself, "I am not going to listen."

When someone shouts and shouts at you on your face, or from your back, and you do nothing, what will happen? Nothing. As Grandshaykh ق said, "Put a dog in a small room with one small window and lock the door, and send smoke inside the room. What will the dog do? He will bark and bark, and go to the window and bark and bark, until he blows out and dies." So that barking is like the barking of the dog: Shayṭān sends smoke to you through your intestine up to your mind and you become drunk, and you shout and shout until you blow up.

What is the benefit? If you answer, you become worse. If not, you take your luggage and go, it's easy. So Shāh Bahāuddīn Naqshband ق said, "I will take my luggage and go, why to answer? I am not going to leave Sayyid Amīr Kulāl, with all his shouting at me, I am going to step on my ego."

Anyone who steps on his ego after fighting and leaves it, if he is right he will inherit by Allāh from Shāh Bahāuddīn Naqshband ق, and that is if he calms down. If he does not calm down the angels will be writing (as bad deeds), because a husband has no right to shout at his wife and the wife has no right to shout at her husband, and the husband and wife have no right to shout at their children except regarding Islamic ways. Children especially don't have the right to shout at the parents! So keep the house clear and everyone is responsible for his doing, if his rights are within the limits of Sharīʿah, or otherwise you have no right to create *fitna* for nothing.

So Sayyīdinā Shāh Bahāuddīn Naqshband ق didn't want to say anything or to tell the students, "This is not fair, this is not true." No, he moved out of the mosque. He said to himself, "Why am I coming out? I am not going to move from this place until my shaykh comes to me." Who is stronger, the one who is thrown out, or the one throwing out? The one being thrown, and so he said, "I want my shaykh to come back to me, that is what is important so I am not moving."

So he put his head on the threshold of the shaykh's *masjid*. That night it was snowing and his head was under the snow and could not been seen. *SubḥānAllāh,* how much these *awlīyāullāh* can take of difficulties! How much Mawlana Shaykh Muḥammad Nazim al-Ḥaqqānī is taking of difficulties from those around him. Sayyid Amir Kulāl ق came out through the door at *Fajr* to go to mosque, and he put his foot on the head of Shah Baha'uddīn Naqshband ق; he knew it was his head and not only that, he pressed on his head and crushed it!

And Shāh Naqshband ق said, "Is that you, *Sayyīdī*?"

Sayyid Amīr Kulāl ق said, "Who is there? Is that you Shāh Bahāuddīn Naqshband ق? *Lā ḥawla wa lā quwatta illa billāhi 'l-'Alīyyu 'l-'Aẓīm*! Come, come," and he took him and cleaned him up and dressed him and gave him all his secrets that Allāh ﷻ gave to him.

This is because by permission of *awlīyāullāh* and permission of Sayyīdinā 'AbdAllāh al-Fā'iz ad-Dāghestānī ق and by permission of Shaykh Muḥammad Nazim al-Ḥaqqānī ق, and Sayyīdinā ' 'Abdu 'r-Raūf al-Yamānī ق who came to all the *ṣuḥbahs* since the beginning of *Ramaḍān* to the end of *Ramaḍān* ! And tonight I was not going to give a lecture, but Sayyīdinā 'Abdu 'r-Raūf al-Yamānī ق indicated to me to make that *ṣuḥbat* to inform them. He was spiritually present every night for these *ṣuḥbats*! *Alḥamdulillāh,* who came got this *barakah* and who came took the benefit, even if they came and went, and he indicated to me to make this *ṣuḥbat*. And we were taken to the presence of the Prophet ﷺ by the *barakah* of Shaykh 'AbdAllāh al-Fā'iz ad-Dāghestānī ق, and Mawlana Shaykh Nazim al-Ḥaqqānī ق, and Sayyīdinā 'Abdu 'r-Raūf al-Yamānī ق. May Allāh ﷻ forgive us! May Allāh bless us!

Bi hurmati 'l-habīb, bi hurmati 'l-Fātiḥah.

Now tomorrow is *'Ēid,* so don't play, go to sleep as *Fajr* is at four o'clock. On the other hand, since it is rejoicing you may also choose to stay up all night rejoicing!

May Allāh forgive us and may Allāh bless us.

Wa min Allāhi 't-tawfīq, bi ḥurmati 'l-ḥabīb, bi ḥurmati 'l-Fātiḥah.
And with Allāh is success. For the sake of the Beloved, for his sake we recite the opening chapter of Holy Qur'ān.

Unite and Do Not Separate

ʿĒid al-Fitr Khutbah

Salāmu ʿalaykum wa raḥmatullāhi wa barakātuh. Alḥamdulillāh for Allāh's Favors on us and for making us from *Ummat an-Nabī* ﷺ and for gifting us the Master of Prophets ﷺ, and *alḥamdulillāh* that Allāh has guided us to Islam. *Ash-hadu an lā ilāha illa-Llāh wa ash-hadu anna Muḥammadan ʿabduhu wa ḥabībuhu wa rasūluh.* We testify there is no god but Allāh, with no partner, we testify that Muḥammad is His Prophet, Servant and Messenger. May Allāh be pleased with his Family ؓ and Companions ؓ and with the Four Rightly-Guided Khalifs ؓ.

O servants of Allāh! *Ramaḍān* has passed us and *Shawwāl* has appeared, the month in which too many changes will be happening on Earth, as the Prophet ﷺ said, there are too many changes on Earth that the killer doesn't know why he killed and the killed doesn't know why he was killed.

وَالَّذِي نَفْسِي بِيَدِهِ لَيَأْتِيَنَّ عَلَى النَّاسِ زَمَانٌ لاَ يَدْرِي الْقَاتِلُ فِي أَيِّ شَيْءٍ قَتَلَ وَلاَ يَدْرِي الْمَقْتُولُ عَلَى أَيِّ شَيْءٍ قُتِلَ

By Him in Whose Hand is my life, a time would come when
the murderer would not know why he has committed the murder
and the victim would not know why he has been killed.[207]

This is what we are seeing today and we have to be away from that and stay with our families and our own communities, and not to go into what is wrong and what is right; we leave it to Allāh's Judgment, *inshā-Allāh*. We ask Allāh ﷻ to accept our fasting and change our imitational fasting into a real fasting, because our fasting is blended with too many bad thoughts and too many sins and too many bad things which we have done that we don't know, but the angels are recording it. Our fasting is becoming a soup, but with Allāh's Greatness and Allāh's Mercy and Prophet's love to his *Ummah*, may Allāh ﷻ accept our *Ramaḍān* and change, as He did in previous

[207] Ṣahih Muslim.

Ramaḍān s, from an imitated *Ramaḍān* to a real *Ramaḍān,* and accept our fasting.

O Muslims! Today is the day of *'Ēid al-Fiṭr* all over the Muslim world and we are celebrating with everyone this day, and it is a day where you don't need to do anything except the five prayers and to remember Allāh ﷻ, and to rejoice and spend it with the family, your children, your relatives, and avoid backbiting and avoid all that Allāh ﷻ does not like. We hope that we will be on the Right Path and we will be toward the love of Prophet ﷺ and love of the *Ṣaḥābat 'l-kirām* ؓ.

Every day we see scholars around the world that, most of them if they are not right scholars, they make up things in order to please others. We call it *muḍāḥala* in Arabic, to pretend you love people; you try to pet them to give them a nice tongue (words), but on their back, on the other side you make a *fitna.* Of those people, we must be careful not to fall into their *fitna* and confusion as the Prophet ﷺ said:

الفتنه نائمه لعن الله من ايقضها

Fitna is dormant and Allāh cursed the one who awoke it.

Fitna is dormant and Allāh curses those who bring it up, and in every community, in every group, there are too many *shayṭāns* making too much *fitna* in order to spoil the unity of that community and divide it and attack it like parasites. Parasites live on the blood of people like bacteria; they don't live by themselves, but have to live off someone else. They are *ṭufaylīyyīn* in Arabic; they don't like to do anything and they live off others and throw words, and in their words is some kind of cheating. And if you are not involved in Islamic knowledge, you will be falling into the trap of these people, who are being pushed by Shayṭān on the last day of *Ramaḍān* to say things that are not accepted and that cause our fasting to be void or null. We have to be very careful, and I will relate this *ḥadīth* of the Prophet ﷺ so you can understand what the Prophet ﷺ said.

Sayyīdinā Jābir ؓ related that the Prophet ﷺ said:

إن من أحبكم إلي، وأقربكم مني مجلسًا يوم القيامة، أحاسنكم أخلاقًا، وإن أبغضكم إلي
وأبعدكم مني يوم القيامة، والثرثارون، والمتشدقون، والمتفيهقون

The dearest and the closest of you to me on the Day of Resurrection will be those who are the best in behavior and the most hateful and the farthest from me on the Day of Resurrection will be the talkative and the most pretentious and the most rhetorical.[208]

"The ones most beloved to me and closest to me on the Day of Judgment and the most I admire are those people with good manners, good characters, good appearance; when they talk they don't talk rudely, they are not speaking with hate, but have *aḥsānakum akhlāqa,* the best of good manners." They make people happy and do not make them divided into *shirdhamah,* small divisions separated from each other, but rather they unite, as Allāh ﷻ said in Holy Qur'an:

وَاعْتَصِمُواْ بِحَبْلِ اللهِ جَمِيعًا وَلاَ تَفَرَّقُواْ

Hold fast to Allāh's rope and don't separate.[209]

So the advice must be to unite, not to separate: to unite, as you know your scholars, as you know your teachers, as you know your guides, to keep the relationship a good relationship and not a divided relationship. So the Prophet ﷺ said, "The most I love among you and most near to me are those with the best of character, people of good characters."

This *Ramaḍān* and every *Ramaḍān* we are taught to polish our egos by keeping our mouth zipped, because every time we open our mouth something will come for sure that Allāh does not like, and angels will convey that *ʿamal* to the Divine Presence. If that *ʿamal* is good and pure, not blended with any impurities, it will go directly and it is accepted, but if not, it is thrown in our faces. We ask Allāh ﷻ to protect us from that!

The Prophet ﷺ continued: *wa inna abghaḍakum,* and Arabs know the meaning of *abghaḍakum,* "the worst, most disgusting people"! "The worst of people despised by me and the people who are very far from me on the Day of Judgment, I will not look at their faces, and they are at the back rows when I do *shafaʿah,*" although they will enter Paradise.

من قال ال اله الا الله دخل الجنة

---

[208] Tirmidhī.

[209] Sūrat Āli-ʿImrān, 3:103.

Whoever says, "Lā ilāha illa-Llāh" enters Paradise.

"But those whom I hate," who are those people? "They don't know what they are saying and they make the devil as an honorable image of human beings and in the image of *awlīyāullāh*," to make devils the worst that you can imagine. Those people the Prophet ﷺ called *falfarkhūn*, they don't know what they are saying: they fabricate things, they falsify and make mistakes when they talk to people, they repeat a phrase they said again and again, and don't remember what they said at the beginning, and attribute it to *Rasūlullāh* ﷺ! They make things up and Prophet ﷺ prohibited us to make things up.

You know today's strategy, they make things up in order to attack as that is the strategy of war: you cheat the enemy, you trick the enemy in order to attack. These people trick honest people, as it is said in Arabic, *farriq tasud*, "divide and conquer." These people divide and conquer even though they are dressed in *Sunnah* clothes and wearing a big turban and in *jubbah*; they are even dressed in traditional clothes, but whatever they are saying they are lying. We have to be very careful. They are the *munāfiqūn*, the hypocrites, as the Prophet ﷺ described them: *idhā ḥadhatha kadhdhab*, "When they speak they lie," *wa idhā w'ada akhlaf*, "When they are entrusted they betray," *wa idhā w'ada akhlaf*, "If he promised he does the opposite."

So be careful from these people, O human beings! That is a general message and not only for us here, but for everywhere it is a general message, and especially those who, at the end of *Ramaḍān*, are putting things on the Internet that are not correct in order to divide the *Ummah* against each other.

وعن جابر رضي الله عنه أن رسول الله صلى الله عليه وسلم قال: إن من أحبكم إلي وأقربكم مني مجلسا يوم القيامة أحاسنكم أخلاقا وإن أبغضكم إلي وأبعدكم مني يوم القيامة الثرثارون والمتشدقون والمتفيهقون قالوا يا رسول الله قد علمنا الثرثارون والمتشدقون فما المتفيهقون ؟ قال المتكبرون رواه الترمذي وقال حديث حسن

The Prophet ﷺ said, "The farthest ones from me on the Day of Judgment are those who speak too much and they don't know what they are saying." *Wa 'l-mutashadiqūn hum al-mutatāwilūna 'alā 'n-nāsi bi 'l-kalāmi*, "Those who don't keep the honor of Allāh's servants; they go up and they say things that are fascinating, and behind it they are tricking you in order to divide and conquer, *farraq tas'ud*."

And the *mutafayhiqūn,* "Those who fill their mouth," prepare to speak complete garbage, "and when they speak people recognize their words are not correct but for the division of the *Ummah.*"

And finally, the *mutakabirrūn,* "The arrogant ones, those who are proud, they say, "We are already dead, we are walking with our spirits, we are already dead," which means "we are not responsible, our spirit is what is making us to do something." They imagine things in their mind as they are bi-polar (a form of mental illness) and spread it among the *Ummah.* And those who don't have a background in Islam or any Sufi order, they will divide the *Ummah* and they begin to fight. Even the four *Madhāhib,* if you study the history of Islam, the students used to fight each other, from Imam Abū Ḥanīfa ﵁, Imam Shafiʿī ﵁, Imam Ibn Ḥanbal ﵁ and Imam Mālik ﵁, their students were fighting with each other. It is well known that those who are arrogant in their knowledge will begin to fight the others who are doing different from them, who follow a different way, because they don't understand what they say. But all roads are leading to one place in Allāh's Divine Presence, in Allāh's Forgiveness, as all Muslims are going to be moved under the *shafaʿah* of Prophet ﷺ, so the goal is the same but the roads are different, so you must respect each other's *madhhabs.* If you are Māliki or Ḥanafi or Ḥanbal ﵁i, you must respect the Shafiʿī.

Islam Does Not Teach to Divide and Conquer

When Imam Shafiʿī ﵁ went to visit a Baghdad mosque, at the grave of Sayyīdinā Imam Abū Ḥanīfa ﵁ he prayed according to how Imam Abū Ḥanīfa ﵁ was praying out of respect to his school, where they don't do the *Duʿā Qunūt* in *Fajr,* so he avoided doing that. We cannot say that Imam Abū Ḥanīfa ﵁ is wrong or Imam Shafiʿī ﵁ is wrong; no, we trust in their *ijtihād* and follow because the Four *Madhhabs* are guiding us to one place at the end and that is what Islam teaches, *ḥusnu 'l-akhlāq,* good manners. Islam does not teach to divide and conquer! You cannot divide people or you will have bloodshed. Those who are posting (falsehood) on the Internet, trying to make one group look bad, that is not accepted and they are lying on the Prophet ﷺ! They are saying the Prophet ﷺ is making his signature on it! If you are seeing this, we are not, and if you are correct, show us that signature. Where is it?

O Muslims! Don't listen to those who are *mutashadiqūn* as they say things with a mouth open so wide that it makes people look crazy! May Allāh ﷻ keep us according to that *ḥadīth,* in order to be saved in *dunyā* and *Ākhirah.*

إِنَّ اللهَ أَوْحَى إِلَيَّ أَنْ تَوَاضَعُوا حَتَّى لاَ يَبْغِيَ أَحَدٌ عَلَى أَحَدٍ وَلاَ يَفْخَرَ أَحَدٌ عَلَى أَحَدٍ

Allāh has revealed to me that you must be humble, so that no one oppresses another and boasts over another.[210]

"Allāh has revealed to me to be humble to each other," not to be arrogant, and not to divide people and the *Ummah* into two or three or four, it is against the teachings of Islam. It is against all the teachings of good manners to go to people who are sheep, who have no background of Islam, and give them something and they think you are *walīullāh,* but you are deceiving them, you are dividing them and taking them to Shayṭān. Be humble, don't say, "I am receiving from the Prophet ﷺ," as you are lying. Don't say you receive from the *Ṣaḥābah* ؓ as you are lying. I don't say there are no *awlīyāullāh* who receive Heavenly Inspirations from the Heavenly Message of the Prophet ﷺ, and from the *Ṣaḥābah* ؓ, but not to say that "the Prophet ﷺ is signing," and, "I am telling you what he ﷺ is signing just now," and spreading rumors around the world by posting this on the Internet!

Ḥattā lā yafkharu āḥadun ʿalā āḥad, not to say, "We are the inner circle, the core of what we believe, and the others are the outer circle." No, every Muslim is in the core and every Muslim is in the presence of the Prophet ﷺ, every Muslim is in the Divine Presence! *Wa lā yabghī āḥadun ʿalā āḥad,* no one should attack the others to show himself higher than the others as we are all from the Children of Ādam ؑ, and the best of those are from the *Ummat an-Nabī* ﷺ.

The Prophet ﷺ said:

لا يدخل الجنة نمام

The person who goes about with calumnies will never enter Paradise.[211]

---

210 Sunan Abi Dāwūd, Muslim.

211 Bukhārī and Muslim.

A Namām Will Not Enter Paradise

Who is a *namām*? That is the one in the group who sees how he can penetrate through the heart of a group to bring them on his side and then divide the rest, to make it two groups by spreading false rumors and false accusations. Allāh is going to punish those who spread *fitna* around the *Ummah* and oppress innocent people as they are doing that in order to impress others. May Allāh ﷻ, on this *ʿĒid* day, save us from this!

And finally, this *ḥadīth* is important, for you will be asked about this on the Day of Judgment, especially regarding your children:

خَرَجَ النَّبِيُّ صلى الله عليه وسلم مِنْ بَعْضِ حِيطَانِ الْمَدِينَةِ، فَسَمِعَ صَوْتَ إِنْسَانَيْنِ يُعَذَّبَانِ فِي قُبُورِهِمَا فَقَالَ " يُعَذَّبَانِ، وَمَا يُعَذَّبَانِ فِي كَبِيرَةٍ، وَإِنَّهُ لَكَبِيرٌ، كَانَ أَحَدُهُمَا لاَ يَسْتَتِرُ مِنَ الْبَوْلِ، وَكَانَ الآخَرُ يَمْشِي بِالنَّمِيمَةِ ". ثُمَّ دَعَا بِجَرِيدَةٍ فَكَسَرَهَا بِكِسْرَتَيْنِ أَوْ ثِنْتَيْنِ، فَجَعَلَ كِسْرَةً فِي قَبْرِ هَذَا، وَكِسْرَةً فِي قَبْرِ هَذَا، فَقَالَ " لَعَلَّهُ يُخَفَّفُ عَنْهُمَا مَا لَمْ يَيْبَسَا ".

Once the Prophet went through the graveyards of Madīnah and heard the voices of two humans who were being tortured in their graves. The Prophet ﷺ said, "They are being punished, but they are not being punished because of a major sin, yet their sins are great. One of them used to not save himself from (being soiled with) the urine, and the other used to go about slandering (namīma)." Then the Prophet asked for a green palm tree leaf and split it into two pieces and placed one piece on each grave, saying, "I hope their punishment may be abated as long as these pieces of the leaf are not dried."[212]

And the Prophet ﷺ passed by two graves on his way and both the dead bodies were being punished, he was hearing the punishment and he was seeing it. And the Prophet ﷺ said, *"yuʿadhibān wa mā yuʿadhibānu fī kabīrah,* they are in punishment and it is not for something big, but despite that, it is big. Allāh is punishing them by burning them."

There was a cemetery I know that was full and someone had died and they needed the grave, and they opened and saw the bodies there were as if they have been burnt, full of ashes!

The Prophet ﷺ said, "These two are being punished and under the *ʿadhāb,* not because of something big, yet it is something big. *Amma Āḥadun*

---

[212] Bukhārī.

fakāna yamshī bi 'n-namīma, one due to spreading false rumors and lies everywhere," like our friend spreading false rumors everywhere, and the second one, especially for parents, to be careful about this for your children. I see many people like that and we have to take it into consideration. "The second was punished because it is not big, but it is big, and Allāh does not like it. *Lā yastatirū min bawlihi,* he doesn't cover himself when urinating and his clothes get full of that urine, and also he doesn't put water to clean himself."

Many Muslims today don't wash with water after their pee (perform *ṭahārah*), but pull up (their clothes) and go and make *wuḍū* and pray (although they remain impure)! You have to teach your children how to clean themselves from urine. It is on your neck! May Allāh open our eyes! You are responsible on the Day of Judgment.

May Allāh forgive us and may Allāh bless us.

Wa min Allāhi 't-tawfiq, bi ḥurmati 'l-ḥabīb, bi ḥurmati 'l-Fātiḥah.
And with Allāh is success. For the sake of the Beloved, for his sake we recite the opening chapter of Holy Qur'ān.

Islamic Calendar and Holy Days

The Islamic calendar is lunar based, with twelve months of 29 or 30 days. A lunar year is shorter than a solar year, so Muslim holy days cycle back in the Gregorian (Western) calendar. This is how *Ramaḍān* is celebrated at different times of the year, as the annual Islamic calendar is ten days shorter than the Gregorian calendar.

Four Islamic months are sacred: Muharram, Rajab, Dhū 'l-Q'adah and Dhū 'l-Hijjah. Holy months include "God's Month" (Rajab), "Prophet's Month" (Sha'bān) and the "Month of the People" (*Ramaḍān*), in which pious acts are rewarded more generously.

Months of the Islamic Calendar

- Muḥarram
- Ṣafar
- Rabīʿ ul-Āwwal (Rabīʿ I)
- Rabīʿ uth-Thāni (Rabīʿ II)
- Jumāda al-Āwwal (Jumādi I)
- Jumāda uth-Thānī (Jumādi II)
- Rajab
- Shaʿbān
- Ramaḍān
- Shawwāl
- Dhū'l-Qʿadah
- Dhū'l-Ḥijjah

al-Hijrah

The 1st of Muharram marks the beginning of the Islamic New Year, chosen because it is the anniversary of Prophet Muḥammad's ﷺ historic *Hijrah* (migration) from Mecca to Madīnah, where he established the first, preeminent Muslim community in which he introduced unprecedented social reforms, including civil law, human and women's rights, religious tolerance, taxation to serve the community, and military ethics.

'Ashūra

On 10th Muharram, 'Ashūra commemorates many sacred events, such as Noah's ark coming to rest, the birth of Abraham, and the building of the Kaʿbah in Mecca. 'Ashūra is a major holy day, marked with two days of fasting, on the $9^{th}/10^{th}$ or on $10^{th}/11^{th}$ based on a holy tradition (*ḥadīth*) of Sayyīdinā Muḥammad ﷺ.

Mawlid

Mawlid an-Nabī, 12th Rabiʿ al-Āwwal, commemorates Prophet Muḥammad's birth in 570. Mawlid is celebrated globally throughout this month in huge communal gatherings in which a famous poem "Qasīdah al-Burdah" is recited, accompanied by drummers, illustrious poetry recitals, religious singing, eloquent sermons, gift giving, feasts, and feeding the poor. Most Muslim nations observe Mawlid as a national holiday.

Laylat al-ʻIsrā' wa 'l-Miʿrāj

Literally, "the Night Journey and Ascension;" 27th of Rajab is when Sayyīdinā Muḥammad ﷺ physically traveled from Mecca to Jerusalem, ascended in all the levels of Heaven from a rock in the Dome of the Rock, and returned to Mecca—while his bed was still warm. In the Night Journey, Islam's five daily prayers were ordained by God. Sayyīdinā Muḥammad ﷺ also prayed with Abraham, Moses, and Jesus in Jerusalem's al-Aqṣā Mosque, signifying that Muslims, Christians, and Jews follow one god. This holy event designated Jerusalem as the third holiest site in Islam, after Mecca and Madīnah.

Laylat al-Bara'ah

The "Night of Freedom from Fire" occurs on 15th Shaʿbān. On this night God's Mercy is great; hence, the night is spent reciting Holy Qurʿan and special prayers, as well as visiting the deceased.

Ramaḍān

Many regard *Ramaḍān*, the 9th month of the Islamic calendar, the holiest month of the year. Muslims observe a strict fast and participate in pious activities such as charitable giving and peace making. It is a time of intense spiritual renewal for those who observe it. Fasting is meant to instill social awareness of the needy, and to promote gratitude for God's endless favors. The fast is typically broken in a communal setting, and hence *Ramaḍān* is a highly social month. At night, a special *Ramaḍān* prayer known as "*Tarawīḥ*" is offered in congregation, in which one-thirtieth of the Holy Qurʿan is recited by the *īmām* (prayer leader); thus the entire holy book of 6,000 verses is recited in this month.

ʿĒid al-Fitr

"Festival of Fast-Breaking" marks the end of *Ramaḍān* and is celebrated the first three days of Shawwāl. It is a time for charity and celebration with family and friends for completing a month of blessings and joy. In the Last Days of *Ramaḍān*, each Muslim family gives "Zakāt *al-Fiṭr*"(charity of fast-breaking) which consists of cash and/or food, to help the poor. On the first early morning of *ʿĒid*, Muslims observe a special congregational prayer, such as Christmas/Easter Mass or the High Holy Days. After *ʿĒid* prayer is a time to visit family and friends, and give gifts and money, especially to children. Many specialty foods and sweets are prepared solely for *ʿĒid* days. In most Muslim countries, the entire three days of *ʿĒid* is a national holiday.

Yawm al-ʿArafāt

"Day of ʿArafāt," the 9th Dhul-Ḥijjah, occurs just before the celebration of *ʿĒid al-Aḍḥā*. Pilgrims on *Sunnah* assemble for the "standing" on the plain of ʿArafāt, located outside Mecca, where they contemplate the Day of Standing (Resurrection Day). Muslims elsewhere in the world fast this day, and gather at a local mosque for prayers. Thus, those who cannot perform *Sunnah* that year still honor the sacrifice of Abraham.

ʿĒid al-Adha

The "Feast of Sacrifice," celebrated from the 10th-13th Dhul-Ḥijjah, marks Prophet Abraham's willingness to sacrifice his son Ismāʿīl on God's order. To honor this event, Muslims perform *Sunnah*, the pilgrimage to Mecca that is incumbent on every mature Muslim once in their life if they have the means. Celebrations begin with an animal sacrifice to commemorate Sayyīdinā Abraham's sacrifice. In Islam, he is known as *Khalīlullāh*, "God's friend." Many consider him the first Muslim and a premiere role model, for his obedience to God and willingness to sacrifice his only child without even questioning the command.

Glossary

ʿabd (pl. *ʿibād*): lit. slave; servant.
ʿAbdAllāh: Lit., "servant of God"
Abū Bakr aṣ-Ṣiddīq: the closest Companion of Prophet Muḥammad; the Prophet's father-in-law, who shared the *Hijrah* with him. After the Prophet's death, he was elected the first caliph (successor); known as one of the most saintly Companions.
Abū Yazīd/Bayāzīd Bistāmī: A great ninth century *walī* and a master of the Naqshbandi Golden Chain.
adab: good manners, proper etiquette.
adhān: call to prayer.
Ākhirah: the Hereafter; afterlife.
al-: Arabic definite article, "the".
ʿalāmīn: world; universes.
Alḥamdūlillāh: praise God.
ʿAlī ibn Abī Ṭālib: first cousin of Prophet Muḥammad, married to his daughter Fāṭimah; the fourth caliph.
Alif: first letter of Arabic alphabet.
ʿAlīm, al-: the Knower, a divine attribute
Allāh: proper name for God in Arabic.
Allāhu Akbar: God is Greater.
ʿāmal: good deed (pl. *ʿamāl*).
amīr (pl., *umarā*): chief, leader, head of a nation or people.
anā: first person singular pronoun
anbīyā: prophets (sing. *nabī*).
ʿaql: intellect, reason; from the root *ʿaqila*: lit., "to fetter."
ʿArafah, ʿArafāt: a plain near Mecca where pilgrims gather for the principal rite of *Hajj*.
ʿarif: knower, Gnostic; one who has reached spiritual knowledge of his Lord.
ʿĀrifūnʿ bil-Lāh: knowers of God.
Ar-Raḥīm: The Mercy-Giving, Merciful, Munificent, one of Allāh's ninety-nine Holy Names.
Ar-Raḥmān: The Most Merciful, Compassionate, Beneficent; the most repeated of Allāh's Holy Names.
ʿarsh, al-: the Divine Throne.
aṣl: root, origin, basis.
astāghfirullāh: lit. "I seek Allāh's forgiveness."
Awlīyāullāh: saints of Allāh (sing. *walī*).
āyah (pl. *ayāt*): a verse of the Holy Qur'ān.
Āyat al-Kursī: "Verse of the Throne," a well-known supplication from the Qur'ān (2:255).
ʿAzraʿīl: the Archangel of Death.
Badīʿ al-: The Innovator; a divine name.
Banī Ādam: Children of Ādam; humanity.
Bayt al-Maqdis: the Sacred Mosque in Jerusalem, built at the site where Solomon's Temple was later erected.
Bayt al-Mā'mūr: much-frequented house; this refers to the Kaʿbah of the Heavens, which is the prototype of the Kaʿbah on Earth, circumambulated by the angels.
bayaʿ: pledge; in the context of this book, the pledge of initiation of a disciple (*murīd*) to a Shaykh.
Bismillāhi'r-Raḥmāni'r-Raḥīm: "In the name of the All-Merciful, the All-Compassionate"; introductory verse to all chapters of the Qur'ān, except the ninth.

Dajjāl: the False Messiah (Anti-Christ) will appear at the end-time of this world, to deceive Mankind with false divinity.
dalālah: evidence.
dhāt: self / selfhood.
dhawq (pl. *adhwāq*): tasting; technical term referring to the experiential aspect of Gnosis.
dhikr: remembrance, mention of God in His Holy Names or phrases of glorification.
ḍīyā: light.
Diwān al-Awlīyā: the nightly gathering of saints with Prophet Muḥammad in the spiritual realm.
du'ā: supplication.
dunyā: world; worldly life.
'Ēid: festival; the two major celebrations of Islam are 'Ēid al-Fiṭr, after Ramaḍān; and 'Ēid al-Adha, the Festival of Sacrifice during the time of *Hajj*, which commemorates the sacrifice of Prophet Abraham.
farḍ: obligatory worship.
Fātiḥah: Sūratu 'l-Fātiḥah; the opening chapter of the Qur'ān.
Ghafūr, al-: The Forgiver; one of the Holy Names of God.
ghawth: lit. "Helper"; the highest rank of all saints.
ghaybu' l-muṭlaq, al-: the Absolute Unknown; known only to God.
ghusl: full shower/bath obligated by a state of ritual impurity, performed before worship.
Grandshaykh: generally, a *walī* of great stature. In this text, refers to Mawlana 'AbdAllāh ad-Daghestāni (d. 1973), Mawlana Shaykh Nazim's master.
Hā': the Arabic letter ه
ḥadīth Nabawī (pl., *aḥādīth*): prophetic *ḥadīth* whose meaning and linguistic expression are those of Prophet Muḥammad.
Ḥadīth Qudsī: divine saying whose meaning directly reflects the meaning God intended but whose linguistic expression is not divine speech as in the Qur'ān.
ḥaḍr: present
Hajj: the sacred pilgrimage of Islam obligatory on every mature Muslim once in their life.
ḥalāl: permitted, lawful according to Islamic *Sharī'ah*.
ḥaqīqah, al-: reality of existence; ultimate truth.
ḥaqq: truth
Ḥaqq, al-: the Divine Reality, one of the 99 Divine Names.
ḥarām: forbidden, unlawful.
ḥasanāt: good deeds.
hāshā: God forbid.
ḥarf: (pl. *ḥurūf*) letter; Arabic root "edge."
Ḥawā: Eve.
ḥaywān: animal.
Hijrah: emigration.
ḥikmah: wisdom.
ḥujjah: proof.
hūwa: the pronoun "he,"made up of the Arabic letters *hā'* and *wāw*.
'ibādu 'l-Lāh: servants of God.
'ifrīt: a type of Jinn, huge and powerful.
iḥsān: doing good, "It is to worship God as though you see Him; for if you are not seeing Him, He sees you."
ikhlāṣ, al-: sincere devotion.
ilāh: (pl. *āliha*): idols or gods.
ilāhīyya: divinity.

ilhām: divine inspiration sent to *awlīyāullāh*.
ʿilm: knowledge, science.
ʿilmu ʾl-awrāq: knowledge of papers.
ʿilmu ʾl-adhwāq: knowledge of taste.
ʿilmu ʾl-ḥurūf: science of letters.
ʿilmu ʾl-kalām: scholastic theology.
ʿilmun ladunnī: divinely inspired knowledge.
īmān: faith, belief.
imām: leader of congregational prayer; an advanced scholar followed by a large community.
insān: humanity; pupil of the eye.
insānu ʾl-kāmil, al-: the Perfect Man, *i.e.,* Prophet Muḥammad.
irādatullāh: the Will of God.
irshād: spiritual guidance.
ism: name.
isma-Llāh: name of God.
isrāʿ: night journey; used here in reference to the night journey of Prophet Muḥammad.
Isrāʿfīl: Archangel Rafael, in charge of blowing the Final Trumpet.
jalāl: majesty.
jamāl: beauty.
jamaʿa: group, congregation.
Jannah: Paradise.
jihād: to struggle in God's Path.
Jibrīl: Gabriel, Archangel of revelation.
Jinn: a species of living beings created from fire, invisible to most humans. Jinn can be Muslims or non-Muslims.
Jumuʿah: Friday congregational prayer, held in a large mosque.
Kaʿbah: the first House of God, located in Mecca, Saudi Arabia to which pilgrimage is made and to which Muslims face in prayer.
kāfir: unBeliever.
Kalāmullāh al-Qadīm: lit., Allāh's Ancient Words, *viz.* the Holy Qur'ān.
kalīmat at-tawḥīd: lā ilāha illa-Llāh: "There is no god but Al-Lah (the God)."
karāmat: miracles.
khalīfah: deputy.
Khāliq, al-: the Creator, one of 99 Divine Names.
khalq: Creation.
khāniqah: designated smaller place for worship other than a mosque; *zāwiyah*.
khuluq: conduct, manners.
Kirāmun Kātabīn: honored Scribe angels.
lā: no; not; not existent; the particle of negation.
lā ilāha illa-Llāh Muḥammadun Rasūlullāh: There is no deity except Allāh, Muḥammad is the Messenger of Allāh.
Lām: Arabic letter ل.
al-Lawḥ al-Maḥfūẓ: the Preserved Tablets.
Laylat al-Isrāʿ waʾl-Miʿrāj: the Night Journey and Ascension of Prophet Muḥammad to Jerusalem and to the Seven Heavens.
Madīnātu ʾl-Munawwara: the Illuminated city; city of Prophet Muḥammad; Madīnah.
mahr: dowry, given by the groom to the bride.
malakūt: divine kingdom.
Mālik, al-: the Sovereign, a divine name.
Mālik: Archangel of Hell.
maqām: spiritual station; tomb of a prophet, messenger or saint.
maʿrifah: gnosis.
Māshā'Allāh: as Allāh Wills.

Mawlana: lit. "Our master" or "our patron,"referring to an esteemed person.
maẓhar: place of disclosure.
miḥrāb: prayer niche.
Mikā'īl: Michael, Archangel of rain.
mīzān: the scale that weighs our deeds on Judgment Day.
mīm: Arabic letter م.
minbar: pulpit.
Miracles: of saints, known as *karamāt*; of prophets, known as *mu'jizāt* (lit., "That which renders powerless or helpless").
mi'rāj: the ascension of Prophet Muḥammad from Jerusalem to the Seven Heavens.
Muḥammadun rasūlu 'l-Lāh: Muḥammad is the Messenger of God.
mulk, al-: the World of dominion.
Mu'min, al-: Guarḍian of Faith, one of the 99 Names of God.
mu'min: a Believer.
munājāt: invocation to God in a very intimate form.
Munkir: one of the angels of the grave.
murīd: disciple, student, follower.
murshid: spiritual guide; *pir*.
mushāhadah: direct witnessing.
mushrik (pl. *mushrikūn*): idolater; polytheist.
muwwāḥid (pl. *muwāḥḥidūn*): those who affirm God's Oneness.
nabī: a prophet of God.
nāfs: lower self, ego.
Nakīr: the other angel of the grave (with Munkir).
nūr: light.
Nūḥ: the prophet Noah.
Nūr, an-: "The Source of Light"; a divine name.
Qādir, al-: "The Powerful"; a divine name.
qalam, al-: the Pen.
qiblah: direction, specifically, the direction faced by Muslims during prayer and other worship, towards the Sacred House in Mecca.
Quddūs, al-: "The Holy One"; a divine name.
qurb: nearness
quṭb (pl. *aqṭāb*): axis or pole. Among the poles are:
Quṭbu 'l-Bilād: Pole of the Lands.
Quṭbu 'l-Irshād: Pole of Guidance.
Quṭbu 'l-Aqṭāb: Pole of Poles.
Quṭbu 'l-A'dham: Highest Pole.
Quṭbu 'l-Mutaṣarrif: Pole of Affairs.
al-quṭbīyyatu 'l-kubrā: the highest station of poleship.
Rabb, ar-: the Lord.
Raḥīm, ar-: "The Most Compassionate"; a divine name.
Raḥmān, ar-: "The All-Merciful"; a divine name.
raḥmā: mercy.
raka'at: one full set of prescribed motions in prayer. Each prayer consists of a one or more *raka'ats.*
Ramaḍān: the ninth month of the Islamic calendar; month of fasting.
Rasūl: a messenger of God.
Rasūlullāh: the Messenger of God, Muḥammad ﷺ.
Ra'ūf, ar-: "The Most Kind"; a divine name.
Razzāq, ar-: "The Provider"; a divine name.
rawḥānīyyah: spirituality; spiritual essence of something.
Riḍwān: Archangel of Paradise.
rizq: provision; sustenance.

rūḥ: spirit. *Ar-Rūḥ* is the name of a great angel.
rukūʿ: bowing posture of the prayer.
ṣadaqah: voluntary charity.
Ṣaḥābah (sing., *ṣaḥābī*): Companions of the Prophet; the first Muslims.
ṣaḥīḥ: authentic; term certifying validity of a *ḥadīth* of the Prophet.
ṣāim: fasting person (pl. *ṣāimūn*)
sajda (pl. *sujūd*): prostration.
ṣalāt: ritual prayer, one of the five obligatory pillars of Islam. Also, to invoke blessing on the Prophet.
Ṣalāt an-Najāt: prayer of salvation, offered in the late hours of night.
ṣalawāt (sing. *ṣalāt*): invoking blessings and peace upon the Prophet.
salām: peace.
Salām, as-: "The Peaceful"; a divine name. *As-salāmu ʿalaykum:* "Peace be upon you," the Islamic greeting.
Ṣamad, aṣ-: Self-Sufficient, upon whom creatures depend.
ṣawm, ṣiyām: fasting.
sayyi'āt: bad deeds; sins.
sayyid: leader; also, a descendant of Prophet Muḥammad.
Sayyīdinā : our master (fem. *sayyidunā; sayyidatunā*: our mistress).
shahādah: lit. testimony; the testimony of Islamic faith: *lā ilāha illa 'l-Lāh wa Muḥammadun rasūlu 'l-Lāh,* "There is no god but Allāh, the One God, and Muḥammad is the Messenger of God."
Shah Naqshband: Muḥammad Bahaʿuddīn Shah Naqshband, a great eighth century walī, and the founder of the Naqshbandi Ṭarīqah.
Shaykh: lit. "old Man," a religious guide, teacher; master of spiritual discipline.
shifāʿ: cure.
shirk: polytheism, idolatry, ascribing partners to God
ṣiffāt: attributes; term referring to Divine Attributes.
Silṣilat adh-dhahabīyya: "Golden Chain"of spiritual authority in Islam
sohbet (Arabic, *suḥbah*): association: the assembly or discourse of a Shaykh.
subḥānAllāh: glory be to God.
sulṭān/sulṭānah: ruler, monarch.
Sulṭān al-Awlīyā: lit., "King of the *awlīyā;* the highest-ranking saint.
Sūnnah: Practices of Prophet Muḥammad in actions and words; what he did, said, recommended, or approved of in his Companions.
sūrah: a chapter of the Qur'ān; picture, image.
Sūratu 'l-Ikhlāṣ: Chapter 114 of Holy Qur'ān; the Chapter of Sincerity.
ṭabīb: doctor.
tābiʿīn: the Successors, one generation after the Prophet's Companions.
tafsīr: to explain, expound, explicate, or interpret; technical term for commentary or exegesis of the Holy Qur'ān.
tajallī (pl. *tajallīyāt*): theophanies, God's self-disclosures, Divine Self-manifestation.
takbīr: lit. *"Allāhu Akbar,"*God is Great.
tarawīḥ: the special nightly prayers of Ramaḍān.
ṭarīqat/ṭarīqah: lit., way, road or path. An Islamic order or path of discipline

and devotion under a guide or Shaykh; Sufism.
tasbīḥ: recitation glorifying or praising God.
tawāḍa': humbleness.
ṭawāf: the rite of circumambulating the Ka'bah while glorifying God during *Hajj* and 'Umra.
tawḥīd: unity; universal or primordial Islam, submission to God, as the sole Master of destiny and ultimate Reality.
Tawrāt: Torah
tayammum: Alternate ritual ablution performed in the absence of water.
'ubūdīyyah: state of worshipfulness. Servanthood
'ulamā (sing. *'ālim*): scholars.
'ulūmu 'l-awwalīna wa 'l-ākhirīn: knowledge of the "Firsts"and the "Lasts" refers to the knowledge God poured into the heart of Prophet Muḥammad during his ascension to the Divine Presence.
'ulūm al-Islāmī: Islamic religious sciences.
Ummāh: faith community, nation.
'Umar ibn al-Khaṭṭāb: an eminent Companion of Prophet Muḥammad and second caliph of Islam.
'umra: the minor pilgrimage to Mecca, performed at any time of the year.
'Uthmān ibn 'Affān: eminent Companion of the Prophet; his son-in-law and third caliph of Islam, renowned for compiling the Qur'ān.
walad: a child.
waladī: my child.
walayah: proximity or closeness; sainthood.
walī (pl. *awlīyā*): saint, or "he who assists"; guarḍian; protector.
waṣīlah: a means; holy station of Prophet Muḥammad as God's intermediary to grant supplications.
wāw: Arabic letter و
wujūd, al-: existence; "to find," "the act of finding," and "being found."
Y'aqūb: Jacob; the prophet.
yamīn: the right hand; previously meant "oath."
Yawm al-'ahdi wa'l-mīthāq: Day of Oath and Covenant, a Heavenly event before this Life, when all souls of humanity were present to God, and He took from each the promise to accept His Sovereignty as Lord.
yawm al-qiyāmah: Day of Judgment.
Yūsuf: Joseph; the prophet.
zāwiyah: designated smaller place for worship other than a mosque; also *khāniqah*.
zīyāra: visitation to the grave of a prophet, a prophet's companion or a saint.

Other Publications (available at www.isn1.net)

Shaykh Muhammad Nazim Adil al-Ḥaqqānī

- New Day, New Provision (2014)
- We Have Honored the Children of Ādam (2013)
- Heavenly Counsel: from Darkness into Light (2013)
- In the Mystic Footsteps of Saints (eBooks) (2 volumes) (2013)
- Heavenly Showers (2012)
- The Sufilive Series (2010-12))
- Breaths from Beyond the Curtain
- In the Eye of the Needle
- Eternity: Inspirations from Heavenly Sources
- The Healing Power of Sufi Meditation
- In the Mystic Footsteps of Saints (2 volumes)
- Liberating the Soul (6 volumes)

Shaykh Muhammad Hisham Kabbani

- The Fiqh of Islam, 2 vols (2014/15)
- Benefits of Bismillāhi 'r-Raḥmāni 'r-Rahīm & Sūrat al-Fātiḥah (2013)
- The Importance of Prophet Muhammad in Our Daily Life
- The Hierarchy of Saints (2013) (also in French)
- The Heavenly Power of Divine Obedience and Gratitude (2013)
- *Salawat* of Tremendous Blessings (also Turkish/ Spanish)
- The Dome of Provisions (2012)
- The Prohibition of Domestic Violence in Islam (2011/*Fatwa*, also in Spanish, French)
- The Sufilive Series (6 vol. 2010-12)
- Jihad: Principles of Leadership in War and Peace
- Cyprus Summer Series (2 vol.)
- The Nine-fold Ascent
- Who Are the Guides? (2008)
- Illuminations (2007)
- A Banquet for the Soul (2006)
- Symphony of Remembrance
- The Healing Power of Sufi Meditation
- In the Shadow of Saints
- Keys to the Divine Kingdom
- The Sufi Science of Self-Realization (also in French)
- Universe Rising: the Approach of Armageddon?
- Pearls and Coral
- Classical Islam and the Naqshbandi Sufi Tradition
- The Naqshbandi Sufi Way
- Links of Light: The Golden Chain
- Encyclopedia of Islamic Doctrine (7 volumes)
- Angels Unveiled, a Sufi Perspective
- Encyclopedia of Muḥammad's Women Companions and the Traditions They Related

Hajjah Amina Adil

℘ Muhammad: the Messenger of Islam (2001)

℘ The Light of Muḥammad

℘ Lore of Light / Links of Light

℘ My Little Lore of Light (3 vol.)

Hajjah Naziha Adil Kabbani

℘ Heavenly Foods (2011)

℘ Secrets of Heavenly Food (2009)

www.ingramcontent.com/pod-product-compliance
Lightning Source LLC
Chambersburg PA
CBHW021143080526
44588CB00008B/194